SCALIA SPEAKS

SCALIA SPEAKS

Reflections on Law, Faith,

and Life Well Lived

ANTONIN SCALIA

Edited by Christopher J. Scalia and Edward Whelan

CROWN
FORUM
NEW YORK

Published in the United States by Crown Forum, an imprint of the Crown
Publishing Group, a division of Penguin Random House LLC, New York.
crownpublishing.com

CROWN FORUM with colophon is a registered trademark of Penguin
Random House LLC.

Library of Congress Cataloging-in-Publication Data
Names: Scalia, Antonin, author. | Scalia, Christopher J., author. |
Whelan, Edward, author.
Title: Scalia speaks : reflections on law, faith, and life well lived /
Antonin Scalia, Christopher J. Scalia, Edward Whelan ; foreword by
Ruth Bader Ginsburg.
Description: New York : Crown Forum, 2017. | Includes bibliographical
references and index.
Indentifiers: LCCN 2017034660 (print) | LCCN 2017035374 (ebook) |
ISBN 9780525573333 (el) | ISBN 9780525573326 (hardback)
Subjects: LCSH: Scalia, Antonin—Political and social views. | Judicial
opinions—United States. | Judges—United States. | United States.
Supreme Court—Officials and employees. | Speeches, addresses, etc.,
American. | BISAC: BIOGRAPHY & AUTOBIOGRAPHY / Lawyers &
Judges. | POLITICAL SCIENCE / Government / Judicial Branch. |
BIOGRAPHY & AUTOBIOGRAPHY / Political.
Classification: LCC KF213.S32 (ebook) | LCC KF213.S32 S32 2017 (print) |
DDC 081—dc23
LC record available at https://lccn.loc.gov/2017034660

ISBN 978-0-525-57332-6
Ebook ISBN 978-0-525-57333-3

Printed in the United States of America

Original photograph by Kainaz Amaria/NPR
Jacket design by Darren Haggar

10 9 8 7 6 5 4 3 2 1

First Edition

To Maureen Scalia

———

I have to thank my wife, Maureen, who's an extraordinary woman, and without whom I wouldn't be here—or if I were here, it wouldn't have been as much fun along the way.

—*ANTONIN SCALIA, on being sworn in to the Supreme Court, September 26, 1986*

Contents

FOREWORD

By Justice Ruth Bader Ginsburg

I first met Antonin Scalia when he served on the faculty of the University of Chicago's School of Law. He was in Washington, D.C., to deliver a lecture on an issue generating controversy among scholars of administrative law, a field in which then-Professor Scalia was a widely recognized leader. I disagreed, in considerable part, with the substance of his presentation, but his acumen, affability, and high spirits captivated me.

When Professor Scalia was appointed to the United States Court of Appeals for the D.C. Circuit in 1982, the court on which I had served since 1980, I joined my colleagues in welcoming him with delight. He brought his large family to the immediate pre-formal investiture oath taking, a ceremony needed to place him on the federal judiciary's payroll. I recall being uncertain whether Maureen Scalia was his wife or eldest daughter. He held his partner in life in highest esteem and often referred to her as Maureen, the beautiful. A 1960 Radcliffe graduate, Maureen was super smart, also master of the arts of raising children, managing social calendars, sewing haute couture clothes, and gourmet cooking. She and my husband, Supreme Chef Marty Ginsburg,* were most popular co-caterers of the Supreme Court spouses' quarterly gatherings for lunch in the Natalie Cornell Rehnquist Dining Room (until the addition of two male spouses, the Ladies Dining Room).

My friendship with Judge, later Justice, Scalia was sometimes regarded as puzzling, because we followed distinctly different

---

* See Associate Spouses in Memoriam, *Chef Supreme: Martin Ginsburg* (Supreme Court Historical Society 2011).

approaches to the interpretation of legal texts. But in our years together on the D.C. Circuit, there was nothing strange about our fondness for each other. Best friend of our chief judge, J. Skelly Wright, was Circuit Judge Edward A. Tamm. Wright had served as a federal district court judge in New Orleans endeavoring, against massive resistance, to enforce desegregation in education and public transportation. Ed Tamm had been second in command to J. Edgar Hoover at the FBI. Wright was a registered Democrat, Tamm, a registered Republican. Yet the two were so close, they even shopped for clothes together. So it did not seem unusual that my closest D.C. Circuit colleagues were Carter appointee Harry Edwards and Reagan appointees Robert Bork and Antonin Scalia.

Justice Scalia was known for opinions of uncommon clarity and inimitable style, writings that did not disguise his view of the opposing side. Yet, as he put it, he attacked ideas, not people. He was a well-schooled grammarian. Now and then he would call me, or stop by my chambers, to point out a slip I had made in an opinion draft. He did this, resisting circulation of a memorandum, copies to other justices, that might embarrass me. When we disagreed, my final opinion was always clearer and more convincing than my initial circulation. Justice Scalia homed in on all the soft spots, energizing me to strengthen my presentation.

Unlike my dear colleague Elena Kagan, I never sought to join Justice Scalia on his hunting adventures. But we several times traveled abroad together for exchanges with judges and lawyers in other lands. During a visit to India in 1994, I learned of his skill as a shopper. On a day free from judicial interchanges, our driver took us to his friend's carpet shop in Agra. One rug after another was tossed onto the floor, leaving me without a clue which to choose. Justice Scalia pointed to one he thought Maureen would like for their beach house in North Carolina. I picked the same design in a different color. It has worn very well.

We shared a passion for opera and were twice supernumeraries at the Washington National Opera. Talented composer, librettist, pianist, and lawyer Derrick Wang wrote a comic opera titled *Scalia/Ginsburg,* which has been performed, in full or in part, in various venues. In his preface to the published libretto,* Justice Scalia described as a high point in his life a spring 2009 evening at the Washington National Opera's Ball held at the British Ambassador's Residence. In an elegant and spacious room, Justice Scalia joined two professional tenors at the piano for a medley of songs. He called it the famous Three Tenors performance. Both on and off the bench, Justice Scalia was a convivial, exuberant performer.

Most of all, I prized the rare talent Justice Scalia possessed for making even the most sober judge smile. When we sat side by side on the D.C. Circuit, I occasionally pinched myself hard to avoid uncontrollable laughter in response to one of his quips. On the Supreme Court, where we were separated by a few seats, notes he sent my way elicited a similar reaction.

This collection of speeches and writings captures the mind, heart, and faith of a Justice who has left an indelible stamp on the Supreme Court's jurisprudence and on the teaching and practice of law. The work of his fine hand will both inspire and challenge legions of judges and advocates. If our friendship encourages others to appreciate that some very good people have ideas with which we disagree, and that, despite differences, people of goodwill can pull together for the well-being of the institutions we serve and our country, I will be overjoyed, as I am confident Justice Scalia would be.

Ruth Bader Ginsburg
Associate Justice
Supreme Court of the United States
July 2017

---

* The libretto, as originally written, appears in 38 *Columbia Journal of Law & the Arts* 237 (2015).

INTRODUCTION

By Christopher J. Scalia

The speaker at my high school graduation was my father, Justice Antonin Scalia. Although he delivered a fine speech, one that's included in this collection, he did not deliver the line I remember most vividly from that day—I did.

It was my responsibility to introduce him with a brief speech of my own, a task I approached with all the intensity you'd expect from an eighteen-year-old determined to impress his classmates. I told the assembled throng about my father's personal life: his immigrant father, his schoolteacher mother, his marriage to Maureen McCarthy, their nine children (gasps from the crowd!). I covered his degrees from Georgetown and Harvard Law School, his work for presidential administrations, his time as a law professor at the University of Virginia and the University of Chicago. I may have mentioned in passing that he'd been nominated to the United States Supreme Court by President Ronald Reagan in 1986 and confirmed by the Senate, 98–0. I cracked a joke about him gaining an unparalleled knowledge of the Constitution from his eighth child (that would be me).

I felt pretty good about the performance as I came down the final stretch. All that was left was to say his name and shake his hand as he approached the lectern.

"Ladies and gentlemen," I said, "please join me in welcoming Justice Anto—." Suddenly my tongue swelled up, my mouth tightened, and I couldn't control what either did as I heard myself mispronounce my own father's first name. I don't even remember how I mispronounced it, because I've never rewatched the speech.

At the time it felt like I turned his first name into a ten-syllable tongue twister.

My only consolations are that I managed to get his last name right and that President Reagan also mispronounced "Antonin" when he nominated my father to the Court. Dad himself sometimes said that he wasn't really sure how the name was supposed to be pronounced. "That's why my nickname is Nino." (For the record, he pronounced it "AN-tuh-nin.")

If I remember correctly, my father began his speech by returning the favor, pretending to forget my name. At least I think he was pretending. It's not easy remembering the names of nine children.

The rest of my father's speech proceeded without incident, which was no surprise. Steve Martin once observed, "Some people have a way with words. Other people, um . . . not have way." Dad had a way.

I heard him deliver a handful of speeches and was always entranced by just how good he was from the podium. The speech I remember most vividly was the one he delivered during his visit to the University of Wisconsin–Madison in the spring of 2001, when I was a graduate student there. This was only a few months after *Bush v. Gore*, and leading up to the event the local progressive paper ran an editorial condemning his role in the decision. This was when Tony Soprano was still a waste management consultant in New Jersey, so the paper decided it would be clever to call Justice Antonin Scalia, the first Italian American on the Supreme Court, "Tony the Fixer." A few protesters gathered outside of the lecture hall holding large pictures of Hitler, Stalin, and Scalia. Not too bad by Madison standards.

The speech itself was packed, of course. My father spoke about the failings of the so-called living-Constitution theory as well as the strengths (and shortcomings) of his own originalist interpretation. It included one of my favorite passages, which I transcribe roughly here:

> To take another example from popular culture, there was a while back an ad on television for Prego tomato sauce. The

husband in this ad asks his wife, "Are you gonna use this store-bought sauce? Aren't you gonna make it yourself? Does it have oregano in it?"

"It's in there!"

"Yeah, but does it have pepper?"

"It's in there!"

"Does it have olive oil?"

"It's in there!"

"What about basil?"

"It's in there!"

We got that kind of a Constitution now. You want a right to an abortion? It's in there! You want a right to die? It's in there! Whatever is good and true and beautiful, it's in there! Never mind the text, it's irrelevant.

This analogy is custom-made for someone like me, who never studied law and spent a lot of time camped out in front of the television. It was an effective way to lighten the mood while conveying a serious point and to reassure non-experts that this was a topic they could understand.

Dad delivered hundreds of speeches over his career, around the United States and across five continents. (The trips he and my mother made to foreign countries over the summer were big events in my family: prime opportunities for my brothers and sisters to "have a few friends over.") He spoke to legal organizations, of course, and those speeches include some of the sharpest and most concise articulations of his legal philosophy. These are speeches that lawyers still talk about, and that helped change the course of American jurisprudence. Shortly after my father died, Neil Gorsuch recalled hearing him speak nearly thirty years before, "remember[ing] as if it were yesterday sitting in a law school audience." One year after he shared that memory, Gorsuch filled my father's vacancy on the Supreme Court.

But my father didn't speak only to lawyers. And even when his subject was the law, his language was tailored to lay audiences in a way that his court opinions, as readable as they are, simply could not be. Opinions are written in large part for specialists, laden with notes and references. My father's speeches are more intimate and direct. Speeches also allowed him to reveal insights into his personal feelings and tastes in ways that legal opinions never can, or at least never should.

Of course, my father's speeches were excellent in part because he was such a good writer. His legal opinions are often cited, studied, and quoted because they are remarkably direct and accessible. He explained the complex clearly, and that helped him influence the direction of American jurisprudence. The journalist Andrew Ferguson has said that "anyone who has spent pleasant hours with his judicial opinions will find it possible to imagine Scalia, in another milieu, becoming a distinguished writer of almost any kind." One of the most significant literary scholars of the past half century, Stanley Fish, analyzed one of Dad's zingers in a book that also included analysis of Jane Austen, Laurence Sterne, and other literary greats.

I once asked my father if writing was easy for him. "No," he said. "It's hard as hell." That was a relief. If even he struggled with the craft, then maybe there's hope for all of us. In a speech he delivered to a group of legal writers ("Writing Well"), my father elaborates on the answer he gave me. The main things separating ordinary writing from good writing are indeed "time and sweat"— writing, revising, rethinking, and writing again.

There is also what he calls "writing genius," which includes the ability to understand one's audience. This isn't the same as aiming to please. He once gave my brother Paul some counterintuitive public speaking advice: "Never tell them what they want to hear." Paul, who was deciding whether to study for the priesthood when my father said that, suspects that this was Dad's way of telling him how to be a good priest. Of course, Dad lived by this counsel, joking even before he was on the Supreme Court that the "endearing quality of saying the right thing at the wrong time is the secret of my popularity." Shortly before he passed away, for example, he delivered a speech to Dominican friars at a celebration of their eight-hundredth anniversary ("Natural Law"). The Dominicans count among their order the great St. Thomas Aquinas, author of the magisterial tract *Summa Theologiae* and one of the most important theologians in the history of the Catholic Church. Naturally, my father took the opportunity to criticize the saint's approach to legal interpretation, going so far as to read a passage from Aquinas and comparing it to something an activist judge would have written.

My father's approach wasn't contrarianism for its own sake. The point was to challenge listeners out of complacency, to inspire them not by affirming what they knew to be true, but by provoking them into reconsidering their preconceptions. It was the public-speaking equivalent of the Socratic method, which he applied as a law professor. Even my father's commencement addresses challenged in this way: they gave good advice, as such speeches should, but more importantly they aimed to dispel misperceptions and illusions, to feed students something more substantial than the empty calories of most graduation speeches.

As my father explains in this collection's "Original Meaning," he often would choose a topic to explore in speeches over the course of a year or so, refining it over time and adapting it for different audiences. These speeches, then, were opportunities for him to think through new areas of interest. They were also chances to convey his most deeply held legal theories and judicial philosophies to a variety of audiences. Some of the points you'll find in these speeches are ones he also made in his opinions: for example, his arguments about the separation of powers and proper role of judges appear in some of his best-known dissents. In speeches, though, he could convey his arguments more directly and more concisely, which makes them an ideal way for the people who don't read every Supreme Court opinion—that is, well-adjusted, normal people—to encounter the ideas that helped shape American legal thought.

Finally, Dad's speeches provided a chance for him to perform. My father was a ham. In his high school's production of *Macbeth* his senior year, he played the title role. As an undergraduate at Georgetown, he was president of the student theater group. (Other club alumni include John Barrymore, Eileen Brennan, and Bradley Cooper.) Along with his friend Justice Ginsburg, in 1994 and again in 2009 he appeared as an extra in the Washington National Opera's performance of Richard Strauss's *Ariadne auf Naxos*. He sang and played the piano at parties and was one of the best story and joke tellers I've ever heard. Giving speeches catered to those strengths and loves in a way that opinions never did. The charm and gregariousness that drew so many people—including ideological adversaries—to him are prominent throughout this collection.

READING THESE SPEECHES often brought me a welcome sensation of déjà vu. I heard him retell his favorite stories, ones he was always happy to share at the dinner table, like the Shakespeare principle he proposes in "Natural Law." He often told me about his freshman composition teacher, Professor Orr, when I complained about teaching my own freshman composition courses. Again, he knew his audience: it was his way of encouraging me to maintain high standards and reminding me of the importance of a good teacher's influence. And when I mentioned that I was studying Ralph Waldo Emerson, he gave me a copy of his speech about legal canards to help me understand the shortcomings of the transcendentalist's famous remark about a foolish consistency.

Other passages I had heard from my siblings before encountering them here. My father had often told my older siblings about his muffed answer during his oral exams at Georgetown. And the professional disappointment he recounts in "Religious Retreats"— being passed over for solicitor general, a blessing in disguise—is something he also related to my brother Matt to cheer him up after a letdown of his own. I didn't know the story myself until Matt shared it with me right after Dad's funeral, as he, my sister, and I stood with our hands on Dad's coffin, unwilling to leave it, trading accounts of how his advice and encouragement had shaped our lives.

Working on this book, I encountered experiences I didn't know my father had and interests I didn't realize we shared. While reading speeches for consideration I discovered one in which he described the excitement he felt conducting legal research: "the process of *looking* for that answer, the process of *research*, is a process that stimulates the mind. New analogies occur, new avenues of inquiry come to mind, new insights are afforded." This passage struck me because it was so like a lecture I used to deliver to my own students when I was a professor. Some similarities between law and literature had always been clear to me (the attention to language, the importance of writing, the lucrative hourly rates), but I'd never considered that my father and I also shared a love of research. That realization thrilled me—until it saddened me that I had never talked to him about that shared joy.

I also learned about his childhood. Although he had shared stories about playing stickball in Queens, he never went into much detail about the different ways he and his neighborhood friends entertained themselves. Perhaps, like me, you'll see these scenes play out in black and white, like something from a classic film. And perhaps, like me, you'll find his tributes to departed friends especially powerful. In those, my father conveys what he admired in other people and what he most appreciated in personal relationships. His sorrow at the death of one friend particularly moved me, as my father expresses regret at "not . . . say[ing] goodbye. But I have the sure hope that I will see him again where old friends will have an eternity to catch up and make amends." These words mirror my own feelings after the death of the man who wrote them.

MY PARTNER IN the editorial process, Edward Whelan, clerked for my father on the Supreme Court during the 1991–92 term. He knows my father's legal opinions as well as anyone and has long admired him as a man. (The admiration was mutual.) We were eager to work on this collection because we think it's important that Americans have an accessible way to encounter Justice Scalia's ideas and personality. Ed and I sorted through hundreds of files and documents, as well as dozens of floppy disks, that we received from Dad's secretary. We were surprised by the number of speeches, the breadth of their subject matter, and their consistently high quality. Neither of us knew that he'd delivered so many speeches that weren't about legal subjects, or to so many groups unassociated with the law. The sheer variety of the material and the many surprises we encountered made the process a joy.

When I began reading through Dad's speeches, I was eager to find the one he delivered in Madison, and assumed that would be an easy task, as he delivered variations of it from the mid-1990s through the early 2000s. I dug through every address about constitutional interpretation, used every relevant search term I could imagine ("Prego," "Ragu," "store-bought tomato sauce"), to no avail. It turned out that he wasn't speaking from a prepared text.

As with his legal opinions, clerks would sometimes conduct the research and write initial drafts—though they would often require more guidance with the speeches than with the opinions, as they would typically know less about my father's desired approach to the subject matter going into the drafting process. My father would then substantially revise the drafts into his own voice and argument before giving his speech.

For the speech he gave in Madison, though, he used only a bare-bones series of prompts—known simply as The Outline, though that's giving it too much credit—which he took to every speaking engagement, even if he was delivering a different, unrelated set of remarks. His assistant Angela Frank still laughs at the idea of Justice Scalia taking this security blanket with him, but she was always sure to have multiple copies available and a copy ready for every trip he took.

"You have The Outline?" he'd ask.

"Of course," she'd say, and show him where.

Ed and I could hardly believe The Outline when we saw it for ourselves. As we explain in the headnote to "Interpreting the Constitution," it was only a single sheet of paper with a few words typed (and one misspelled) on it—in a font that suggests it had originally been composed on a typewriter—and a series of fragmented scribbles and names of people. It definitely did not include any notes about tomato sauce or television commercials.

Most of the speeches we read were already quite polished, and a handful had been previously published, so the most challenging task for us was choosing which ones to include. Once we had a long list of contenders, we corrected glitches and typos (as Ed pointed out, Dad never won any spelling bees). There was also some overlap between speeches, as Dad often referred to stories, speeches, or writings of which he was especially fond. You'll find that he more than once discusses advice his father gave him, the Soviet Union's bill of rights, George Washington's Farewell Address, and passages from Robert Bolt's play about Thomas More, *A Man for All Seasons*. We have maintained some repetition, both so that we don't mar the speeches and so that they convey what really mattered to him.

We organized the speeches thematically, beginning with a series about national and ethnic character. These touch on his thoughts about immigration, assimilation, and American exceptionalism. Far afield, perhaps, from the subject matter for which he is best known, but which demonstrate his deep love for America and the many peoples who compose it.

In the speeches collected in "On Living and Learning," my father discusses some of his favorite pastimes and pursuits, his childhood, and his legendary (or is it mythical?) "athletic prowess." A former professor, he also discusses the importance of different types of education: civic, legal, liberal, and religious. The original audiences for these ranged from turkey hunters in Nashville to performing artists and students at the Juilliard School in New York City. This section demonstrates the breadth of his interests, as well as the variety of people whose company he enjoyed, and vice versa.

My father's deep Catholic faith and his articulate explanations of the proper role of religion in American life were a significant reason many people—not only Catholics—admired him, and why many others did not. The speeches in "On Faith" cover the role of religious belief in public life, the separation of church and state, and the place of Christians in the sophisticated modern world. Throughout, he expounds upon his simultaneous beliefs that religion plays an honored and important role in American democratic life, but that it is not the role of a judge to apply his religious (or other) convictions.

The "On Law" section naturally takes up the most real estate in this collection, but we were careful to select only speeches that we thought nonlawyers would appreciate. Here he grapples with some of the most significant topics he faced in his career as a judge and clarifies his understanding of the Constitution and the law. This section includes a number of speeches in which Dad explains originalism and textualism—the twin methods of jurisprudence he was instrumental in returning to the mainstream of American legal thought—and others that deal with those intruders he sought to expel: the "living Constitution," foreign law, and legislative history. He also discusses the role of dissents, the place of the Court in American society, the qualities of a good judge, what he calls the "wondrous durability of the Constitution," and the dangers of judges as "pioneering policymakers." Throughout this section, Dad articulates his admiration for America's institutions, his concern for its legal system, and his humble opinion of his own vocation.

"On Virtue and the Public Good" explores the qualities that ennoble human behavior and sustain societal health, including tradition, courage (a trait he had in abundance), and what he calls "the triad of human perfection": knowledge, judgment, and character. He emphasizes the last as the most significant trait throughout these speeches. Here is also a moving reflection on the Holocaust, in which he reminds us that there exist "absolute, uncompromisable standards of human conduct."

The collection ends with speeches about individuals familiar and obscure. His remarks about major figures in American history demonstrate his profound admiration for them. His touching (and sometimes funny) tributes to dear friends illustrate the variety of remarkable people he was fortunate to know.

It's worth mentioning that my father didn't always stick to the text of his speeches. The videos we've seen indicate that he was happy to improvise and would sometimes use the text more as a guide than as a script. Fidelity to text, I'm sure he would say, is a judicial duty that flows from separation-of-powers principles, but not a rigid principle binding the speech giver.

A brief note on citations: my father prepared few of these speeches for publication, so many of them had only informal citations. Because this volume is not aimed at an academic audience, we have tried to declutter the text by eliminating unnecessary citations. We trust that the reader will recognize that my father was drawing on secondary sources, rather than doing his own original research, in, for example, his biographical details on George Washington, Abraham Lincoln, and William Howard Taft.

SEVERAL MONTHS BEFORE my father died, I dropped by my parents' house to borrow something. He was in the basement, watching an old western.

"Sit down," he said from his recliner. "Join me for a cigar."

It was a tempting offer, but I couldn't. Besides, there would be other opportunities—I had just moved back to the D.C. area and would see him often.

"Take a cigar with you," he said. I did.

Although reading through these speeches doesn't quite make up for that missed opportunity to spend more time with him in what turned out to be his final months of life, it did make me hear his voice again in all its warmth, wisdom, and humor. I think I speak for Ed when I say that working on this collection has been a moving experience. It has been an honor to help family, friends, and colleagues re-experience a man they admired, and to allow others to encounter for the first time someone whose influence they have heard about and whom they want to understand for themselves. Regardless of our own contributions, we know that these speeches will help his great American legacy endure.

On the American People and Ethnicity

"What makes an American . . . is not the name or the blood or even the place of birth, but the belief in the principles of freedom and equality that this country stands for."

What Makes an American

In October 1986—one month after he became the first Italian American to sit on the Supreme Court—Justice Scalia received the National Italian American Foundation's award for public service. In the course of explaining why he was proud of his Italian heritage, he drew a broader lesson about what makes an American.

My fellow Italian Americans:

I am happy to provide the occasion for this celebration of our common Italian ancestry. You do me great honor this evening—and it is an honor that by all rights I must share with many others. My parents and relatives, of course—my teachers (some of whom are here this evening)—all of those who have had an influence on my life. One debt I would like particularly to acknowledge is to the many Italian Americans in many fields of endeavor, but particularly in politics, who by their example of ability and integrity made it easy for someone with an Italian name to be considered for high office. Even the most successful of us are midgets standing on the shoulders of others—and I want to acknowledge my special indebtedness to the Peter Rodinos and Frank Annunzios and John Volpes who made my path an easy one. It is a great responsibility to be readily identifiable with a particular ethnic group. I am where I am in part because my predecessors bore that responsibility well. I hope to do the same.

I want to say a few words this evening about why we are proud of our Italian heritage—and about why that pride makes us no less than 100 percent Americans.

Three of the world's great civilizations flourished in the lands you and I came from. The southern part of Italy, Magna Grecia, was one of the most important parts of ancient Greece—and Syracuse was the largest city of that civilization. The Roman Empire began on the Italian peninsula and spread its influence throughout the Western world. And the Italian city-states of the Renaissance were the beginning of the modern world. We are also a race that has lived under many foreign rulers—the Normans, the Saracens, the French, the Spanish, and the Austrians. So we bear with us the knowledge, learned the hard way, of how difficult it is to create a great society, and how easy it is, through foolish discord at home or failure to confront threats from abroad, to lose it.

The Italian immigrants who came to this country possessed, it seems to me, four characteristics in a particularly high degree—characteristics that continue to be displayed, by and large, by their descendants. First, a capacity for hard work—whether on the lines of the railroads whose construction brought many of them here, or in the machine shops and garment factories of the industrial East, or in the fisheries and vineyards of California. They were successful in that work, as is evident from the fact that the last time I looked at the figures their descendants have the highest per capita income of any ethnic group (including Anglo-Saxons) except the Chinese and Japanese. Second, a love of family. The closeness of the Italian family is legendary—it is one of our great inheritances. Third, a love of the church. Italian American priests and Italian American parishioners have—with a good deal of help, it must be acknowledged, from our Irish co-religionists in the East and Hispanic Americans in the West—made Roman Catholicism one of the major religions in a country where it began as a tiny minority. And fourth, perhaps arising from the first three—the product of hard work, a secure family environment, and a confident knowledge of one's place within God's scheme of things—a love of the simple physical pleasures of human existence: good music, good food, and good—or even pretty good—wine.

We have shared those qualities with our fellow Americans—as they have shared the particular strengths of their heritages with us. And the product is the diverse and yet strangely cohesive society called America. It is a remarkable but I think demonstrable phenomenon that our attachment to and affection for our particular heritage does not drive our society apart, but helps to bind it together. Like an intricate tapestry, the fabric of our society is made up of many different threads that run in different directions, but all meet one another to form the whole. The common bond I have with those who share my Italian ancestry prevents me from readily being drawn into enmity with those people on the basis of, for example, politics. If I were, for example, a Republican, I could not think *too* ill of Democrats—because, after all, Pete Rodino is a Democrat and he's a *paisan*. And of course we all have loyalties based on factors other than our ethnic heritage that bind us together with other Americans—we go to the same church as they, or belong to the same union, or went to the same college. It is these intersecting loyalties to small segments of the society that bind the society together.

So I say you can be proud of your Italian heritage—as the Irish can of theirs, and the Jews of theirs—without feeling any less than 100 percent American because of that.

While taking pride in what we have brought to America, we should not fail to be grateful for what America has given to us. It has given us, first and foremost, a toleration of how *different* we were when we first came to these shores. What makes an American, it has told us, is not the name or the blood or even the place of birth, but the belief in the principles of freedom and equality that this country stands for.

There have, to be sure, been instances and periods of discrimination against Italian Americans, just as there have been against all other new arrivals. But that was the aberration, the departure from the norm, the failure to live up to the principles on which this republic was founded. If you do not believe that, you need look no further than the actions of the greatest American of them all, the Father of our Country, George Washington. During his first term in office as president, Washington wrote a letter that is a model of Americanism, addressed to the Hebrew Congregation of Newport,

Rhode Island. This blue-blooded, aristocratic Virginian assured that small community that his administration, his country, would brook no discrimination against that small and politically impotent community. And that the children of Abraham, as he put it, were welcome in this country, to live in peace and never to have fear.

Italian View of the Irish

Justice Scalia liked to joke that, with his Irish American wife, Maureen, he had a mixed marriage. In these St. Patrick's Day remarks to the Society of the Friendly Sons of St. Patrick in New York City in 1988, he celebrated the appealing qualities of the Irish.

———

I notice that this assembly is in good spirits, and I cannot help observing that that may be attributable in part to the fact that a fair quantity of spirits has been externally applied. Being in the midst of such spirituous conviviality has, of course, placed a special burden on me—not only because I am supposed always to be sober as a judge (or indeed, sober as a justice, which is presumably soberer), but also because I have carried throughout the entire evening the knowledge that I was supposed to stand up and demonstrate that quality by delivering a coherent address. Frankly, I have felt like the only designated driver for this entire assembly of partygoers—with the exception, of course, of the clergy.

I was frankly somewhat puzzled when I received the invitation to this august event. It is true that my aunt Rose married a man named O'Brien—who, I am sorry to say, is dead or I would have a much better collection of Irish stories for you this evening. It is also true that I myself married a McCarthy and have four-and-a-half Irish children, at last count. But still and all, that is a fairly tenuous Irish connection. I have concluded that the reason you invited me, instead of the Brennan, the O'Connor, or the Kennedy you fellows already have on the Supreme Court, is to get me to take my wife's name, so that you can claim four out of nine. Tomorrow the world. Well, now that you have seen me, I am sure you are persuaded of the folly of this project. No one will believe it.

But having undertaken to give this address, I had to figure out what to talk about. I quickly decided, of course, to talk about . . . twenty minutes—the best formula for after-dinner speeches being what one of the Jesuits I had in high school advised was the best advice regarding kissing among unmarried couples: *leviter, breviter.* For the younger clergy in the audience, that is Latin for "lightly and briefly." I have reason to believe that that advice has been no more effective for after-dinner speakers than it has been for unmarried couples.

Anyway, having resolved the time issue I still needed an appropriate subject. I went across the street to get some advice from my friend Daniel Patrick Moynihan, who seemed to me a likely source of expertise. He recommended that I discuss the application of the negative Commerce Clause in recent Supreme Court jurisprudence. I told him only an Irishman could make that subject interesting. I decided, instead, that what I would talk about is the Irish, seen from an Italian point of view.

Now that might not be as useless an enterprise as you might think. You people are really too close to yourselves to understand you; a view from a distance is sometimes more informative. I am not at too great a distance, of course, having grown up in New York and gone to high school at Xavier down on 16th Street— where the Regiment trooped out every St. Patrick's Day to be the second unit (after the Fighting 69th) in the parade. Just for fun I got out my old yearbook to look at the class of 1953. There were a fair number of names like Armentano and Antonicelli, Bonomo, Bugoni, and Cercio. But when you get to the Ms it reads Mahaney, Mahoney, McAvoy, McCarthy, McCorry, McGroddy, McGuire, McGurn, McHugh, McMahon, McNierney, and McNulty. Sounds like McNamara's band. So I know whereof I speak.

Now, the first thing you Irish should know about yourselves is that you're what are called *ethnics.* A lot of us didn't even realize this when we were growing up in New York. We thought we were just Greeks and Italians and Jews and Irish and all the wonderful diversity of Americans that made for good Pat O'Brien, William Bendix–type war movies. But all the time we were ethnics. Now there is not a whole lot of use in being an ethnic, unless you're running for office or perhaps going through a confirmation hearing. But if you are one, I think you will agree that you ought to know it. So what we are talking about here is really that subspecies of *Homo ethnicus* known as *Homo hibernicus.*

The first appealing quality about the Irish, as seen by us subtle Italians, is their bluntness. There is very little beating about the bush with them. You always know where you stand. My wife, Maureen, has this endearing quality to a preeminent degree. An example that occurs to me is not really Maureen's own line, but a cartoon obviously inspired by an Irishman, which she left on the breakfast table shortly after I had been confirmed to the Supreme Court. It shows a stern-looking, paunchy fellow (which increasingly fits my description) sitting at the breakfast table across from his wife, reading the paper, and Maureen—or I mean the wife in the cartoon—is saying, "While you *are* a conservative jurist who believes in judicial restraint, you are also a louse."

Bluntness is important not only because it lets people know where they stand, but also because it toughens them up. Life is not an enterprise for sissies; the Irish know that, and they treat both themselves and others with a kind of benevolent roughness designed to prepare them for the world. This was brought home to me on the first day of my exposure to what might be called a substantially Irish world—my first day in class at Xavier. Scalia, then a thirteen-year-old, had taken the subway from Queens, walked into a strange classroom with a lot of strange faces, wearing a strange military uniform of dress blues. My new homeroom teacher, Father Tom Matthews, an Irishman if there ever was one, went down the roster of the class, calling out each cadet's name to see what he looked like. He came to Antonin Scalia. He mispronounced the "Antonin"; everybody does; actually, I'm not sure how it should be pronounced. Anyway, I shall never forget the first benevolently toughening Irish words he said to me: "Who's your patron saint?"

Another characteristic of the *Homo hibernicus* is his constancy, in both friendships and in enmities. If I may be permitted a political observation, that is one of the problems Republicans have had in weaning the Irish away from the Democratic Party. The story is told of a speech Teddy Roosevelt was once giving, in which he was repeatedly heckled by an Irishman standing in the back, who kept shouting, "I'm a Democrat!" Teddy, who was pretty quick-witted, finally decided he would engage the fellow, so he asked, "Why are you a Democrat?" And the heckler replied, "My grandfather was a Democrat, my father was a Democrat, and I'm a Democrat!" "Well," said Teddy, "if your grandfather was a jackass, and your father was a jackass, what would you be?" "A Republican," came the reply.

This constancy is, as I say, displayed toward enemies as well as toward friends. One of the most characteristic Irish prayers is the following:

> *May those who love us love us,*
> *And those that don't love us,*
> *May God turn their hearts.*
> *And if He doesn't turn their hearts,*
> *May He turn their ankles,*
> *So we'll know them by their limping.*

Another characteristic of the Irish—perhaps their most endearing—is their lightheartedness. A result, no doubt, of the depth of their belief in the hereafter. It's only a short time here, so there's no use taking it all too seriously. This attitude causes them to be quite careless of time. The story is told of a tourist in Dublin whose watch had stopped. He asks several passersby for the time, but none of them has a watch. Finally he goes up to a policeman and says, "Excuse me, Officer, could you tell me the exact time?" The policeman says, "The exact time, sir?" "Yes, the exact time." The policeman ponders a minute, looks skyward, and asks, "Was it the exact time you wanted?" "Yes, that's right, the exact time." "Well, sir, it's exactly between one and two."

This same attitude accounts for the uncanny Irish attitude toward illness and death. You know the sort of thing: "It wasn't the cough that carried him off, it was the coffin they carried him off in." There is surely no other race that has so many jokes about bodies and coffins and such. Because, as I say, it's only natural and no big deal. When they had the wake for my wife's uncle Dave in South Boston a few years back, my wife's mother, Mary Fitzgerald McCarthy, was sitting in the home when one of Dave's elderly friends came in, obviously somewhat confused and befuddled about where he was to go. Before he could even say, "I'm sorry for your trouble," Mary McCarthy said, as natural as could be, "Ah, you'll be lookin' for Dave—he's up front."

Another characteristic of *Homo hibernicus*—I know you would be annoyed if I did not mention it—is quickness of intellect. Now I must admit that on this point you Irish may be better judges of yourselves than an outsider like me would be. Because the Irish have all sorts of ways of seeming to be knowledgeable when they are not. One, of course, is lying. Any other group would take offense at that—but I am sure that this gathering will proudly agree that nobody in the world can tell a glorious, toweringly false tale as well as an Irishman. An Italian lie is often more subtle and deceptive, more likely to be believed. But if it is *not* believed, it is seen as a sneaky, unworthy, disreputable thing. The wonderful thing about a proper Irish lie is that it does not *matter* if it is believed. It is such a bold, courageous, imaginative invention that, even when you see through it, you are so impressed with the quality of mind that could concoct such nonsense that it is impossible to have anything but admiration for the author. That is the great strength of the Irish lie: It does not matter whether it is believed or not.

Another reason I think I am unqualified to gauge precisely the quickness of Irish intellect is that when an Irishman does not know the answer to a question, he is most unlikely to admit that. If all else fails, he will simply ask a question in return. I once asked Chief Judge Howard Markey of the Federal Circuit, "Why does an Irishman always answer a question with a question?" And Markey said, "Why do you say that?"

Of course the questioner is sometimes fortunate to receive only

a question in response. Another device that *Homo hibernicus* sometimes employs to avoid an answer is to suggest the absurdity of the
question. The story is told of the Irish litigator, in the days of occupation, arguing a weak case before an English judge. "Counsel,"
intoned the judge, "have you never heard of the maxim *'Ratio est
legis anima. Ratione legis mutata, mutatur et lex'*?" "Sure, me lord," said
the Irishman, "in the hills of Kilkenny we talk of little else."

The last notable thing I want to mention about the Irish is their
way with words. I've always wondered if they spoke Gaelic as well
as they speak English. It is a beauty to hear. First of all, just the
sound of the words. One of the great tragedies of modern America
is the disappearance of the Irish brogue. When I was growing up
in New York, it was all around. I recall in particular a fellow who
used to be on the radio often, Michael Quill, head of the New York
Transport Workers Union. He had a brogue so thick that we Italians could scarcely make out what he was saying, though it was
clear that he cared a lot about it and it was important. Nowadays
the genuine Irish accent is so rarely encountered that the comedi-
ans can't even mimic it very well anymore. I suggest the Congress
should look into this important matter.

It's not only the Irish's way with the sound, of course, it's also
their way with the content. What is technically known as the Blarney touch. Perhaps some of you do not know the origin of the term
"blarney." It is the name, of course, of a castle near Cork, built
in 1446 by Cormac McCarthy and containing the famous Blarney
stone, reputed to confer eloquence upon all who kiss it. But the use
of the term to mean smooth, wheedling flattery comes, I am told,
from—of all people—Queen Elizabeth I, who had some dealings
with one of the descendants of Cormac McCarthy, Cormac Mac-
Dermott McCarthy, Lord of Blarney. The Queen had repeatedly
pressed the lord to abandon the traditional system whereby Irish
clans elected their chiefs, and to take tenure of his lands from the
Crown. While seeming to agree, the Lord of Blarney postponed
fulfillment of his promise from day to day with "fair words and soft
speech," causing Queen Elizabeth to snort, "This is all Blarney.
What he says he never means."

ONLY IN AMERICA

Justice Scalia "greatly revered Jews and Jewish tradition," observes Nathan Lewin, an Orthodox Jew who was a Harvard law school classmate and good friend of the justice. That admiration is evident in this excerpt from a March 1987 speech to the Jewish organization B'nai B'rith in Washington, D.C.

Lewin was struck by Scalia's "keen interest in Jewish learning" and "the frequent references in his opinions to the Talmud and other Jewish sources." For example, Scalia wrote in one opinion:

A Talmudic maxim instructs with respect to the Scripture: "Turn it over, and turn it over, for all is therein." Divinely inspired text may contain the answers to all earthly questions, but the Due Process Clause most assuredly does not.

Scalia was also the first justice to use the familiar Yiddish word chutzpah *in an opinion.*

———

I am delighted to be here this evening. Washington is becoming more and more like New York. Just last Wednesday I was at the dinner of the Friendly Sons of St. Patrick, and here I am at B'nai B'rith. As Irving Kristol said some years ago, in reference to the election of a Jewish mayor of Dublin, "Only in America!"

Last year, in cleaning out the attic of my parents' home after their deaths, I came across the graduation photo from P.S. 13, Queens. It had to be there, of course. I was the only child, and my mother saved anything I had ever come near. She was the prototypical Italian Mother, which you should all be familiar with because it is a species of the genus Mediterranean Mother, to which the Jewish Mother also belongs. Anyway, I had forgotten what a melting pot of kids that school was: Irish and Italian and German and Jewish and Greek. It was a wonderful way to grow up, and about that one can truly say "only in America."

One of the strengths of this great country, one of the reasons we really are a symbol of light and of hope for the world, is the way in which people of different faiths, different races, different national origins, have come together and learned—not merely to tolerate one another, because I think that is too stingy a word for what we have achieved—but to respect and love one another.

Without pretending that all vestiges of anti-Semitism have been eliminated from our society (they assuredly have not been), I think it is fair to say that we have made enormous strides since the days before Louis Brandeis was appointed to the Supreme Court in 1916. It would be foolish to think, however, that it doesn't take an effort to retain the progress we have made (never mind to improve upon it). Modern man—perhaps mesmerized by the phenomenon of constant progress in the physical sciences— tends to think that constant progress in morality and ethics is also inevitable. That education will inevitably produce virtue, and every day in every way we will get better and better. One would think that Nazi Germany was a sufficient demonstration of the fallacy of that thinking. In the 1920s and 1930s Germany was the leader of the world in most areas you could name—the physical sciences, historical scholarship, music, philosophy, public education. The most sobering fact about the Holocaust is that it was *there*, and not in some backward, underdeveloped country, that it occurred.

And the fact is, of course, that in this country as well, toleration for Jews, and for other minority groups, has not been a record of unremitting progress. I don't know how many of you are familiar with George Washington's Letter to the Hebrew Congregation in Newport, Rhode Island. Every American—and especially every American Jew—should be, because it demonstrates what a spirit of toleration animated the beginnings of our nation. It's a short letter and—with apologies if I'm repeating something you already know by heart—let me read it to you.

To the Hebrew Congregation in Newport, Rhode Island

[August 18, 1790]

Gentlemen:

While I receive with much satisfaction your address replete with expressions of affection and esteem, I rejoice in the opportunity of assuring you that I shall always retain a grateful remembrance of the cordial welcome I experienced in my visit to Newport from all classes of Citizens.

The reflection on the days of difficulty and danger which are past is rendered the more sweet from a consciousness that they are succeeded by days of uncommon prosperity and security. If we have the wisdom to make the best use of the advantages with which we are now favored, we cannot fail, under the just administration of a good government, to become a great and happy people.

The Citizens of the United States of America have a right to applaud themselves for having given to Mankind examples of an enlarged and liberal policy, a policy worthy of imitation. All possess alike liberty of conscience and immunities of citizenship. It is now no more that toleration is spoken of, as if it was by the indulgence of one class of people, that another enjoyed the exercise of their inherent natural rights. For happily the Government of the United States, which gives to bigotry no sanction, to persecution no assistance requires only that they who live under its protection should demean themselves as good citizens, in giving it on all occasions their effectual support.

It would be inconsistent with the frankness of my character not to avow that I am pleased with your favorable opinion of my administration, and fervent wishes for my felicity.

May the children of the Stock of Abraham, who dwell in this land, continue to merit and enjoy the good will of the other inhabitants, while everyone shall sit in safety under his own vine and fig tree, and there shall be none to make him afraid.

May the Father of all mercies scatter light and not darkness in our paths, and make us all in our several vocations useful here, and in his own due time and way everlastingly happy.

One wonders if some later presidents, after the era of the Know-Nothings in the mid-nineteenth century, would have written such a letter. I doubt it.

So that is one message I would like to leave with you—that it's a constant struggle which cannot be neglected, and that backsliding is possible. For this group, that is probably preaching to the choir (if I may use a peculiarly inapt metaphor).

AMERICAN VALUES
AND EUROPEAN VALUES

Founded in the 1950s by West German chancellor Konrad Adenauer and French prime minister Antoine Pinay, Le Cercle is a group of European and American parliamentarians, diplomats, intelligence officials, bankers, and business leaders. Speaking at a meeting of Le Cercle in Washington, D.C., in June 2007, Justice Scalia sketched some fundamental differences between Americans and Europeans.

———

The question I have been asked to address today is: "Does America have different values from Europe?" My answer is simple: "Absolutely." But since I am supposed to speak for closer to an hour, allow me to elaborate. Before I do, though, let me make two more prefatory remarks: First, I am an American. Thus, the remarks that I make unapologetically favor my own country's ways, so you might want to take them with the appropriate grain of salt. Nothing in my speech, nor the blunt manner in which I deliver it, should detract from the centuries of warm relations our countries have enjoyed. Second, I would like to point out that I am far from the first person to address the topic at hand. My speech will therefore borrow the ideas of others, including in particular one perceptive Frenchman who visited the United States in the early 1800s.

Many Americans like to think of the United States as the prototypical Western nation, the culmination of centuries of European experience and wisdom. And many Europeans like to think of Americans as their close cousins—albeit reckless, loudmouthed cousins they're embarrassed to talk about at dinner parties. It is easy to forget, however, that the United States was settled primarily by people seeking, in one way or another, refuge from the ways of Europe. The men who founded our republic did not aspire to emulating Europeans at all—to the contrary, the project of drafting the American Constitution was largely about ensuring that the American people would never languish under the yoke of a European-style government. Our Founding Fathers collaborated to correct the numerous abuses and excesses they saw as plaguing the monarchies of the Old World, codifying the uniquely American values the settlers brought with them across the ocean.

Tocqueville explained this phenomenon back in 1835, in *Democracy in America*:

> [T]he origin of the Americans, or what I have called their point of departure, may be looked upon as the first and most efficacious cause to which the present prosperity of the United States may be attributed. The Americans had the chances of birth in their favor; and their forefathers imported that equality of condition and of intellect into the country whence the democratic republic has very naturally taken its rise. Nor was this all; for besides this republican condition of society, the early settlers bequeathed to their descendants the customs, manners, and opinions that contribute most to the success of a republic. When I reflect upon the consequences of this primary fact, I think I see the destiny of America embodied in the first Puritan who landed on those shores, just as the whole human race was represented by the first man.

If there was any thought absolutely foreign to the Founders of our country, surely it was the notion that we Americans should be governed the way Europeans are. And since our Constitution's ratification more than two hundred years ago, Americans' belief in the overarching values underlying that document has changed remarkably little. In those same two hundred years, European monarchies have been transformed into republics and parliamentary democracies, but the core values underlying those societies have remained worlds apart from those of Americans. To be sure, at a superficial level, we share many of the same goals: liberty, human rights, rule of law. But it's easy to agree on labels; the devil is in the details. And when it comes to the substance underlying those lofty ideals, Americans and Europeans are often hopelessly divided.

One need look only as far as the American Bill of Rights, which reads like a veritable laundry list of ways in which American values—primarily legal values—have differed from their European counterparts. The First Amendment, often considered by Americans to be the proverbial jewel in the crown that is the U.S. Constitution, staunchly defends freedom of speech. Americans have proven themselves to be willing to protect that freedom against all manner of detractors; willing to display the thick skin the First Amendment requires, and to recognize that the right to speak is far more important than a right not to be offended by what is spoken. Thus, when the Nazi Party of America planned to march through the streets of Skokie, Illinois, in 1977, its right to do so was supported by the American Civil Liberties Union and protected by the courts despite the repugnancy of its message.

To be sure, Europeans also value the freedom of speech and its importance to a functioning democracy. But they are far more willing to suppress a speaker's message when it might prove inflammatory to the populace at large, or even when it might be thought to erode national culture. Thus, laws such as those banning pro-Nazi propaganda that would never pass constitutional muster in the United States are not atypical in Europe. In November 2002, the Council of Europe approved an "Additional Protocol to the Convention on Cybercrime" that would make it illegal to distribute anything online which "advocates, promotes or incites hatred [or] discrimination." A spokesman for the United States Department of Justice said (quite correctly) that this country could not be a party to such a treaty because of the First Amendment.

The First Amendment also staunchly protects the freedom to practice one's religion, and freedom from the governmental establishment of religion. Thus, while Americans tend to believe strongly that religious *values* undergird government, and should be acknowledged to do so, they simultaneously believe that the government should play no role in *controlling* religion, either at the individual or institutional level. Europeans tend to invert these two positions, believing that politicians should keep their religious beliefs to themselves while (paradoxically) turning a blind eye to state/church institutional entanglement—hence, the Church of England and the Concordat between the Vatican and Italy favoring the Catholic Church. And when it comes to the individual freedom to practice one's religion, Europeans are less inclined to oppose laws denigrating that right, such as laws preventing Muslim women and girls from wearing headscarves in school.

The Second Amendment, which protects the right to bear arms, is another source of vast cultural difference between Americans and Europeans. Our Founders, having witnessed firsthand the indignities and abuses that overeager governments can impose on their own citizens, believed in a citizen's right to bear arms for protection against, among other things, the state itself. In number 46 of the *Federalist Papers*, James Madison speaks contemptuously of the governments of Europe, which are "afraid to trust the people with arms." Even today, whether for hobby, hunting, or self-defense, Americans believe strongly in the right to own a gun. There are nearly two hundred million guns in private American hands, or roughly one per person, dispersed among one-third to one-half of American households. By contrast, Europeans have largely abandoned their guns, preferring to trust the state with a monopoly on weaponry.

The Third Amendment says that soldiers should not be quartered in a citizen's house without the owner's consent. Okay, maybe we can all agree on that one.

But our differing values are front and center once again in amendments Four through Six, which outline various bedrock American principles of criminal procedure: right to a jury trial, right against self-incrimination, right against unreasonable searches or seizures, right to compulsory process, right to confrontation of adverse witnesses. I wrote an opinion for the Court a few years ago overruling an earlier case which had held that the Confrontation Clause is satisfied so long as the unconfronted testimony has "particularized guarantees of trustworthiness." The opinion points out that the Confrontation Clause was designed precisely to *prevent* a procedure considered trustworthy by continental European nations and others that followed the civil-law tradition. "Examinations of witnesses upon Interrogatories," wrote John Adams, "are only by the Civil Law. Interrogatories are unknown at common Law, and Englishmen and common Lawyers have an aversion to them if not an Abhorrence of them." As recently as 1993, France was still defending its use of *ex parte* testimony before the European Court of Human Rights, arguing that the defendant's accusers in a drug trafficking case had a "legitimate interest in remaining anonymous" and that the defendant's rights were adequately protected so long as the "judge held hearings which enabled him to satisfy himself" that the witnesses stood by their statements. I say with the utmost confidence that few Americans would want our life or liberty subject to the disposition of French or Italian criminal justice—not because those systems are unjust, but because we think ours is better.

The Seventh Amendment, providing for juries in civil trials, is another source of considerable difference between American and European legal values. Of all the values enshrined in the American Bill of Rights, the right to a lay civil jury has probably been the one least adopted by other nations. Europeans—even the British, who despite their common-law tradition have largely abandoned the practice—find lay civil juries to be outright untrustworthy (or at a minimum distasteful), preferring that their lawsuits be decided by judges and/or professional jurors. But the American legal culture is steeped in the belief that our conflicts should be resolved by our peers, those half a dozen to a dozen earnest men and women with somewhat confused-looking faces, sitting in the jury box, conscientiously trying to sort out the evidence and answer the questions that need no professional jurist to resolve: Who's telling the truth and who's lying? Who's been treated unfairly? Who's entitled to how much compensation? Indeed, American litigants who grew up watching *Perry Mason*, *L.A. Law*, or *Law & Order* would likely be shocked and dismayed if they were prevented from presenting their case to a lay jury and instead were forced to plead before a European-style professional venire.

Finally, we come to the Eighth Amendment, which protects Americans from cruel and unusual punishment. Surprisingly, for all the scorn that European governments show toward the United States' use of capital punishment, this is one area where the values of the American populace do not seem to differ greatly from their European counterparts: studies have shown that "[a]ctual public opinion in Europe . . . tends to *favor* capital punishment, in some countries at about the same rate as in the United States." The only reason the United States permits capital punishment while European nations prohibit it is that the predominant values of Americans have prevailed on this issue through the democratic process, whereas European governments have enforced the countermajoritarian values of the governing elite.

Outside of *legal* values, I believe there are three core social values that represent fundamental differences between Americans and Europeans: religious belief, reliance on the state, and belief in true democracy.

The most pronounced difference between European and American values, outside the legal context, arises in the area of faith. Many settlers who came to this continent were devoutly religious, searching for freedom to practice their particular brand of religion without interference from the state. They were not, however, in search of freedom *from* religion; quite to the contrary, Americans, from the settlers to the founding generation, believed vehemently in the importance of religion to the welfare of democracy and stressed the civic importance of passing religious values on to future generations. Benjamin Rush wrote that "[t]he only foundation for a useful education in a republic is to be laid in RELIGION. Without this, there can be no virtue, and without virtue, there can be no liberty, and liberty is the object and life of all republican governments." He continued:

> The complaints that have been made against religion, liberty
> and learning, have been, against each of them in a separate

state. Perhaps like certain liquors, they should only be used in state of mixture. They mutually assist in correcting the abuses, and in improving the good effects of each other. From the combined and reciprocal influence of religion, liberty and learning upon the morals, manners and knowledge of individuals, of these, upon government, and of government, upon individuals, it is impossible to measure the degrees of happiness and perfection to which mankind may be raised.

John Adams wrote that a republic "is only to be supported by pure Religion or Austere Morals. Public Virtue cannot exist in a Nation without private [Virtue], and public Virtue is the only Foundation of Republics." And, famously, George Washington's Farewell Address warned that our political prosperity depends on religion and morality:

Of all the dispositions and habits which lead to political prosperity, Religion and morality are indispensable supports. In vain would that man claim the tribute of Patriotism, who should labour to subvert these great Pillars of human happiness, these firmest props of the duties of Men and citizens. The mere Politician, equally with the pious man ought to respect and to cherish them. A volume could not trace all their connections with private and public felicity. Let it simply be asked where is the security for property, for reputation, for life, if the sense of religious obligation *desert* the oaths, which are the instruments of investigation in Courts of Justice? And let us with caution indulge the supposition, that morality can be maintained without religion. Whatever may be conceded to the influence of refined education on minds of peculiar structure, reason and experience both forbid us to expect that National morality can prevail in exclusion of religious principle.

As America's religiously grounded democracy developed and flourished over the ensuing two hundred years, Europeans began taking a very different tack. Out of the oppressively religious societies that many American settlers sought to escape developed a staunchly secularist continent, committed to the principle of an absolute separation of church and state (if in practice more than in name) and increasingly populated by people who do not believe in any religion. The modern-day statistics bear out these vast differences: In the United States today, 45 percent of people attend religious services at least once a week, compared to only 14 percent in the U.K., 8 percent in France, 40 percent in Italy (that estimate strikes me as very high), 25 percent in Spain, and 11 percent in Germany. And a remarkable 96 percent of Americans report a belief in God, compared to an average of only 67 percent in the European nations I just named. This fundamental disconnect in the importance that each society places on religion, the faith that each society places in God, permeates our social interactions and social policies.

Unlike our differences in religious values, which have deepened over time, the differences between Americans and Europeans regarding their attitude toward the state have existed ever since America's founding. For one thing, Americans take a far more active role in politics—not just voting but taking action to elect their candidates and foster their political views. Once again, Tocqueville observed the phenomenon most astutely:

> [T]he political activity that pervades the United States must be seen in order to be understood. No sooner do you set foot upon American ground than you are stunned by a kind of tumult; a confused clamor is heard on every side, and a thousand simultaneous voices demand the satisfaction of their social wants. Everything is in motion around you; here the people of one quarter of a town are met to decide upon the building of a church; there the election of a representative is going on; a little farther, the delegates of a district are hastening to the town in order to consult upon some local improvements; in another place, the laborers of a village quit their plows to deliberate upon the project of a road or a public school. . . . In some countries the inhabitants seem unwilling to avail themselves

of the political privileges which the law gives them; it would seem that they set too high a value upon their time to spend it on the interests of the community; and they shut themselves up in a narrow selfishness, marked out by four sunk fences and a quickset hedge. But if an American were condemned to confine his activity to his own affairs, he would be robbed of one half of his existence; he would feel an immense void in the life which he is accustomed to lead, and his wretchedness would be unbearable.

Where Europeans are often willing to wait for the state to take care of their needs and sort out their problems, Americans are far more likely to take action themselves—and to take it in concert. Tocqueville once again:

> The political associations that exist in the United States are only a single feature in the midst of the immense assemblage of associations in that country. Americans of all ages, all conditions, and all dispositions constantly form associations. They have not only commercial and manufacturing companies, in which all take part, but associations of a thousand other kinds, religious, moral, serious, futile, general or restricted, enormous or diminutive. The Americans make associations to give entertainments, to found seminaries, to build inns, to construct churches, to diffuse books, to send missionaries to the antipodes; in this manner they found hospitals, prisons, and schools. If it is proposed to inculcate some truth or to foster some feeling by the encouragement of a great example, they form a society. Wherever at the head of some new undertaking you see the government in France, or a man of rank in England, in the United States you will be sure to find an association.

Finally, I focus your attention on one last value, adherence to which has diverged only over the last fifty years: the belief in democracy. Various commentators have pointed out that Americans and Europeans took away sharply different lessons from World

War II. Whereas Europeans saw the rise to power of Hitler and Mussolini as representing the failures of democracy, the danger that can result from the tyranny of the majority, Americans saw their defeat of fascism as a great victory for democracy, proof that democracy is the path of greatest virtue. In the post-war world, Americans took it upon themselves to spread the bounties of democracy to the world. Europeans, much to the contrary, set out to create international organizations and supranational regulatory bodies to constrain democracy, with the hope of establishing universal norms that a nation's majority would be powerless to trump.

This project began within Europe itself, with the establishment of the European Union. To be sure, the EU has an elected parliament, but as a practical matter it suffers from a serious democracy deficit; its edicts are determined by an unelected commission and interpreted and enforced by an unelected court. As Professor Jeremy Rabkin explains, the member states of that organization must

> submit to rules and regulations drawn up by the European Commission in Brussels and enforced by the European Court of Justice in Luxembourg. The ECJ even claims (and exercises) the authority to invalidate enactments of national parliaments if they conflict with European law, in a process the ECJ itself describes as developing "constitutional norms" for Europe.

In this system that Rabkin terms "EuroGovernance," even the national constitutions of member states "can now be overridden by bureaucratic directives, resting on nothing more than the say-so of officials in Brussels."

In recent years, the European drive toward dictating what national democracies can and cannot do—how sovereign governments must treat their own citizens—has expanded beyond the bounds of Europe, with advocacy of organizations such as the International Criminal Court. To be sure, my own court is often justly accused of playing the same anti-democratic role in American society, invalidating the decisions of political majorities based on the policy preferences of nine unelected judges. But that is precisely why the judicial nomination process in the United States has of late become so politicized—a polity as fiercely democratic as America's will find a way to have its voice heard one way or another.

Do not mistake me. I am all in favor of human rights and living in a perfect society; but Europeans have far more confidence than Americans that they know what a perfect society entails, and that their own policy preferences should therefore trump majority will around the world. As Professor Jed Rubenfeld explains:

> European diplomats and politicians not only excoriate the United States for allowing the death penalty but even call for our expulsion from international organizations such as the Council of Europe. The American view holds that democratic nations can sometimes differ on matters of fundamental rights. For example, freedom of speech is stronger in America than in many other nations; an individual has the constitutional right in the United States to make statements in favor of Nazism that might land the person in jail in Germany. Yet the United States does not demand that Germany change its law on this point or risk expulsion from international organizations. Again, in America today, it's a bedrock principle of constitutional freedom that there be no established church at any level of government. But the American position does not require every nation with an established church—such as England or Italy—to disestablish.

Of course, all the differences in values I have discussed today are relatively minor; overall, Americans and Europeans probably share more common values than any two continents of people on Earth. Indeed, it is largely for this reason that we have become so mutually frustrated with one another in recent years: we tend to *believe* we are essentially the same, to *perceive* a common set of values, and we are left quite disappointed when we begin to realize how different we truly are.

On Living
and Learning

"It is a belief that seems particularly to beset modern society that believing deeply in something, and following that belief, is the most important thing a person can do. . . . I am here to tell you that it is much less important how committed you are than what you are committed to."

THE ARTS

Joseph Polisi, president of the Juilliard School in New York City, invited Justice Scalia to participate in the school's Symposium on the Arts and American Society because he knew of the justice's love of opera and because his "views on the subject might be quite different from the day-to-day discourse that we experience in New York City." Held on September 22, 2005, the symposium boasted an impressive lineup: the other participants on his panel were Tony Award–winning composer Stephen Sondheim (who co-wrote "Gee, Officer Krupke" from West Side Story, *a song that Scalia enjoyed and even worked into a dissent), renowned opera singer Renée Fleming, and Pulitzer Prize–winning historian David McCullough. Polisi reports that the audience of nearly one thousand musicians, dancers, and actors, as well as law students from around the city, received Scalia warmly and "once he started speaking, [they] fell in love with him." Polisi calls it "one of the high points of my thirty-three years" at the school. It was an honor for the justice, too.*

———

I am happy to be here this afternoon—and to tell you the truth somewhat surprised to be here this afternoon. Today's program reads like some sort of IQ test: "Which of the following is out of place? Diva, Author, Composer, Lawyer." It is certainly true that lawyers (and by extension judges) are rarely associated with the arts. In fact, it might be said with some degree of truth that the main business of the lawyer is to take the imagination, the mystery, the romance, the ambiguity, out of everything that he touches. It is not for nothing that the expression is "sober as a judge," rather than "exciting as a judge" or "inspiring as a judge."

So I view as my first task this afternoon to explain what I am doing here. Well, the reason is this: if lawyers do not produce art, neither do they produce much of anything else. They do not dig serviceable ditches, do not produce consumable goods, do not increase physical well-being, do not enlighten, entertain, or inform. Or at least they do none of that directly. They are an entirely ancillary profession—by which I mean that they, and the law that they serve, perform the humble but essential function of establishing and preserving the social conditions that enable the work (and the play) of the world to be conducted smoothly, harmoniously, and consistently with the values (such as individual freedom) that the society considers important.

Thus, while lawyers do not sing grand opera, they provide the conditions for those who have that talent to make a living at it. One of the famous old cases in the development of Anglo-American law is *Lumley v. Wagner*, decided by the lord chancellor of England in 1852. The plaintiff, Mr. Lumley, was the proprietor of the Drury Lane Theater. The defendant was a popular diva of the day, Johanna Wagner. (She, by the way, was the niece of Richard Wagner—and was good enough that Franz Liszt wrote about her "great and rare distinctions" as an artist, and also about "her charming and simple personal qualities.") Ms. Wagner had contracted with Mr. Lumley to sing at Drury Lane for three months, and had promised that, during that time, she would not "use her talents at any other theatre . . . without the written authorization of Mr. Lumley." Shortly after that contract was signed, however, Ms. Wagner received a better offer—from one of Lumley's competitors, Mr. Gye, to sing at the Royal Italian Opera in Covent Garden. Lumley sued to have her perform her contract, and the case was ultimately appealed to the lord chancellor. He stated that under the contract, "[i]t was clearly intended that [Johanna] was to exert her vocal abilities to the utmost to aid the theatre to which she agreed to attach herself." But what could Lumley do about it? Could he use the law to drag her to the stage? No. The chancellor held that Lumley could not obtain what lawyers call "specific performance" of the contract—in other words, making Johanna show up and sing, whether she wanted to or not. The case is famous for establishing the proposition that personal-service contracts are not specifically enforceable.

But the chancellor also said that while he couldn't *force* her to sing for Lumley, he could give her a nudge. "It is true, that I have not the means of compelling her to sing, but she has no cause of complaint, if I compel her to abstain from the commission of an act which she has bound herself not to do, and thus possibly cause her to fulfill her engagement." In other words, he immobilized her: break your contract if you want to, but don't plan to sing elsewhere. The point of the story, for present purposes, is that without an elaborated law of contracts, the intricate arrangements and expectations that attend production of an opera could not be assured.

Of course the law of contracts facilitates all sorts of work—the digging of ditches no less than the writing and singing of arias. One area of the law, however, is devoted exclusively to the protection of creative talent, including artistic creativity. And one of the many remarkable things about the Constitution of the United States is that that very brief and concise document (one could commit it to memory—I suspect it is no longer than the lines of the prince in *Hamlet*)—provided for federal protection of creativity. The relevant clause in Article I reads, "The Congress shall have Power . . . [t]o promote the Progress of Science and useful Arts, by securing for limited Times to Authors and Inventors the exclusive Right to their respective Writings and Discoveries." This wasn't just talk, either. The importance that the Framers attached to the Patent and Copyright Clause is demonstrated by the fact that the first Patent Board consisted of Thomas Jefferson, Henry Knox, and Edmund Randolph—our first secretary of state, our first secretary of war, and our first attorney general.

Two and a quarter centuries later, the Founders' wisdom continues to be vindicated. Intellectual property—the stuff of patents, copyrights, and trademarks—is in the current age perhaps *the most valuable kind* of property. You can tell by the hourly rates of lawyers in the patent and copyright bar. A term rarely passes in which a significant intellectual-property case does not reach the Supreme Court. I will describe a few from recent years.

One of the exceptions from the copyright protection that Congress has enacted is the so-called "fair use" exception, which sometimes brings the creativity of two artists into conflict. A case my court decided in 1994 involved Roy Orbison's hit song "Oh, Pretty Woman." In the late 1980s, the rap group 2 Live Crew wrote a song—"Pretty Woman"—which member Luther Campbell said was intended to satirize the original. 2 Live Crew offered to pay a fee to the owner of Orbison's song (he had sold his rights), but that entity refused the offer. 2 Live Crew proceeded anyway and found themselves named as defendants in a lawsuit. To cut a long story short, the Supreme Court found that parody—even when it has a commercial purpose, as 2 Live Crew certainly did—can fit within the Copyright Act's "fair use" exception, so long as it *is* a parody. That means that you can't rip off somebody else's idea and pass it off as your own, later protecting yourself by calling it a "parody." Rather, it must be clear that you are evoking the earlier work and commenting on it by, perhaps, making fun of it (or of other subjects).

The protection of copyright poses a never-ending dilemma as technology changes. In June of this year my court decided a prominent case (prominent among recording artists, at least) involving an online entity called "Grokster." Grokster's software enabled individuals to share recorded songs—*copyrighted* recordings—with each other by use of peer-to-peer networks. (You don't have to know what that means.) Indeed, the overwhelmingly predominant use of Grokster, and the source of the lion's share of its profits, was the unauthorized copying of copyrighted material. Grokster itself, of course, was not the immediate violator of the copyright; that was the individual user who made the unauthorized copy. Suing the literally hundreds of thousands of individual users (many of whom were perhaps teenyboppers with few assets, financial or otherwise) was obviously impractical. So the copyright owners went after Grokster for facilitating and inducing the copyright violation. Without going into the details of the matter, suffice it to say that the copyright owners won. Another victory for the protection of artistic creativity. The matter was not, I may add, as black and white as it might seem, since Grokster was a creator as well: its peer-to-peer network was an ingenious and useful device, and we would not want to discourage *that* sort of creativity by threatening its inventor with liability if someone uses it for unlawful purposes. But our opinion concluded that Grokster itself induced and encouraged the violation.

Well, I have come this far into my talk and haven't even mentioned the subject that most of you—including, I must say, the sponsors of this event—expected me to address: the First Amendment. I put it last intentionally, to give it some perspective. The First Amendment is of course not absolute. It guarantees not "freedom of speech" but "*the* freedom of speech"—which means that freedom which was the right of Englishmen when the First Amendment was adopted. It does not include, for example, the freedom to libel, or the freedom to publish obscenity—though it would certainly make life easier for authors if those limitations did not exist. It also does not include the right to use so-called "fighting words"—insults likely to produce physical assault.

With regard to the First Amendment, as with regard to the other provisions of the Constitution, I am not a strict constructionist. Though it literally protects only "the freedom of speech and of the press," I believe the most reasonable understanding of it is that speech and press represent all means of communicating ideas. Thus, handwritten letters are protected, even though they are not speech or press. So also are communicative acts—such as raising a clenched fist in the black power salute, or burning an American flag to symbolize disgust with the government.

There is, however, this difference between government prohibition of conventional means of communication—writing, speech, printing, even semaphore—and government prohibition of actions that are not inherently communicative, but that someone chooses to use for communicative purposes. The former prohibition— prohibition of conventional means of communication—always has as its purpose the suppression of communication, whereas the latter may have some other, entirely benign, purpose. For example, a community may have a safety ordinance prohibiting sticking arms or legs outside a moving vehicle; it does not offend the First Amendment to fine someone for violating that ordinance by giving the black power salute out of the window of a moving car. Nor does it violate the First Amendment to fine the burning of an American flag in violation of a municipal ordinance prohibiting the burning of *any* materials—leaves, garbage, rags, and flags—in the public streets. And it does not in my view violate the First Amendment (and here is where I find myself in disagreement with the most avid artistic invokers of the First Amendment, and, I am sorry to say, with a peculiar opinion of my court) to fine nude dancers for violating a municipal ordinance against public nudity. The actions that you choose as communicative symbols must be actions that are themselves lawful.

This assumes, of course, that dancing (in the nude or otherwise) implicates the First Amendment at all. The First Amendment says what it says, not what we lovers of the arts would like it to say. And frankly, I find it impossible to stretch "the freedom of speech and of the press" beyond those symbols (including even symbolic actions) that convey thought as opposed to aesthetic, or for that matter erotic, emotion. This means, I am sorry to say, that in my view even music (as opposed to lyrics) is not covered. The First Amendment forbids the censoring of operas because their librettos are revolutionary, as the kings of Europe used to do; but it does not forbid censoring them because their music is lousy. It forbids censoring sculpture or painting that promotes socialist ideals; but it does not forbid censoring sculpture with ugly form, or painting with ugly colors. Would I favor such censorship? Maybe if you let me pick the operas, the sculpture, and the paintings. No, of course I would not. Nor would almost all Americans. But not everything that is stupid is unconstitutional.

If you go down the list of guarantees in the Bill of Rights, you will find that some of them are really quite insignificant, compared to the much more important matters that are omitted. You are assured, for example, trial by jury in all matters at common law involving more than $20. Who cares? But you are not assured the right to raise and educate your children according to your wishes, rather than according to the wishes of Big Brother. How can you explain this discrepancy? The answer is simple. The Bill of Rights was designed to cover those rights that a tyrant was most likely to infringe. George III doesn't care how I raise my kids. But he might try to suppress speech, especially political speech, to impose religion, to confiscate arms, to quarter troops in homes, to conduct unreasonable searches and seizure, to prevent juries rather than his own judges from determining whether his agents are liable for damages, and so forth. Given the criterion for selection of the guarantees in the Bill of Rights, it surprises me not at all that forbidding the censorship of music, dancing, painting, and sculpture is not included. Indeed, it would have been remarkable if it *was* included. Many of the Framers, bear in mind, were not such patrons of the arts as you and I. In 1800, when John Marshall told John Adams that a recent immigration of Frenchmen would include talented artists, Adams denounced all Frenchmen, but most especially "schoolmasters, painters, poets, &c." He warned Marshall that the fine arts were like germs that infected healthy constitutions.

Of course the usual battleground, insofar as censorship of the arts is concerned, relates to the definition of obscenity—which, as I have said, has no First Amendment protection. The Supreme Court has not done a very good job of framing that definition. The line between protected pornography and unprotected obscenity lies, judging from the swing opinion in one of the important cases, between appealing to a good, healthy interest in sex and appealing to a depraved interest—whatever that means. The result is that every little town in America must tolerate the existence of a porno shop. I would prefer to draw the line where Justice William Brennan once drew it—though he later recanted. A work is not obscene merely because it portrays nudity or sexual activity; but it becomes so when it is designed or marketed to pander to the sexual appetite. This is not to say that the marketing of sex must be forbidden; many communities will want their porno shops. It is only to say that it *may* be forbidden; the First Amendment does not take it out of the realm of democratic debate.

Another common battleground relates to funding of the arts. Congress has created institutions, like the National Endowment for the Arts, that pass tax dollars to organizations or individuals for use in various artistic projects. Can the government require the artist receiving the money to use it in ways approved by the government? *Of course it can.* Unless you think that NEA funds must be distributed pro rata to all artists, or on the basis of some random lottery. To say that the government may fund the arts is necessarily to say that the government may decide what art is deserving of public funding. Just as to say that the government may run a school system is necessarily to say that the government may decide what ought to be taught. Congress found that paying $15,000 for a grant that produced a photograph of a crucifix immersed in the artist's urine—brilliantly entitled *Piss Christ*—was a waste of public money. It did not pass a law to throw this modern-day da Vinci in jail or stop him from displaying his world-class art. It just didn't want to *pay* for it. The NEA similarly did not want to fund a project consisting of a woman's "stripping to the waist and smearing chocolate on her breasts," using profanity all the while.

I can entirely understand discomfort with the government making artistic choices. But the only remedy for that discomfort is to get the government out of the business of funding the arts. The First Amendment does not repeal the ancient verity that he who pays the piper calls the tune. By refusing to *pay* for art or speech that it does not like, Congress does not abridge—restrict—penalize—that speech.

As I intimated earlier, I suspect—no, I am sure—that many of you would *like* the First Amendment to cover some of the things I have said it does not cover. To tell you the truth, so would I. But it is the beginning of wisdom in this area to acknowledge that the Constitution says what it says. And the *fullness* of wisdom is to recognize that the crowning achievement of America is not the Bill of Rights (every modern banana republic has one) but rather the structure of government and the democratic tradition that make a Bill of Rights enforceable according to its terms, and not according to the wishes of the ruler—be that ruler a generalissimo or a majority of the electorate. Pursuant to that structure of government and democratic tradition, subjects not covered by the Constitution's words—even subjects on which people have passionately held opposing views—are to be resolved by open debate, rational persuasion, and prudent compromise. That process produces a body of laws—laws like the law of contracts and the law of copyrights—that may seem dull beside the inspiring provisions of the Bill of Rights, but that provide the conditions essential to the flourishing of the arts.

GAMES AND SPORTS

Even though he made his name by sitting on a bench, Justice Scalia was given a sports award by the University Club of Washington, D.C., in June 1997. In his acceptance speech, the justice described the games of his youth, offering a fascinating look into the childhood of a Queens kid in the mid-twentieth century.

———

I have been asked many, many times to what do I attribute my well-known athletic prowess. I have always given an evasive answer, but I have decided on this solemn occasion—and on the understanding that this is all off the record and no reporters are present—to give the true answer. The answer is intensive cross-training. Beginning early in my youth, I played a great diversity of games and sports. As a result, I never got to be really good at anything, but I developed a lot of different muscles.

I grew up in New York City, in the Borough of Queens, in an era when college admissions were based on either academic ability, family background, or money. There was consequently no need for parents to ensure that their child was the striker on a traveling soccer team, or a lacrosse star, or a state cross-country finalist. In those days, as far as I can recall, only Notre Dame gave a damn about hand-eye coordination. It is impossible to describe what a difference this made in the ordering of young people's lives. The principal difference it made is that their lives were not ordered. Or at least not ordered after school. So long as you did your homework, kept your grades up, stayed out of trouble—and in my case practiced the piano, which was a form of self-discipline and penance—parents did not care how you spent your leisure time. Much less did they feel any obligation to arrange it for you.

There were no such things as soccer moms, for a number of reasons. First of all, soccer-momming is impossible without a car, and only a couple of people in our neighborhood had cars, mainly for show. I remember how we used to watch the neighbor a few houses down wash and wax his Packard on weekends. Second, family life did not revolve about the child's extracurricular activities to such a degree that fathers would be willing to postpone 6:30 dinner, or go to a Saturday evening instead of a Sunday morning Mass, in order to accommodate their kids' game schedule. Come to think of it, there were no Saturday evening Masses, the Third Commandment in those days not yet having been revised to read "Remember that thou keep holy the weekend." And third and most conclusively, there were no soccer moms because there was no soccer. Americans overwhelmingly preferred baseball, a game in which a lot of players stand around while not much happens, to soccer, a game in which people run back and forth furiously while not much happens.

Anyway, the consequence of all this is that kids were left pretty much to decide for themselves what games they would play— indeed, even to invent their own games. And the result of that, in turn, is that I played an awesome variety of sports that developed every muscle of my body. First of all, there was marbles, also known as "mibs." This was played in the dirt on the tree-lawn between the curb and the sidewalk on 92nd Street. It was a good game for a hot day, because it was in the shade. It did not put a premium on upper-body strength, to which I attribute the fact that the neighborhood champ was a tomboy named Vivian Weaver.

Closely related to marbles, because it could be played on the same tree-lawn, was a game whose name I am not sure of—it might have been mumblety-peg—which consisted of throwing a penknife into a square marked off in the dirt, and then drawing a line from where the knife landed so as to claim for yourself a piece of your opponent's territory. (In those days nobody worried about kids carrying knives.) The game was terrific for developing the right wrist.

Utterly central to my youthful athletic training was a piece of athletic equipment called a spaldeen. I have not seen one of these for many years. I think they have been banned by the Consumer Product Safety Commission. The spaldeen was a lively, pink rubber ball, fabricated by vulcanizing together two pink rubber hemispheres. It had many advantages over tennis balls: it was lighter, livelier, cheaper, and you knew when its useful life was over because its two hemispheres would simply fall asunder and go careening off in opposite directions.

Spaldeens were used in a game indigenous to New York City—or indeed, perhaps only to Queens—called stoop ball. The requisite playing field for this sport was a fairly tall, brick front stoop facing the street and not too far from it. (There were plenty of those in our neighborhood.) The object of the game was to throw the ball against the stoop in such fashion that it would bounce over or past your opponents, who were fielding out in the street. You aimed for the point of the brick. The game developed sharp eyes and quick hands.

Spaldeens were also used in a game called "War," in which a large circle was drawn in chalk on the street, divided into pie-slice segments, each of which bore the name of a country. One player would approach the center of the circle, while each of the others stood in the segments representing the countries they had chosen, and the lead player would announce "I declare war on" and then he would shout out the name of one of the countries, as he did so smashing the ball into the center of the circle. The player for the country named would have to chase down the ball; as soon as he got it everyone else would have to freeze; and then, after taking no more than ten steps, the person warred upon would have to hit one of the other players with the ball.

Spaldeens were also used in the quintessential game of my youth, stickball. Queens stickball, I should point out, is quite different from the more effete game of the same name that was played in Brooklyn. It was not played in the street, but in a schoolyard, usually against a handball court that nobody ever used for handball. Whereas in Brooklyn the ball was thrown in on a bounce, with a catcher behind the batter, in Queens the ball was thrown into a box drawn on the wall, the width of home plate and extending from the knees to the shoulders of an average batter. The pitch was a strike if it went in the box. (If the player was shorter than the average batter, tough luck; get used to a bigger strike zone; we learned in Queens that the world ain't always fair.) The equipment was a broomstick or, even better, a mopstick (for some reason they were heavier), and, of course, the spaldeen.

Another game we played bore the unlikely name Ringalevio. (I don't know how to spell it; I actually don't think it has ever been written down.) This consisted of chasing down members of the opposite team and putting them into a marked-off jail called the "den." Captives could be liberated from the den if one of their team made it in without being caught and shouted "Free Den Rest." (Den rest allowed the liberating player a respite while his freed teammates ran off.) Ringalevio was good for the wind.

And of course there was street hockey. This was played like regular hockey, only on roller skates. It totally obstructed traffic, so could be played only on streets that the New York cops now and then sealed off with signs marked PLAY STREET. When I see kids skating around today with elbow pads, knee pads, and helmets, I remember those rough-and-tumble hockey games played without any protective equipment. Come to think of it, to get to and from all of these activities we used to ride balloon-tire bikes—and nobody ever heard of a bicycle helmet. How the blood has thinned.

And of course there were the more standard games: baseball and football were usually pickup games. You would go over to the field on a Saturday morning or Sunday afternoon and choose up sides. No adult supervision. No conceivable financial liability. In the winters, when there were not many hours of daylight after school was out, we used to play basketball, two or three to a side, out in the street under an old-fashioned streetlight—the kind with a shade over the top. The backboard had been nailed to the wooden light pole.

When I was in high school (I rode the subway to school in Manhattan, to a Jesuit military school called Xavier, just above the

Village), I earned the only school-team appointment I ever received during my long athletic career: I was on the junior-varsity rifle team. How different the New York of then was from the New York of now can be appreciated by imagining me traveling back and forth on the subway from Queens to Manhattan with a .22 rifle over my shoulder (in a carrying case, of course). The Xavier varsity team was really pretty good; it used to beat the West Point plebes.

That was, as I say, my only formal team appointment—only JV, at that—though later on, in law school, I was a member of the *Harvard Law Review* touch football squad, known as the Fungibles.

WRITING WELL

Scribes, an organization that "seek[s] to create an interest in writing about the law and to promote a clear, succinct, and forceful style in legal writing," honored Justice Scalia with its lifetime achievement award in August 2008. The award declared that the justice "has done as much as anyone in the modern era to promote clear, robust expression in a field often lacking in these qualities." The speech offers some insights into how he did that.

———

Having anticipated that in accepting this award I would be expected to say something more than thank you, I have prepared a few observations.

The first is that you gotta get a new name for this award. Lifetime Achievement Awards are best known at the annual Oscar ceremonies, where they are given to some old-time actor who never won an Oscar but should have, just for sheer persistence and endurance. The awardee usually crosses the stage on a cane. I assume that your award has none of these connotations, and therefore accept it with great pride. But get a new name.

The rest of my observations pertain to legal writing. The first and most important is that I do not believe legal writing exists. That is to say, I do not believe it exists as a separate *genre* of writing—alongside, for example, poetry and playwriting, children's stories and murder mysteries. Rather, I think legal writing belongs to that large, undifferentiated, unglamorous category of writing known as nonfiction prose. Someone who is a good legal writer would, but for the need to master a different substantive subject, be an equivalently good writer of history or economics or indeed even theology. (Had he been a lawyer, C. S. Lewis would have been a magnificent legal writer.) Indeed, in the days before economic scholars turned from writing for a general intellectual readership to writing for one another (with esoteric regression analyses and mathematical formulas), I used to ask myself why legal articles could not be as clear and uncluttered as the lucid economic articles written by Ronald Coase or John Kenneth Galbraith.

Oops, I said the word *uncluttered*, which has set my esteemed co-author Bryan Garner a-twitching—he who has embarked upon a campaign to eliminate from the text of briefs and banish to footnotes the case citations that so disrupt the flow of thought. This is indeed one respect in which legal writing, or at least legal writing that purports to describe the law in a common-law system based upon precedent, differs from almost all other writing. Because the points to be made depend not only upon fact and reason, but must also—yea, even at the expense of fact and reason!—rest upon authority, allusions to the relied-upon case precedents must be scattered throughout the piece. The only other type of writing coming to mind that is similarly afflicted is theological writing in a religion based upon revelation. There also, reason is well and good, but it must be consistent with and affirmed by the Book. This necessity of constant appeal to authority does not make common-law legal writing a different *genre*, but it does require the mastery and intelligent use of a different technique—much as writing in the field of anatomy requires intelligent use of illustrations.

I learned that there is no such thing as legal writing during my first two years of teaching, when I taught classes in (supposedly) legal writing at the University of Virginia Law School. It became immediately clear to me—as I think it must become clear to anyone who is burdened with the labor-intensive job of teaching legal writing—that what these students lacked was not the skill of legal writing, but the skill of writing at all. To tell the truth, at as late a stage as law school I doubt that skill can be taught. What I hope to have taught (in one semester) were the prerequisites for self-improvement in writing, which are two things: (1) the realization (it came upon some of my students as an astounding revelation) that there is an immense difference between writing and good writing; and (2) the recognition that it takes time and sweat to convert the former into the latter.

Time and sweat. I believe I was set on the road to good writing during my first year at Georgetown College. I had a young professor for English Composition whose name I still remember, so much angst did he bring to my freshman year. P. A. Orr was a Canadian, and a damned hard grader; and he gave a writing assignment every weekend. I was not accustomed to getting the B minuses that I received on my first few assignments, and as a consequence every weekend of my first semester I devoted many nervous hours to writing and rewriting. I am grateful to this day.

Time and sweat. To tell you the truth, I was never sure the game was worth the candle until I sat on the D.C. Circuit. After all, I thought, judges don't read your brief, or even lawyers your legal publications, to get an aesthetic high. They want information, and it does not make a heck of a lot of difference whether it is conveyed as gracefully as might be, so long as the point comes through. I knew judges—facile writers—who applied this sort of cost-benefit analysis to their opinions. The game is not worth the candle.

I was disabused of that belief during a case that came before the D.C. Circuit involving, as I recall, federally prescribed automobile emission standards. There were many amicus briefs—quite common in the Supreme Court, but fairly unusual, in those days at least, in the D.C. Circuit. I was getting quite punchy slogging through them and, frankly, absorbing less and less of what they said. Then, quite far along in the process, I picked up a brief that woke me up and grabbed my attention—so clear, so precise, so well organized, so elegantly expressed it was. I turned to the front cover to see who had written this, and—oh, joy!—I was delighted to learn that talent and hard work pay off. The author was one of the members of the bar whom I knew well and greatly respected for his writing ability and his dedication. Of course it might be true that only judges who care about good writing are impressed by good writing. But I doubt it.

Finally, rather than making a last point, I want to raise a departing question—a question that has long intrigued me: Is high intelligence a prerequisite for great legal writing? It is surely not a sufficient condition. When I made the *Harvard Law Review* many years ago (we used to refer to it as "making" the *Review*), I remember being overawed at the raw brainpower of the students with whom I was now spending much of my life. But I was not impressed, by and large, with their writing ability. I thought I could write rings around many people who were much smarter than I.

But if high intelligence is not a sufficient condition, is it at least a *necessary* condition of great legal writing? You know, I think not—unless you are evaluating legal writing in part by its content rather than exclusively by its form. To be sure, much of what it takes for good legal writing can be learned; the less-than-brilliant mind may take longer to master those elements (good grammar and good Latin, for example), but it is doable. There is, however, a certain quality possessed by the really great writer—legal or otherwise—that has nothing to do with brainpower and probably cannot be taught. The same phenomenon exists in other fields of human endeavor. The ability to speak foreign languages, for example, has nothing to do with IQ. And in the field of music—the other principal means of human communication—there is no reason to believe that Mozart was a genius in the ordinary sense of being brainy. He was a musical genius. I think there is writing genius as well—which consists primarily, I think, of the ability to place oneself in the shoes of one's audience; to assume only what they assume; to anticipate what they anticipate; to explain what they need explained; to think what they must be thinking; to feel what they must be feeling.

I do believe, however, that there is at least this connection between good writing and intellect: it is my experience that a careless, sloppy writer has a careless, sloppy mind.

TURKEY HUNTING

The National Wild Turkey Federation might not be on every justice's speaking circuit, but it was on Justice Scalia's. Scalia delivered this speech at the NWTF's 2006 convention, which drew an audience of forty thousand. When he returned six years later, he received thunderous applause as he was awarded the group's coveted Grand Slam for successfully hunting each of the four U.S. subspecies of wild turkey: Eastern, Osceola, Rio Grande, and Merriam's.

———

It is true. I confess it: I'm a turkey hunter. Many of you have better excuses for that than I do. How many turkey hunters out there grew up in New York City? I did, and you would have thought I'd have been spared the turkey addiction. But, I later discovered, it apparently can just skip a generation.

My grandfather, my aunt told me, used to disappear into the mountains of Sicily for a week, and his family would get very upset not knowing where he was. He was off hunting. My last recollection of him is hunting rabbits on Long Island. He finally grew too old to go out in the woods, so he would sit on the back porch of the bungalow—or in the vegetable garden nearby—that we had out there. In those days, Long Island was still the country. He would sit there holding his L.C. Smith side-by-side. Since he couldn't get to the rabbits, he'd wait for the rabbits to come to him. I still have his gun. It is entirely corroded about six inches down from the end of the barrel, from him holding it every evening.

So, I guess that's how it started. Then, years later, my eldest son married a young lady from Covington, Louisiana, whose father was a hunter, and he got me into deer hunting. A little after that, I became the circuit justice for the Fifth Circuit, which covers Louisiana, Mississippi, and Texas, and bad went to worse. I got into duck hunting, and then boar hunting, and finally, as I say, I got addicted to the worst of all—turkey hunting.

Now there are a lot of good things about turkey hunting. Of course the best thing is it gets you outside the Beltway. It also gives you a lot of time alone, out in the woods. Even if you have a hunting companion, if he knows anything, he will shut up and not call too often. Those of us who are religious—and most turkey hunters, in my experience, are—value that time alone. There's just something spiritual about it. You can pray to the Creator out there, even while you're hunting.

The man who most got me into turkey hunting—Charles Pickering, one of the judges on the Fifth Circuit—presented me recently with a volume called *The Outdoorsman's Bible*. Maybe some of you have it. It has a few pages at the beginning that contain certain quotations from the Bible about hunting. Most important of all, it's a camo Bible. Or at least the cover is camouflage. The pages aren't, so the turkeys might see you if you actually open it.

Another good friend of mine, Louis Prejean, is a Cajun, and of course he's Catholic. When he prays out there he has a rosary, and a rosary is much better: it's not camouflage but the turkeys still won't see it, and you don't have to turn any pages. You just hold it in your left hand and your shotgun in your right hand. Now, that alone is no reason to change your church.

One of my most humbling moments came while turkey hunting. I took a shot at a gobbler and he went right down—flapped a little and went down. I was so excited, I jumped out of the box stand and hurried to him. I got about five feet away and he lifted his head, looked up at me, and ran away. And I had left my gun back in the box stand.

Just to be serious for a couple of minutes: I first of all want to commend the National Wild Turkey Federation for the terrific job of conservation that it has done, spreading the wild turkeys around the country. I mentioned growing up in New York City, but

I was born in Trenton, New Jersey—the most densely populated state in the Union—and my mother's sister still lives just outside of Trenton. I saw a flock of about eight hens when I was there a couple of years ago. I would never have imagined that there were any turkeys left in New Jersey, at least not near the state capital. I've also seen a wild turkey inside the Beltway, right on my property, twenty minutes from the nation's capital. There are a lot of other turkeys inside the Beltway, but this one was wild.

How could you explain our hunting culture to someone from another country? I'm not sure you can. Your president-elect was referring a little earlier to the need to preserve that hunting culture. I hope it can be preserved.

The hunting culture begins, of course, with a broader culture that is not hostile toward firearms. When I was growing up in New York City, people were not afraid of people with firearms. I lived in Queens and took the subway to my military high school in Manhattan. We had a pretty good rifle team that used to compete against the West Point plebes. So I used to travel on the subway from Queens to Manhattan with a .22 carbine target rifle. Can you imagine doing that today? In New York? "Look out—There's a man with a gun!"

That attitude of associating guns with nothing but crime is what has to be changed. It's not necessarily a matter of getting your friends into hunting. If you can't get them into hunting, get them into skeet shooting, or anything that shows that guns are not things that are used only by bad people.

In the *Federalist Papers,* James Madison spoke contemptuously of the countries of Europe, which he said "are afraid to trust their people with arms." I hope this country never falls into such a state.

One of the things I've loved—and I think it's what everybody loves—about turkey hunting is the people you hunt with. I've enjoyed being here. Thank you for having me.

CIVIC EDUCATION

On February 14, 2014, Justice Scalia spoke at the Union League Club of Chicago's annual George Washington's Birthday Gala. Illinois supreme court justice Anne Burke, in introducing Scalia, praised him as "a product of the great American immigrant experience unique to our nation" and as someone who "embodies the goals and dreams of the Founding Fathers." In his speech, Scalia lamented that our country has lost the founding generation's vision of civic education.

———

I am truly delighted to help the Union League Club continue its almost 150-year-old tradition of marking the birthday of George Washington. Washington is my favorite of the Founders—the one I would most have liked to meet. Not just because he was the indispensable man—the man without whom the American Revolution would not have succeeded. But also because he is a puzzlement. He was not a great intellect; indeed, he was quite sensitive about his relative lack of formal education. (He was not even, to tell the truth, that skilled a military tactician, as the New York campaign demonstrated.) And he was surrounded by great intellects, who produced great writings—Hamilton, Madison, and Jefferson, to name the most prominent. Washington himself wrote not much of note, beyond his famous First Thanksgiving Proclamation and his Farewell Address. (One is reminded of the response of one college professor to the assertion that Jesus Christ was a great man: "Bah, what did he write?") Yet all those well-published, intellectual geniuses looked up to, deferred to, stood in awe of George Washington. What *was* there about the man that produced that result?

It must have been character. Washington was a man of honor, of constancy, or steady determination. A man who could be believed, trusted, counted on. A man who would step down as president after two terms, though he could have been re-elected for life, because that is what he believed a democratic republic required. (Has any national leader with the exception of Cincinnatus so willingly stepped down?) He was, as I have said, the indispensable man.

I want to speak this evening about a subject that Washington would have approved of: the education of the citizenry to render it capable of democratic self-governance. According to a study released a few years ago by the Intercollegiate Studies Institute, American college students are woefully uninformed about this nation's history and its founding principles. The study warns of a "coming crisis in citizenship"—which may not be an exaggeration. To recount my own admittedly episodic observation: When I teach a class on constitutional law (I did this frequently, at the University of Chicago and Stanford, before becoming a judge, and I continue to do it in one-shot appearances even today), I usually ask how many of the students have read, cover to cover, the *Federalist Papers*. I have never seen more than about 5 percent of the students raise their hands. These are students at the nation's elite law schools, the best and the brightest men and women, who have a *particular* interest in law and government. It is truly appalling that they should have reached graduate school without having been exposed to that important element of their national patrimony—the work that best explains the reasons and objectives of the Constitution, and a contribution to human knowledge so profound that it is studied in political-science courses in foreign countries.

One of the ISI study's findings in particular caught my eye: at several elite schools, including Yale and Georgetown, seniors know less than freshmen about America's history, government, foreign affairs, and economy. The study calls this "negative learning," which is of course a euphemism for "getting dumber." To be fair, one could put an optimistic face upon the finding: perhaps today's freshmen arrive better educated than the freshmen of three years ago. But even if that were true (and I have no reason to believe it is), it would at least mean that three years of college have not made up for the deficit.

Tonight I want to comment on two aspects of the civic-education issue. First, I shall describe the Founders' views on civic education, to help evaluate how our performance has lived up to expectation. Second, I shall comment on the Supreme Court's contribution to the crisis.

Views representative, I think, of the Founders can be found in Noah Webster's 1790 essay, "On the Education of Youth in America." Webster, a zealous patriot, famous lexicographer, and educator (a Yale graduate, by the way), stated that American students must "know and love the laws." "This knowledge," he wrote, "should be diffused by means of schools and newspapers; and an attachment to the laws may be formed by early impressions upon the mind." More particularly, Webster prescribed a course of study rich in American history and government:

> [E]very child in America should be acquainted with his own country. He should read books that furnish him with ideas that will be useful to him in life and practice. As soon as he opens his lips, he should rehearse the history of his own country; he should lisp the praise of liberty, and of those illustrious heroes and statesmen, who have wrought a revolution in her favor. A selection of essays, respecting the settlement and geography of America; the history of the late revolution and of the most remarkable characters and events that distinguished it, and a compendium of the principles of the federal and provincial governments, should be the principal school book in the United States. These are interesting objects to every man; they call home the minds of youth and fix them upon the interests of their own country, and they assist in forming attachments to it, as well as in enlarging the understanding.

A similar approach was recommended by the other prominent founding-era writer on civic education, Benjamin Rush. Rush, signer of the Declaration of Independence, doctor, educator, and prominent essayist, wrote the following: "From the observations that have been made it is plain, that I consider it is possible to convert men into republican machines. This must be done, if we expect them to perform their parts properly, in the great machine of the government of the state." (Webster and Rush, by the way, did not agree about everything. As noted by the editor of a volume of essays on education in the early republic: "In their disagreement on the role of the Bible in the public schools and in the suitability of instruction in French and the harpsichord for young ladies, Webster and Rush suggest that some educational questions may indeed be eternal.")

It is fairly clear that what Webster and Rush were recommending was nothing short of indoctrination in republican principles, at least for the young. Thus, a widely shared view of civic education in the early republic was that our system of education should stop glorifying European culture. Before a broad system of education is to succeed, wrote Webster, "Americans must *believe* and *act* from the belief that it is dishonorable to waste life in mimicking the follies of other nations and basking in the sunshine of foreign glory." The fear was that educators would glorify a corrupt European culture and would fail to develop our own. Far from mimicking the customs, manners, and intellectual fashions abroad, our Founders expected us to serve as a model for other nations' improvement. As Madison explained,

> [t]he American people owe it to themselves, and to the cause of free Government, to prove by their establishments for the advancement and diffusion of Knowledge, that their political Institutions, which are attracting observation from every quarter, and are respected as Models by the new-born States in our own Hemisphere, are as favorable to the intellectual and moral improvement of Man as they are conformable to his individual & social Rights. What spectacle can be more edifying or more seasonable, than that of Liberty & Learning, each leaning on the other for their mutual & surest support?

How politically incorrect these ideas seem in an age that worships diversity and moral relativism. To be willing to train the young in American principles, one must believe, first, that there is such a thing as distinctive American principles (which is necessarily to say that contrary principles are *not* American), and second, that those distinctive American principles are superior to those of other societies. Would anyone, nowadays, expect to hear a public grammar-school principal voicing these exclusionary and un-PC sentiments?

Another focus of the Founders' writings on education was the importance of discipline. The Founders believed that discipline was a necessary ingredient of civic education not just because it created a proper environment for learning, but because it taught respect for the rule of law. "In the education of youth," Benjamin Rush explained, "let the authority of our masters be as *absolute* as possible. The government of schools like the government of private families should be *arbitrary*, that it may not be *severe*. By this mode of education, we prepare our youth for the subordination of laws and thereby qualify them for becoming good citizens of the republic." Webster shared these views: "Here children should be taught the usual branches of learning; submission to superiors and to laws; the moral or social duties; the history and transactions of their own country; the principles of liberty and government."

And discipline, naturally, required effective punishment. Webster minced no words:

> The rod is often necessary in school, especially after children have often been accustomed to disobedience and a licentious behavior at home. All government originates in families, and if neglected there, it will hardly exist in society, but the want of it must be supplied by the rod in school, the penal laws of the state, and the terrors of divine wrath from the pulpit.

Few of us today would reintroduce the rod (and, I may add parenthetically, few pulpits dwell upon the terrors of divine wrath). But swift and effective punishment of even the nonphysical sort is imperiled in today's public-school classrooms, because of the application of the Due Process Clause to school affairs (about which more later) and the *in terrorem* effect of litigation.

It should be apparent from several of the passages quoted above that the Founders were as interested in teaching virtue as in teaching civics. This is apparent from Article III of the Northwest Ordinance, enacted by the Continental Congress and reenacted by the First Congress. It read in part: "Religion, morality, and knowledge, being necessary to good government and the happiness of mankind, schools and the means of education shall forever be encouraged." As Webster put it, "[t]he *virtues* of men are of more consequence to society than their *abilities*; and for this reason, the *heart* should be cultivated with more assiduity than the *head*." And this could not likely be done, the Framers believed, without religion.

I have often thought that one of the foundations for the relative political stability of the West has been the Our Father—and in particular its avowal that we forgive those who have trespassed against us. When I was in high school in New York City, there existed an organization called the Catholic Forensic League, in which many of the Catholic high schools would compete in various categories of public speaking: debate, extemporaneous speaking, and oratorical declamation, among others. This last category included famous speeches, such as the speech (if I recall its title correctly) of Telemachus to the Gladiators. One of these set pieces re-enacted a conversation between a noble Roman and the bishop of Rome. The Roman, a convert to Christianity, had seen his mother and brother slain before his eyes when Christians who had been invited on some pretext to the Colosseum saw imperial archers swarm into the arena and let loose a hail of arrows into the crowd. The bishop tells the Roman to fall to his knees and say the Our Father—which he does, haltingly when he comes to "as we forgive those who trespass against us." I remember being mightily impressed by that bit of theater. Now to be sure, Christians have not always honored that avowal, just as they have often disobeyed other injunctions of their faith. But they have often observed it, so that slaying twentieth-century Moslem Kosovars because of a

Moslem slaughter of Serbs that occurred at Kosovo Polje in 1389 seems to most of us beyond the pale. And of course St. Paul's letter to the Romans gives the same message: "Vengeance is mine, saith the Lord." Is there any other good reason—a reason that will appeal to the heart—not to avenge past wrongs?

The Founders stressed that a civic education required the teaching of religious values. Benjamin Rush wrote that "[t]he only foundation for a useful education in a republic is to be laid in RELIGION. Without this, there can be no virtue, and without virtue, there can be no liberty, and liberty is the object and life of all republican governments." He continued:

> The complaints that have been made against religion, liberty and learning, have been, against each of them in a separate state. Perhaps like certain liquors, they should only be used in state of mixture. They mutually assist in correcting the abuses, and in improving the good effects of each other. From the combined and reciprocal influence of religion, liberty and learning upon the morals, manners and knowledge of individuals, of these, upon government, and of government, upon individuals, it is impossible to measure the degrees of happiness and perfection to which mankind may be raised.

John Adams wrote that a republic "is only to be supported by pure Religion or Austere Morals. Public Virtue cannot exist in a Nation without private [Virtue], and public Virtue is the only Foundation of Republics."

In his Farewell Address, issued before his retirement to Mount Vernon, George Washington famously declared that "Religion and morality are indispensable supports" of "all the dispositions and habits which lead to political prosperity":

> In vain would that man claim the tribute of Patriotism, who should labour to subvert these great Pillars of human happiness, these firmest props of the duties of Men and citizens. The

mere Politician, equally with the pious man ought to respect and to cherish them. A volume could not trace all their connections with private and public felicity. Let it simply be asked where is the security for property, for reputation, for life, if the sense of religious obligation *desert* the oaths, which are the instruments of investigation in Courts of Justice? And let us with caution indulge the supposition, that morality can be maintained without religion.

All this was written, of course, in a day when education was generally not a function of the state, but of parents and churches—though it must be noted that even so adamant a separationist as Thomas Jefferson provided for clergymen on the faculty of his state-funded University of Virginia.

Lest I be misunderstood, let me make clear that I am *not* saying that every good American must believe in God. Certainly not. I am sure that some of the Founders—including, perhaps, some of those who spoke favorably of the necessity of religion to a successful republic—were atheists or at least agnostics. What I am saying, however, is that it is contrary to our founding principles to insist that government be hostile to religion, or even to insist (as my court, alas, has done in word though not in deed) that government cannot favor religion over nonreligion. It is not a matter of believing that God exists (though personally I believe that); it is a matter of believing, as our Founders did, that belief in God is very conducive to a successful republic. Believe, if you wish, that religion is, as Marx said, the opiate of the masses—so long as you acknowledge it to be our tradition that it is better for the republic that the masses be thus opiated. Or believe, with Voltaire, *si Dieu n'existait pas, il faudrait l'inventer*—if God did not exist, we would have to invent Him.

The Founders did not believe in education for education's sake. They believed in education for *civil government*'s sake. Even those Founders who spent more time thinking about constitutional government than civic education shared these views: "A popular Government," James Madison wrote, "without popular information, or the means of acquiring it, is but a Prologue to a Farce or a Tragedy; or, perhaps both. Knowledge will forever govern ignorance: And a people who mean to be their own Governors, must arm themselves with the power which knowledge gives." Indeed, in Massachusetts, the connection between civic education and the republican experiment was made a matter of constitutional law: Chapter VI of that state's 1780 constitution provided that "[w]isdom, and knowledge, as well as virtue, diffused generally among the body of the people [are] necessary for the preservation of their rights and liberties." This is, of course, "Republicanism 101."

IF WE HAVE lost sight of the founding generation's vision of civic education, I think it is fair to say that, of late, the Supreme Court has been a factor in the obfuscation.

The Court is partly to blame for law students' failure to study our legal history and traditions. When we live under a so-called living Constitution whose content is determined by current popular preferences (or more precisely current judicial preferences) rather than the dispositions solemnly adopted by prior generations, law students have little incentive to study our history and traditions. Who cares what Hamilton, Madison, and Jay thought?

As for grade-school and high-school students: Here the Supreme Court has had a more direct role in making civic education more difficult—though some of that role, I expect, is inevitable in a system of public education. As mentioned, the Court has subjected public-school discipline to due-process review. That was probably not necessary. The Due Process Clause prevents the deprivation of "life, liberty, or property without due process of law." I doubt that depriving a student of an A grade is a deprivation of property, or that holding a student after school is a deprivation of liberty in the relevant sense. In any case, swift and certain punishment in public school is a thing of the past; the process has been subjected to law and to lawyers.

The Court has invoked the First Amendment to restrict public educators' ability to determine what students should learn. In one case, the Court held that a school board's decision about what books to hold in its library is subject to federal-court review. Once a school has placed a book in its library, the Court held, the First Amendment prohibits the school from removing that book because of *its content*—which is of course the only sound pedagogical reason for either acquiring or getting rid of a book.

But perhaps the Court's most destructive line of decisions relating to civic education is the line of decisions involving the Religion Clauses. As I have mentioned, the Founders believed morality was essential to the well-being of the republic, and that religion was the best way to foster morality. Religious values were therefore central to the Founders' aspirations for civic education. This is not an anachronistic view, either; it is well reflected in the current sense of society. When the Ninth Circuit Court of Appeals struck down the "under God" portion of the Pledge of Allegiance as unconstitutional under the Religion Clauses, the Senate unanimously, and the House with only five dissenters, strongly criticized the decision. (My court subsequently vacated the Ninth Circuit's decision on standing grounds.)

Yet the Supreme Court has adopted the demonstrably unhistorical view that the Constitution forbids not merely the favoring of one religion over another but even the favoring of religion in general over irreligion. In fact, it forbids the former, but not the latter—and to know what that means in practice you need only consult George Washington's First Thanksgiving Proclamation, issued at the direction of the same First Congress that proposed the First Amendment. It is deeply religious but assiduously nondenominational. No mention of Jesus Christ. I have always been impressed, by the way, with its genuinely religious conclusion—which, instead of expressing the hope that God will grant this new country prosperity (as any modern politician would do), expresses the hope that He will grant "such a degree of temporal prosperity as he alone knows to be best."

Nonetheless, despite Washington's example, the Court repeatedly says that government cannot favor religion over nonreligion. To tell the truth, it does not really *apply* that principle, since when push comes to shove, it has shrunk from disapproving such long-standing historical practices favorable to religion as the granting of real-estate exemptions for houses of worship, and the opening of federal and state legislative sessions with prayers led by a chaplain—in the case of the federal Congress, a paid chaplain. But despite the reality of its decisions, the Supreme Court constantly repeats the mantra: the state cannot favor religion over nonreligion.

And I think that mantra has had its effect upon our decisions regarding religious observance in state schools. In *Lee v. Weisman*, the Court held that a principal could not invite a rabbi to deliver a benediction at a middle-school graduation—a rigorously nondenominational benediction, given that the rabbi was speaking to a middle school in the Bible Belt—because of the "subtle coercive pressure[s]" (in favor of religion, presumably) that such a benediction would produce. Never mind that the practice is as old as public graduation ceremonies themselves. In *Santa Fe Independent School District v. Doe*, the Court held that student-led, student-initiated prayers at a high school football game violated the Establishment Clause. In short, the Court has rejected as an establishment of religion a public preference for religion over irreligion, when a preference for religion over irreligion is central to our history and traditions.

IT IS A requirement of a talk like this one to quote at least once from *Democracy in America*. So I shall conclude with some Tocqueville. Tocqueville observed:

> [T]he origin of the Americans, or what I have called their point of departure, may be looked upon as the first and most efficacious cause to which the present prosperity of the United States may be attributed. The Americans had the chances of birth in their favor; and their forefathers imported that equal-

ity of condition and of intellect into the country whence the democratic republic has very naturally taken its rise. Nor was this all; for besides this republican condition of society, the early settlers bequeathed to their descendants the customs, manners, and opinions that contribute most to the success of a republic. When I reflect upon the consequences of this primary fact, I think I see the destiny of America embodied in the first Puritan who landed on those shores, just as the whole human race was represented by the first man.

I'm with Tocqueville, in that I attribute the success of America to our forefathers' virtue and intellect being passed down from generation to generation—passed down even to those many immigrants and their descendants who did not share the English background and the Protestant religion of the first Pilgrim. I hope that our educators can manage, despite formidable obstacles, to impress upon today's students a better knowledge and appreciation of our civic heritage.

COLLEGE EDUCATION

Justice Scalia balked when Father David M. O'Connell, the new president of Catholic University, asked him to speak at the school's commencement ceremonies in May 1999. Scalia explained that he had long fended off such invitations by declaring that he didn't do commencement speeches unless his own children were graduating, so saying yes to O'Connell would "make a liar out of me." O'Connell was ready:

> *I looked as disappointed as I could and replied, "But this is my first graduation as president; I need it to be a really memorable one . . . for the students." Scalia grimaced slightly—I knew I had him from the smile in his eyes—and said "OK."*

———

The subject matter of commencement addresses, those of you who have not been exposed to them should know, is pretty much *ad libitum.** Perhaps no other genre of human discourse covers such a range. Many of them are, or seek to be, quite educational—so that I could talk to you, if I wished, about the Ex Post Facto Clause of the Constitution. You will be relieved to know that I have decided not to do that. Partly because I suspect you have had, for the moment, quite enough education. But mostly because of my philosophy about commencements—which is that they are not for the enlightenment, or even at all for the benefit, of the graduates, who would probably rather have their diplomas mailed to them at the beach; but for the pleasure and satisfaction of the

---

* At one's pleasure.

graduates' families and friends, who take this occasion to observe and celebrate a significant accomplishment on the part of those whom they love. In that respect a commencement is like a wedding or baptism; the primary participants in those events would rather be elsewhere as well.

Given, then, what I consider to be the nature of the event, I thought I would make a few remarks about what it is you have accomplished primarily, as I say, for your friends' and relatives' benefit—though it may be of interest to you as well, since sometimes (as in that great movie *The Bridge on the River Kwai*) one gets so involved in achieving something that he forgets what it is he is achieving. I will be addressing primarily the college graduates, who are the most numerous here—but what I have to say will apply as well, *mutatis mutandis*, to those of you receiving graduate degrees.

My father used to enjoy telling an old Sicilian story about a ferryman who was rowing a priest across a river. As he is sitting in the back of the rowboat, watching the ferryman bend over the oars, the priest asks, "Tell me, my good man, have you studied any philosophy?" The ferryman answers, "No, no philosophy." "A pity," the priest replies, "you've wasted a quarter of your life." The ferryman keeps on rowing. "What about history, have you learned any history?" "No," says the ferryman, "no history." "What a shame," says the priest, "you've wasted half your life." The ferryman keeps on rowing. "Mathematics," says the priest, "surely you've learned some mathematics!" "No," says the ferryman, "no math." "A tragedy," says the priest, "you've wasted three-fourths of your life." About this time they are in the middle of the river, the ferryman looks down and sees water filling the bottom of the boat. "Tell me, Father," he says, "have you learned how to swim?" "No," the priest says. "A pity, you've wasted all your life."

Indeed, what good is all the philosophy and history and math you've acquired over the past four years—and the languages and accounting and economics as well? It is traditional, at commencements, for the person conferring degrees to say something like "Welcome to the community of scholars." Well, that's something, I suppose; but it really only postpones the question. What good is it to be a scholar, if that's what a college education makes you?

Let me begin by saying what good it is *not*. The bad news is that your four years of college have not made you *experts* on almost anything. There is almost (if not entirely) *no* field that you have mastered so intensively as to be able to make significant advances in the state of human knowledge. (I know this from having read your transcripts.) But the good news is that if you have understood the bad news, you are an educated person. One of the values of college education—especially a liberal college education—is to make the mind aware of the immeasurable immensity of human knowledge, and the even greater immensity of things still unknown. One can be *told* that, but one cannot really appreciate it until he has researched some infinitesimal recondite point in some specialized field and has seen how many fine minds have been over that territory before—some of them two thousand years ago, and seemingly no more stupid than we are today. Thus, the educated man or woman is not a know-it-all. This attitude of humility before the breadth of knowledge mankind has accumulated, and before the even greater breadth of the unknown, is the beginning of wisdom. The know-it-all has nothing to learn.

The second thing you have *not* acquired in college—I do not care how specialized the course of study you took—are the narrow skills that will ultimately make you a success in whatever business or profession you choose. You may have acquired what are called entry skills—business accounting, or computer programming, or whatever. But they are good only for what the name "entry skills" suggests: to get you in the door, which you would not even *need* if you have an uncle in the business. How you ultimately succeed, I guarantee you—no matter *what* field you are entering—will depend very little upon the specific items of knowledge you now have crammed into your heads. That will be true even if you go on to take an advanced degree in a subject such as law. I expect I have forgotten 90 percent of the legal "rules" I learned in law school; and half of what I do remember from that time is now *wrong*. The world changes quickly, and today's important knowledge is tomorrow's trivia.

Does that mean that your Catholic University education has only a two-year warranty? Not at all. My father—whose wisdom continually came to mind as I prepared this talk because he was a college professor—used to teach Romance languages: Spanish, French, and Italian. He knew that the vast majority of his students would never really use the language he taught them after they left the ivy halls. But that did not bother him. The raw material of the language was to the mind, he used to say, what chewing gum is to the jaw. It is a means of exercising the faculties in a particular way, after which it can be spit out. The good it has done will endure. Just as there are separate exercises—separate Nautilus machines, if you will—for developing the individual muscles of the body, so also there are separate disciplines for developing the various faculties of the mind: precision, logic, subtlety, adaptability. In four years you will have had a thorough workout. But I am beginning to sound like Francis Bacon.

My point is that, insofar as future practical utility is concerned, education is not *merely*, and not even *primarily*, the imparting of a body of specialized knowledge, which will soon enough be forgotten or even be superseded by more accurate data. Rather it is largely the teaching of a process. The practical skill you have principally acquired from your years here is learning how to think, learning how to learn. That skill will never go stale, and it is marketable anywhere.

A third thing you have acquired in four years of college—perhaps the most important thing, from a purely secular point of view—is the knowledge of who you are. That requires some explanation: When I was a college student, I spent my junior year abroad, at the University of Fribourg in Switzerland. During my time there, I recall being deeply offended by the habit the French-speaking professors had of lumping together Great Britain, the United States, Canada, and Australia as "*les pays anglo-saxes*"—the "Anglo Saxon countries." Wait a minute, I thought, you have it all wrong. I am as much an American as anyone else. But my name is Scalia and my ancestors are Italian. I ask you, is this an Anglo-Saxon face? I didn't realize until the end of the year, when I visited England on the way back, how right they were. I felt infinitely more at home. It wasn't the language—for I spoke French pretty well by then. But it was the attitudes, the assumptions, the shared literature, political traditions, and even social conversations of the people. God help me, I thought, I *am* an Anglo-Saxon, whether the rest of them realize it or not!

My point is that, as you have come to learn during your four years here, you are not just the child of your parents who are here today. Physically you are totally theirs, to be sure. But intellectually, attitudinally, culturally, you are a child of the West, and of that particular *part* of the West that is the United States—which is close to, but not quite the same as, the part that is England, and a little bit further from, but not *very* far from, the part that is France, and so forth. You are, to mention only a few of your forebears, a child of Homer and Alcibiades, Cicero and Caesar, Dante and the Medici, Alfred and Chaucer, Joan of Arc and Louis XIV, Elizabeth and Shakespeare, Milton and Cromwell, Carlisle and Edmund Burke, Hamilton and Jefferson, Nathaniel Hawthorne, Abraham Lincoln and Mark Twain. Many of your contemporaries, who have not had the benefit of a college education, are as much their children as you are—*but they do not know it*. They do not really know what they come from, *WHO they ARE*.

I will mention only one more value of your Catholic University education, before I let this commencement address fade into the obscurity that embraces its millions of predecessors. As I have just observed, it is good to know where you came from. It is even better to know where you are going.

A friend of mine once told me of his experience in returning to a boys' boarding school in England—a monastery school—that he had attended many years ago. Most of his teachers were gone, but one elderly brother was still there, the headmaster of the place. After speaking with him at some length about old times, he asked the brother how the school was faring today. "Oh, I think we are preparing our boys quite well," he said. "And what are you preparing them *for?*" my friend asked. A puzzled look came over the old man's face, as though he was surprised by a question that had such an obvious answer. "Why," he said, "for death." A very Catholic—a very Christian—response.

If a Catholic educational institution does not have *that* sort of preparation, moral formation, as a part—indeed, as a principal part—of its mission, it may as well not be a Catholic educational institution. Let me quote from one of the greatest Catholic educators, Cardinal John Henry Newman:

> Knowledge is one thing, virtue is another; good sense is not conscience, refinement is not humility, nor is largeness and justness of view faith. Philosophy, however enlightened, however profound, gives no command over the passions, no influential motives, no vivifying principles. Liberal Education makes not the Christian, not the Catholic, but the gentleman. It is well to be a gentleman, it is well to have a cultivated intellect, a delicate taste, a candid, equitable, dispassionate mind, a noble and courteous bearing in the conduct of life;— these are the connatural qualities of a large knowledge; they are the objects of a university; I am advocating, I shall illustrate and insist upon them; but still I repeat, they are no guarantee for sanctity or even for conscientiousness; they may attach to the man of the world, to the profligate, to the heartless. . . . Quarry the granite rock with razors, or moor the vessel with a thread of silk; then may you hope with such keen and delicate instruments as human knowledge and human reason to contend against those giants, the passion and the pride of man.

And of course in the hands of "the man of the world, the profligate, the heartless," the education you have received produces, in the end, nothing but an increased capacity for evil. Which is why the Romans said *corruptio optimi pessima est*: the corruption of the best is the worst.

The time was—not so long ago—when all educational institutions took moral formation as a serious part of their mission.
Thomas Jefferson, for all his insistence upon a wall of separation
between church and state, provided for chaplains at the University
of Virginia. Today, sad to say, not only is moral formation not an
objective of higher education; it is virtually a forbidden topic. For
to have strong views of right and wrong is to be discriminating,
which is the only sin left on campus; just as toleration is the only
universally acknowledged virtue. The object is to place all options
before young men and women—from Jesus Christ through Larry
Flynt—so that they may choose for themselves, and not (heaven
forbid) be criticized for their choice.

There are a few exceptions to abdication of responsibility for
moral formation. The service academies still do it: Duty, Honor,
Country is still taught at West Point. And some (though by no
means all) religiously affiliated institutions—which are under
constant pressure in academic circles to display their sophistication by abandoning their principles. May it not happen here.

Lest it be thought that, by adhering staunchly to its religious
beliefs, the Catholic University of America becomes more Catholic
but less American, let me conclude by reading a few words from
the greatest American of them all, the indispensable man, the Father of His Country—who, by the way, was not half the intellectual
of Jefferson or Madison or Hamilton, but by his force of character
placed them all in awe (and there is a lesson there). In his farewell
address to the nation, when he declined (can you imagine it?) to
wear the mantle of power for a third term, George Washington
wrote the following:

> Of all the dispositions and habits which lead to political pros-
> perity, Religion and morality are indispensable supports.
> In vain would that man claim the tribute of Patriotism, who
> should labour to subvert these great Pillars of human happi-
> ness, these firmest props of the duties of Men and citizens. The
> mere Politician, equally with the pious man ought to respect
> and to cherish them. A volume could not trace all their con-

nections with private and public felicity. Let it simply be asked where is the security for property, for reputation, for life, if the sense of religious obligation *desert* the oaths, which are the instruments of investigation in Courts of Justice? And let us with caution indulge the supposition, that morality can be maintained without religion. Whatever may be conceded to the influence of refined education on minds of peculiar structure, reason and experience both forbid us to expect that National morality can prevail in exclusion of religious principle.

Ladies and gentlemen of the Class of 1999: With the other parents and friends here, I congratulate you on the achievement you complete today. As with all genuine achievement, in the very grasping of it there is a tinge of regret. The race is over, and you will never, ever, run a race as exciting as this one again.

LEGAL EDUCATION

George Mason Law School in Arlington, Virginia, invited Justice Scalia to celebrate the dedication of its new building in March 1999. Scalia's remarks illustrate that he always remained a teacher in spirit.

In November 2016—nine months after the justice's death—George Mason Law School was rechristened Antonin Scalia Law School.

———

Despite the remnants of my New York accent, I am at heart a Virginian, and so am especially pleased to be present at the dedication of this splendid new law building for the commonwealth. I remember—not so long ago—when George Mason Law School was first established. And behold what a mighty oak that acorn has already produced. Located in a state that has demonstrated its support for higher education, and within a population center that has an unusual concentration of talented people who make their living writing the law, interpreting the law, applying the law, or figuring out how to get around the law—there is every reason to believe that the future of this institution will display the same extraordinary growth and progress as its brief past.

I have only a few words to say to you this afternoon—some directed to the faculty, some to the students, and some to the friends of this institution.

To the faculty: Before I became part of the problem in Washington, I used to do what you do—and I miss it. Allow someone who is now at a sufficient distance from his teaching years that he can see rather more clearly what he did right and what he did wrong to give you advice.

During the last few years of my academic career, I had become—or at least thought I had become—something of an expert in my chosen field of administrative law. It was easy to get what I wrote published, and I had a lot of insights I thought worth writing about. I reached the point (which I had seen some of my older colleagues reach, but thought I would never experience) of begrudging the time that I had to take away from my research and writing to devote to teaching class, and to the preparation for teaching class. (The preparation, as you all know, takes much more time than the teaching itself: at least three hours of the one for each hour of the other—unless you have not taught the course before, in which case the spread is much greater.)

When I look back at those feelings now, I think what a fool I was. The Great American Law Review Article—let's face it—has a shelf life of at most ten years, after which it is of little more than historical interest. And the Great American Law Treatise endures not much longer. But I still encounter students whom I do not remember, but whom I taught at Chicago and Stanford between 1976 and 1981, and indeed whom I taught at Virginia between 1967 and 1971, who come up to me with great warmth and affection, and say what a lasting impact I had upon their love for, and their approach to, the law. And many of them, I assume, have similarly infected others. In fact, I occasionally encounter students who were taught by my father at Brooklyn College in the 1940s and 1950s, who come up to tell me what a terrific teacher he was, and how he affected their intellectual life.

So do not delude yourselves. Research and writing is of course a part of the academic life—and perhaps the part that makes you best known, for the time being, beyond the walls of your own institution. But the reality is that the part of your academic career that will have the most lasting impact—and that will be remembered after you are gone—is those hours that you spend producing a living intellectual legacy, in the classroom. Of course administrators ought to be aware of this as well as faculty. Some law schools value teaching more than others; I hope George Mason will always be a teaching law school.

To the students: The law is, we used to be told when I was a student at Harvard, a stern mistress. (I suppose that formulation is sexist, if not indeed unlawful, today—but you get the point.) The sheer body of law that there is to learn increases mathematically every year. And large portions of that corpus ought to be known, at least in its general outlines, by any member of the profession, whatever the particular specialty he or she practices. You cannot negotiate resolution of a contract dispute, for example, unless you know the strength of your client's position—which involves not only knowing contract law, but also knowing the law of evidence, since points that cannot be brought forward in litigation (the moment of truth, so to speak) are points that are useless. You cannot negotiate a settlement of a tort claim unless you are familiar with the law of contracts—and probably federal income tax as well.

During the three years I spent at law school, I pretty much stuck to what are called the bread-and-butter courses. Indeed, in those days there were not many courses that weren't bread and butter. Even so, I could not take all the courses I wanted to, and I feel deeply the existence of some gaps in my education as a lawyer— gaps that I probably never will be able to fill.

It is only in this place—in a law school—that you will have the opportunity to study an entire body of law not haphazardly, or episodically, but systematically. You have the great luxury, for example, of studying the entire Bankruptcy Code, and seeing how all the pieces fit together (or in some cases don't fit together). If you haven't taken bankruptcy law—as I, alas, did not—later in life you will get thrown at you one isolated provision of the Code, and be asked to decide, or to advise a client, how it applies. You will always have the feeling, as I certainly do, that you are not quite sure what will be the overall consequences of coming out this or that way. You're not quite sure what this particular string is attached to, if you should pull it. (I have to judge that by reading the predictions made by the briefs for both sides and deciding which of them exaggerates the more.)

So I advise you students to make the best use of your time here, and not to give short shrift to that aspect of legal education that the law schools do best: the conveying of a systematic body of knowledge concerning discrete areas of the law. There is some time for trial practice, of course—and the law schools have gotten better and better at teaching that. There may even be a little time for more pizzazzy courses. But I assure you that if you spend too much of your time here in courses on Law and Ice Cream, you will live to regret it.

And finally, to the friends and supporters of this law school, most of whom I assume are lawyers: There has been a trend in American legal education that is disturbing to me and many others—the gradual estrangement of the academy from the practice. To confirm it, all you have to do is compare the lead articles in law reviews today to those of forty or fifty years ago. The ones today contain a much higher proportion of philosophy, and a much smaller component of case analysis and empirical inquiry resolving some small but thorny problem of securities law or contracts or tax. In some places—not this one, I am sure—the practice is regarded as a pursuit too crass and mundane to be of interest to the professoriate, despite the fact that most of the tuition-paying students plan to pursue that career.

Perhaps the principal blame for this (I consider it blameworthy, though obviously not all academics would agree) lies with faculty and administration, but surely some of it rests with the bar itself— and especially that portion of the bar which provides generous financial support to the law schools, yet often pays little attention to just what sort of legal education is being supported. Do not mistake me: I do not believe it is the function of the law school to prepare moneymaking associates for the law firms—graduates who can hit the ground running and be billed at high hourly rates from the outset. But I think it *is* the law school's function to provide the broad intellectual and technical grounding that can form the basis of a successful legal career.

How many firms that interview students for summer jobs or for postgraduation employment convey the message that it does make a big difference what particular courses the student has chosen to pursue? How many senior partners, in their frequent hobnobbing with the administrators of their alma mater, display the slightest awareness of, and concern for, the law school's curriculum? And how many members of the bar make it a point to welcome and indeed attract law professors into the valuable projects, such as law reform, that bar associations undertake? Young associates are actively encouraged by their law firms to take an active part in the work of the bar. (Not only is it professionally responsible, it is good for business.) Young law professors do not have that stimulus from above; in the law school, generally speaking, there *is* no above, and the law dean will never be the authority figure that a senior partner is. So the job of keeping the academy close to the bar must fall largely to the bar itself. Take a law professor out to lunch.

Having lectured everybody here—except perhaps the security officers—let me conclude by expressing again the great delight of the legal community at witnessing the flourishing of this much needed institution in Northern Virginia. May it grow and prosper. And may this wonderful new building be replaced 50, 100, and 150 years from now with progressively more wonderful ones.

THE LEGAL PROFESSION

Then a judge on the D.C. Circuit, Antonin Scalia delivered the commence-ment address at the University of Dayton law school's graduation in May 1984. Among the graduating law students was Elizabeth McClanahan, who in 2011 would become a member of the supreme court of Scalia's adopted home state of Virginia. Reviewing his long-ago remarks, Justice McClana-han finds that they remain "sage advice for anyone entering the legal profes-sion."

———

I am a former academic. That means that I have suffered through *many* commencement addresses. But the sad or happy fact is that I have never been on the delivering end before. Needless to say, I do not recall the point or even the subject of any commencement address I have ever heard. So I consulted a number of friends who are experienced in this art form and asked them what I should talk about. The response, I was surprised to find, was unanimous—and here I am not kidding. They all said to talk about . . . fifteen min-utes. Since it is the only advice I received, I promise to stick to it.

I would like to share with you graduates today, and with your parents, friends, and visitors, some thoughts concerning the career you are about to enter upon. Not concerning what that career can do for the world. Let's face it, none of us here is likely to change the world very much. But more important, what the career is likely to do to *you*. One's work is not to be taken lightly. Not only because it is a necessary means of putting bread on the table, but because it is perhaps the single most influential factor (apart from your own free will) in determining what kind of people you will be.

There is a profound spiritual connection between a human being and his or her work. What we do for a living is at once and the same time an *expression* of our identity, and a *formation* of it. It is less true that we are what we eat than that we are what we *do* to eat. The conscientious workman stamps his personality upon his handiwork; but likewise the nature of his work makes its impression upon his personality. Hence, there are certain archetypes that come to mind when one mentions certain occupations and professions: policemen, construction workers, soldiers, cabdrivers, lawyers. I would like to consider with you for a few moments what you have let yourselves in for. What are the distinguishing features of our profession?

At the outset, let me remove a fear that I know many of you and your parents must have prominently in mind—that by accepting this degree and becoming lawyers you have probably lost your immortal soul. In the New Testament there is assuredly no group that comes in for such scathing denunciation. Christ says—to pick one of several such passages at random:

> Woe to you lawyers! because you have taken away the key of knowledge. You have not entered yourselves, and those who were entering you have hindered.

Passages such as this can worry you a lot until you put them in their proper context. The lawyers referred to were the lawyers of a *theocracy*; and the law was the law of Moses rather than of Caesar. In other words, a more accurate translation, taking account of these basic differences, would be "Woe to you, *theologians!*" We have always known that *that* is a troublesome crowd. The proper lawyers who appear in the New Testament are probably tax gatherers—and they fare pretty well.

Having removed the false premise that one of the characteristics of lawyers is damnation, let me turn to what I think the true characteristics are.

First, I suppose, there is a compulsive *precision*. You've already been exposed to that a good deal in law school. Don't think it gets any better when you get out into practice. One of the distinctive skills of our profession is to discern ambiguities, inaccuracies, and insufficiencies that would not occur to the ordinary layman: The term in a draft contract that *seems* clear enough but, when you think about it, could mean either of two slightly different things. The provision in a statute that can be interpreted in two quite different ways. The holding of an opinion based on facts that are just a *little bit* different from the facts in the present case.

It is this particular skill or instinct or habit that has earned us a reputation as hairsplitters and pettifoggers. The reputation is well deserved—though it might be put more nicely. The fact is that we do tend to pick things apart; and that is exactly what the nature of our work requires.

Of course other trades and professions require precision as well—from surgery to diamond cutting. But the difference is that the surgeon deals only with human bodies and the diamond cutter with stones. The entire parade of life comes before the lawyer and must be described precisely in the instruments, the opinions, and the statutes with which he or she deals. So that describing a thing—*any* thing—precisely becomes a habit, a compulsion that tends to spread into all aspects of a lawyer's life.

For you graduates, it is probably already too late to escape this blessing or curse—whichever you choose to regard it.

Have you not been reading a novel or watching a play and been struck with the uninvited thought "That idea was not put quite precisely!"? The question is not *really*, after all, *To be or not to be*—unless one is certain there is no afterlife. Perhaps it might better have been put: "To continue this life, or not to continue this life, *that* is the question!"

This is the reason, by that way, that I am persuaded—despite the evidence to the contrary—that William Shakespeare was not a lawyer. Or in any event not a very good one. Suggestion, allusion, and thus to some extent imprecision is the very life of poetry—and the very death of the law.

Ladies and gentlemen of the Class of 1984, if you aspire to be poets, get out now.

A second characteristic of our profession that must be observed is a certain worldly wisdom—or, if you wish to put it pejoratively, cynicism. Billy Budd, Pollyanna, and Mr. Micawber could never have been lawyers. The thought was put most concisely by Charles Lamb, who wrote: "Lawyers, I suppose, were children once."

How is it that we are this way? I, at least, have led a very sheltered life. The answer, of course, is that we are so worldly-wise because we have seen so much of the world *vicariously*, through the innumerable cases we have read, covering the entire spectrum of human experience. We have learned about mill shafts and exploding squibs and the dangers of grafting skin from the chest onto the palm of the hand. We can make a fair guess concerning the relevant market for beer; and we know that for the owner of a shopping center it is as important for a store to stay open as it is for the store to pay its rent. We even know the meaning of FOB and TOFC. The areas of activity to which we have been exposed in this fashion cover the whole range of human activity. More than a thousand words could ever describe—or would care to.

And we have not just learned about life, we have learned about people. People at their worst. By and large, human fault and human perfidy are what the cases are about. We have seen the careless, the avaricious, the criminal, the profligate, the foolhardy parade across the pages of the case reports. We have seen evil punished and virtue rewarded. But we have also seen prudent evil flourish and foolish virtue fail. We have seen partners become antagonists, brothers and sisters become contesting claimants, lovers become enemies.

It does tend, as Charles Lamb suggested, to shatter the illusions of childhood rather quickly. Hence the image of the lawyer as the skeptical realist. Expect to find here no more a dreamer than a poet.

The image has always been presented most vividly to my mind by the story told of that excellent lawyer, and later secretary of state, John Foster Dulles. Dulles even *looked* the part of the precision-obsessed skeptic I have just been describing. Put a pitchfork in his hand and he could have posed for *American Gothic*. When he was secretary of state, a comedienne—I think it may have been

Carol Burnett—made famous a wonderful spoof of a torch song entitled "I made a fool of myself over John Foster Dulles!" You get the picture.

Anyway, the story is told that Douglas MacArthur visited President Eisenhower on one occasion to induce him to expand the Korean War and invade China. He went on at some length in the eloquent, almost epic manner that MacArthur was able to muster. He concluded with a rousing description of how it was Eisenhower's destiny to alter the course of history, to change the geopolitical map for centuries to come, to enter the list of immortal military leaders alongside Alexander, Caesar, and Napoleon.

When he had finished, the spell of his oratory hung over the room. It was broken by the dry, crackling voice of the lawyer Dulles, who said, "Well, Douglas, you may be right, but you may also be as wrong as you were when you tried to get the Republican nomination for president."

The third and last characteristic of lawyers that needs mention is our *obsession with process*. As a matter of fact, process is what we are all about!

Lawyers really have no more interest than anyone else—and no more expertise than anyone else—in what the *substance* of our laws should be. If you want to know whether deregulation is good or bad, ask an economist. If you want to know whether indeterminate prison sentences are good or bad, ask a criminologist or penologist. What lawyers are good at, what lawyers are *for*, is implementing these decisions in a *manner*, through a *process*, that is fair and reasonable.

I fear that this characteristic of ours, which is perhaps our most distinctive and profound characteristic, will never be understood by the layman. It is the source of the most common criticism of lawyers: that we can argue both sides of a case. *But of course* we can—because except to the extent that a client's interest may be involved, we *as lawyers* have no interest in a particular outcome, but only in assuring that the outcome be fairly and intelligently arrived at and clearly and precisely expressed!

To show you what I mean—to demonstrate how corrupted by

process your thinking has already become—let me read to you a statement, written by the nineteenth-century English essayist Sydney Smith, intended as an indictment of lawyerkind, but which will, I expect, not seem to you much of an indictment at all:

> Can any thing be more preposterous than this preference of taste to justice, and of solemnity to truth? What an eulogium of a trial to say, "I am by no means satisfied that the jury were right in finding the prisoner guilty; but everything was carried on with the utmost decorum. The verdict was wrong; but there was the most perfect propriety and order in the proceedings. The man will be unfairly hanged; but all was genteel!"

Now the lawyer's reaction to that statement is "Good grief, what more can the man expect! If by 'perfect propriety and order in the proceedings' there is included (as there must be) the notion that there was the minimum amount of evidence necessary to enable a reasonable jury to convict, then it is *not my job* to second-guess the jury!"

This attitude which stresses the propriety of process rather than correctness of result is born, of course, of that skepticism I mentioned earlier. We lawyers know from experience that a lot of different people have a lot of different views as to what is a "correct" result. That is what separates the kingdom of Caesar, with which we deal, from the kingdom of God. But for the fact that he was dealing with the wrong kingdom when he asked the question, Pontius Pilate was quite right to inquire "What is truth?" Indeed, in the realm of political science, as opposed to theology, he was ahead of his time. That skepticism is the very basis for preferring democracy to enlightened autocracy. And the paramount truth of democracy is process.

Fealty to process is not a very stirring cause. No crowd has ever formed behind a banner that read "BE FAIR" or "HEAR BOTH SIDES." Yet in the last analysis, there is a certain romance even in that—though it takes a poet rather than a lawyer to describe it.

I would like to conclude by reading a passage (from a play) with which I used to conclude my constitutional law course, in those days of strong feelings not too long ago when young people were certain that they had THE TRUTH and were willing to brook no opposition from existing laws or existing institutions in implementing it. It is especially fitting to reflect on the wisdom of St. Thomas More, as depicted in Robert Bolt's *A Man for All Seasons*:

Exit RICH. All watch him; the others turn to MORE, their faces alert.

ROPER: Arrest him.

ALICE: Yes!

MORE: For what?

ALICE: He's dangerous!

ROPER: For libel; he's a spy.

ALICE: He is! Arrest him!

MARGARET: Father, that man's bad.

MORE: There is no law against that.

ROPER: There is! God's law!

MORE: Then God can arrest him.

ROPER: Sophistication upon sophistication!

MORE: No, sheer simplicity. The law, Roper, the law. I know what's legal not what's right. And I'll stick to what's legal.

ROPER: Then you set Man's law above God's!

MORE: No, far below; but let me draw your attention to a fact—I'm not God. The currents and eddies of right and wrong, which you find such plain-sailing, I can't navigate, I'm no voyager. But in the thickets of the law, oh, there I'm a forester. I doubt if there's a man alive who could follow me there, thank God. . . . (He says this last to himself.)

ALICE (exasperated, pointing after RICH): While you talk, he's gone!

MORE: And go he should if he was the devil himself until he broke the law!

ROPER: So now you'd give the Devil benefit of law!

MORE: Yes. What would you do? Cut a great road through the law to get after the Devil?

ROPER: I'd cut down every law in England to do that!

MORE (roused and excited): Oh? (Advances on ROPER.) And when the last law was down, and the Devil turned round on you—where would you hide, Roper, the laws all being flat? (Leaves him.) This country's planted thick with laws from coast to coast—man's laws, not God's—and if you cut them down—and you're just the man to do it—d'you really think you could stand upright in the winds that would blow then? (Quietly.) Yes, I'd give the Devil benefit of law, for my own safety's sake.

PLATITUDES AND WISDOM

Justice Scalia delivered addresses at high school or college commencements for four of his children and two of his grandchildren. He delivered this speech at his son Paul's graduation from Langley High School in June 1988.

———

Giving a commencement address is not as safe an enterprise as it used to be. I am told that the graduating classes in some schools, to while away the time as the speaker drones on, have devised a kind of contest, with an appropriate prize, to see who can write out in advance the greatest number of the platitudes that the speaker will deliver. Perhaps a speaker should not complain about that, because it at least ensures that everyone will be paying attention. Almost anything beats being ignored.

A few weeks ago, *The Washington Post* published a Bingo card containing some of the most frequently used graduation platitudes— ranging from "This is not an end, it is a beginning," to "You are the future leaders of America." The idea was that you would take the card to the graduation ceremony, and if the speaker is really platitudinous enough that you can check off a whole string of old chestnuts—a whole row up or across—the entire class would stand up in unison and yell, "Bingo!" Your principal, Dr. Manning, is probably angry at me for giving next year's class the idea. I have heard some speeches where I wanted to jump up and yell bingo even without the benefit of a bingo card.

But, in fact, taking some of the available store of platitudes out of circulation is probably a good idea. So good an idea that I intend to make it the subject of my remarks today. My problem with these platitudes is not that they are old and hackneyed, but that a lot of them are wrong. Let me examine a few.

A good one to start with—because it's used not just in graduation addresses but in television news broadcasts, editorials, and all forms of what are meant to be evocative communications—is the old standby "We face unprecedented challenges." Ladies and gentlemen, you should not leave Langley High School thinking that you face challenges that are at all, in any important sense, *unprecedented*. Humanity has been around for at least some five thousand years or so now, and I doubt that the basic challenges it has confronted are any worse now—or, alas, even much different—from what they ever were.

Consider, for example, what is often thought to be a brand-new problem: environmental protection. Not really new. The famous London fogs of the nineteenth century—which make such a wonderful background for Sherlock Holmes and Jack the Ripper movies—turn out to have been not fog at all, but mostly smog, caused by innumerable coal-burning fireplaces. And every ancient city, from Athens to Rome to Venice, had major sanitation and waste problems.

Today, to be sure, we have the capacity to destroy the entire world with the bomb. I suppose you can consider that a new problem, but it is really new in degree rather than in kind. If you were a teenager graduating from the Priam Memorial High School, in Troy, about 1500 B.C., with an army of warlike Greeks encamped all around the city walls, and if you knew that losing the war would mean, as it did, that the city would be utterly destroyed, its men killed, its women and children sold into slavery, I doubt that that prospect was any less terrible to you than the prospect of the destruction of the world. It was all of the world *you* ever used anyway. Your country, your family, your friends, your entire society. The thought that other societies, at least, would go on was of no more comfort to the Trojans—or later, to the Carthaginians, who were also utterly destroyed, or the MacDonald Clan, which was massacred at Glencoe—than it is of comfort to you that if this world is incinerated, well, it's good to know there may be other ones.

The challenges faced by different societies at different times take different forms—defending against the French longbow versus defending against a ballistic missile—but in substance they are always the same: (1) the forces of nature (how to ensure a continuing supply of food, fuel, shelter, and clothing); and (2) the forces of man (how to get along with one another or defend against those we cannot get along with).

It is important not to believe that you face unprecedented challenges, not only because you might get discouraged, but also because you might come to think that the lessons of the past, the wisdom of humanity (there are a couple of good platitudes), which it is the purpose of education to convey, are of not much use. Earlier this year I gave a little talk to Langley High School—not just your class—about the Constitution. In the course of it I discussed, I believe, some of the writings of the Founding Fathers in the *Federalist Papers*. They knew they were facing great challenges in seeking to establish at one and the same time a federation and a democracy. But they did not think for a moment it was an unprecedented challenge. If you read the *Federalist Papers*, you will find they are full of examples to support particular dispositions in the Constitution— from Greece, from Rome, from medieval Italy, France, and Spain. So if you want to think yourselves educated, do not believe that you face unprecedented challenges. Much closer to the truth is a different platitude: There is nothing new under the sun.

The second platitude I want to discuss comes in many flavors. It can be variously delivered as "Follow your star" or "Never compromise your principles" or (quoting Polonius in *Hamlet*—who people forget was *supposed* to be a silly man) "To thine own self be true." Now this can be very good or very bad advice, depending. Indeed, follow your star—if you want to head north and it's the North Star. But if you want to head north and it's Mars, you had better follow somebody else's star. Indeed, never compromise your principles— unless, of course your principles are Adolf Hitler's, in which case you would be well advised to compromise them as much as you can. And indeed, to thine own self be true—depending upon who you think you are.

It is a belief that seems particularly to beset modern society that believing deeply in something, and following that belief, is the most important thing a person can do. Get out there and picket, or boycott, or electioneer, or whatever, show yourself to be a "committed person." (That is the fashionable phrase.) I am here to tell you that it is much less important how committed you are than what you are committed to. If I have to choose, I will undoubtedly take the less dynamic, indeed even the lazy person, who knows what's right, than the zealot in the cause of error. He may move slower, but he's headed in the right direction. Movement is not necessarily progress. More important than your obligation to *follow* your conscience—or at least prior to it—is your obligation to form your conscience correctly. Nobody, remember this, nobody ever proposed evil *as such*. Neither Hitler, nor Lenin, nor any other despot you can name ever came forward with a proposal that read: "Let's create a really oppressive and evil society." Rather, Hitler said, *Let's take the means necessary to restore our national pride and civic order.* And Lenin said, *Let's take the means necessary to ensure a fair distribution of the goods of the world.*

In short, it is your responsibility, men and women of the Class of '88, not just to be zealous in the pursuit of your ideals, but to be sure that your ideals are the *right* ones—not merely in their ends but in their means. That is perhaps the hardest part of being a good human being. Good intentions are not enough. Being a good person begins with being a wise person. *Then* when you follow your conscience you will be heading in the right direction.

The next platitude I want to address is perhaps the most common one—especially at graduation addresses, and most especially at graduation addresses in the nation's capital. I refer to the phrase "The United States is the greatest country in the world." Now I do not intend to contradict that platitude, because I think it to be true. But I would like to explore with you a bit what it is we *mean* when we say we believe it. A few possibilities can easily be rejected. We don't mean the most physically beautiful. Acre for acre, Switzerland has it all over us—and even if you take the total number of scenic wonders I'm not sure we come out first. At least you couldn't be sure unless you've traveled everywhere. Nor do we mean by "the greatest country" the most powerful country—because then we would have to think that next to living in the United States we would like to live in the Soviet Union, which I doubt is the case. Perhaps, then, what we mean when we say our country is the greatest is that it best satisfies both the physical and the spiritual desires of its people. But no, we could not mean that, because on that analysis the nation of Attila the Hun could be considered great: it certainly satisfied the physical desire of its people (to take everything in sight) and the principal spiritual desire of its people (to dominate others).

Perhaps, then, we think it to be the greatest because it is the freest. Now there is a real possibility. In fact, I think that is a platitude derivative of the one I am discussing: "We are the greatest because we are the freest." I have heard that very often, as I suppose you have. But is it really true? If so, then I suppose the *really* greatest nation in the world would be one where there were no laws, and chaos prevailed—the Wild West, perhaps, in the days before the law arrived, where a fella could shoot up a town unless somebody bigger could stop him. No, that can't be the answer either.

Not to keep you in suspense, let me tell you what I think the answer is. We are the greatest, because of the good qualities of our people, and because of a governmental system that gives room for those qualities to develop. I refer to qualities such as generosity. Americans are there not only when their neighbors need help, but even when strangers on the other side of the world do. Qualities such as honesty. Americans are, by and large, people you can trust; George Washington and the cherry tree, Abe Lincoln and returning the book through the snowstorm are part of our tradition. Qualities such as constancy. Americans can be counted on. They are not quitters, even when things look bleak. Valley Forge and Bull Run are part of our tradition, too. Qualities such as tolerance. Americans believe in things—and believe deeply—but will try to persuade others to their way of thinking, and not coerce them. The First Amendment and the Virginia Declaration of

Religious Rights are part of our tradition, too. And I could go on: self-reliance, initiative, civility—these are also qualities we take pride in regarding as somehow especially American, characteristic of our great country. These are what make us the greatest.

The point I am driving toward—and maybe it has taken me too long to get there—is that not only is it not true that we are the greatest because we are the freest, but rather, quite the opposite is true: we are the freest because we have those qualities that make us the greatest. For freedom is a luxury that can be afforded only by the good society. When civic virtue diminishes, freedom will inevitably diminish as well. Take the simplest example. Many municipalities do not have any ordinances against spitting gum out on the sidewalk; as far as the law is concerned, you are "free" to do that. But that freedom is a consequence of the fact that not many people are so thoughtless of others as to engage in that practice. If that behavior becomes commonplace, you can be absolutely sure that an ordinance will be passed, and the "freedom" will disappear.

The same principle applies in larger matters. The English legal philosopher Lord Acton had it right when he said, "That society is the freest which is the most responsible." The reason is quite simple and quite inexorable: legal constraint—the opposite of freedom—is in most of its manifestations a cure for irresponsibility. You are all familiar, I hope, with Madison's famous passage in number 51 of the *Federalist Papers*:

> What is government itself, but the greatest of all reflections on human nature? If men were angels, no government would be necessary.

The same can be said of the *product* of government—laws—and the constraints upon individuals that those laws establish. Law steps in, *and will inevitably step in*, when the virtue and prudence of the society itself is inadequate to produce the needed result. When the society is composed entirely of criminals, only the strict regimentation of a prison will suffice.

If I am right that we are the freest because we are the greatest, the message for your lives should be clear. Do not go about praising our Bill of Rights and the wonderful liberties we enjoy without at the same time developing within yourselves, and within those whose lives you touch, the virtue that makes all that possible.

The last platitude I want to mention—it is appropriately last, because it usually comes toward the end of the commencement address—goes somewhat like this: "This is not an end, it is a beginning." I want to tell you that is not true. I think there is no more significant rite of passage in our society, no more abrupt end to a distinct age of your life, than the graduation from high school, and the departure from home that soon follows. You have been living up to now in a moral environment that could be closely supervised by the people who love you most in the world, your parents. They got to know your friends, your teachers, your school—and did what they could to change or improve them when they thought that was for your good. Most of you will be going off to college, which is not a place where your parents can any longer control the influences upon your character, and which is not, by and large, a place where anybody else seeks to exercise that control as well. From here on out you are, much more than you have ever been—I am groping for a platitude to convey the thought—captains of your own ship, masters of your own destiny. Your moral formation—what makes you a good person or a bad one, a success in all that matters or a failure—is now pretty much up to you. As a parent who is now sending off his sixth child, away from home and into a world that has a lot of wisdom but also a lot of folly, a lot of good but also a lot of bad, I assure you that if you are not at all worried at the prospect, your parents are. But there comes a time to let go, and it is now.

I have high hopes for the Class of '88, because I know a lot of them, I know some of their teachers, and I know the quality of education in knowledge as well as in goodness that Langley has provided. Good luck and—let's see, I had one last platitude around here somewhere; oh, yes—*the future is in your hands*. BINGO.

ON FAITH

"The serious Christian must be a pilgrim, an alien citizen, a bit 'different' from the world around him."

The Christian as Cretin

In 1960, Antonin Scalia graduated magna cum laude from Harvard Law School and married Radcliffe graduate Maureen McCarthy. He also won a fellowship that enabled him to travel with his bride throughout Europe during their honeymoon year. While in London they attended a performance of Robert Bolt's new play A Man for All Seasons. *Mrs. Scalia reports that Bolt's depiction of St. Thomas More—combining a life of faith with a firm commitment to the rule of law—made a strong impression on them and "grew in significance to us over the years."*

Justice Scalia nicknamed this speech "The Two Thomases," after Thomas More and Thomas Jefferson. From 1993 on, he presented it dozens of times to various St. Thomas More societies and other religious groups throughout the country. He delivered this particular version to St. Thomas More societies in Green Bay, Wisconsin, and Richmond, Virginia, in the fall of 2010.

———

The title of my talk today is "Not to the Wise: The Christian as Cretin." The second half of that title, "The Christian as Cretin," is meant, of course, to be a play on words. And it is a wordplay that has some etymological basis. The English word *cretin*, meaning "a person of deficient mental capacity," in fact derives from the French word *chrétien*, meaning "Christian," which was used in the Middle Ages to refer to the short, often grotesque, severely retarded people who were to be found in some remote valleys of the Alps—perhaps the result of excessive inbreeding. These people were called "chrétiens"—Christians—to make the point that they were human souls and not brutes.

It has often occurred to me, however, that for quite different reasons the equivalence of the words *Christian* and *cretin* makes a lot of sense. To be honest about it, that is the view of Christians—or at least of traditional Christians—taken by sophisticated society in modern times. One can be sophisticated and believe in God— heck, a First Mover is at least as easy to believe in as a Big Bang triggered by nothingness. One can even be sophisticated and believe in a *personal* God, a benevolent Being who loves mankind, so long as that Being does not intrude too ridiculously into the world—by working so-called miracles, for example, or by limiting human behavior in inconvenient ways. And one can even be sophisticated and believe in Jesus Christ, as having been in some sense a "son" of God (are we not all children of the Creator?) and as having in some sense triumphed over death (his message, after all, lives on). One can believe all that, I say, and still be considered sophisticated.

But to believe in what might be called "traditional" Christianity is something else. To believe, first and foremost, that Jesus Christ *was God*. (Why, the notion that the Creator should become a man is as unsophisticated as the notion that Zeus should become a bull.) Or to believe that he was born of a virgin. (Well, I mean, really!) That he actually, physically, rose from the grave. That he founded a church with power to bind and loose—to pronounce, authoritatively, the will of God for mankind. That, as he taught, hardship and suffering are not to be avoided at all costs but are to be embraced and indeed even sought after—as penance for sin, and as a means of sharing in the crucifixion of Christ. (How utterly ridiculous to forgo perfectly legitimate pleasures, and to seek discomfort! How absurd the vow of chastity and the hair shirt!) Or the belief in miracles, as at Lourdes or Fatima. Or, finally, the belief that those who love God and obey his commands will rise from the dead, in their bodies, and be happy with him forever in heaven; and that those who do not will burn eternally in hell.

Surely those who adhere to all or most of these traditional Christian beliefs are regarded, within the educated circles that you and I travel in, as—well, simpleminded. The attitude of the wise is well reflected in the statement that appeared in a news story (not an opinion piece) in *The Washington Post* some years ago, stating, matter-of-factly (as though anyone of intelligence knew and agreed with it), that Christian fundamentalists were "largely poor, uneducated and easy to command." The same attitude applies, of course, to traditional Catholics—by which I mean those who do such positively peasant-like things as saying the rosary, kneeling in adoration before the Eucharist, going on pilgrimages to Lourdes or Fatima, and, worst of all, following *indiscriminately* (rather than in smorgasbord fashion) the teachings of the Church. Surely, these people are "uneducated and easy to command." *Chrétien,* cretin.

Let me turn now to the first part of my title: "Not to the wise." I mean that as an allusion to the Gospel passage that you and I have heard read at Mass frequently. As recorded by St. Matthew and St. Luke, Christ said: "I praise thee, Father, Lord of heaven and earth, that thou didst hide these things from the wise and prudent, and didst reveal them to little ones." The same thought appears many other times in the New Testament. St. Paul writes to the Corinthians that "the natural man [i.e., the man of the world] does not perceive the things that are of the Spirit of God, for it is foolishness to him and he cannot understand." And he advises them: "Let no one deceive himself. If any one of you thinks himself wise in this world, let him become a fool, that he may come to be wise. For the wisdom of this world is foolishness with God." In other words, St. Paul quite entirely expected—he *assumed*—that the wise of the world would regard Christians as fools. And from the beginning until now that expectation has not been disappointed.

It is interesting to read of St. Paul's experience in that ancient center of wisdom and intellectuality, Athens. The Acts of the Apostles record some great successes in Paul's preaching; Athens was not one of them. He goes to the Areopagus—where, as the Acts contemptuously describe it, "all the Athenians and the visitors there from abroad used to spend all their leisure telling or listening to something new." Sort of an open-air *Donahue Show,* though perhaps a bit more intellectually elevated. Anyway, Paul goes up there, and he has this really clever speech laid out, in which he says that he knows the people of Athens are very religious, and he has noticed that one of their altars is inscribed "To the Unknown God." It is that God he has come to tell them about. This is a brilliant intro, and Paul gets rolling along pretty well, until he says that this God he has been talking about "will judge the world with justice by a Man whom he has appointed, and whom he has guaranteed to all by raising him from the dead." Well, that breaks it. The wise men of Athens, circa A.D. 50, know just as well as the wise men of America, A.D. 2010, that people don't rise from the dead. As the Acts record it: "Now when they heard of a resurrection of the dead, some began to sneer, but others said, 'We will hear thee again on this matter.'" Paul did not think the prospects of their hearing him again good enough to be worth his time. The next line of the Acts is "So Paul went forth from among them."

Now let me propel you forward in time, from A.D. 50 to A.D. 1804—just yesterday, by comparison—to the study of another wise man, a worthy successor of those of Athens, and one of our nation's greatest political figures, Thomas Jefferson. Jefferson is creating the work that he would call "The Life and Morals of Jesus of Nazareth," known more familiarly as the Jefferson Bible. As one historian [Jaroslav Pelikan] describes the scene:

> There has certainly never been a shortage of boldness in the history of biblical scholarship during the past two centuries, but for sheer audacity Thomas Jefferson's two redactions of the Gospels stand out even in that company. It is still a bit overwhelming to contemplate the sangfroid exhibited by the third president of the United States as, razor in hand, he sat editing the Gospels during February 1804, on (as he himself says) "2. or 3. nights only at Washington, after getting thro' the evening task of reading the letters and papers of the day." He was apparently quite sure that he could tell what was genuine and what was not in the transmitted text of the New Testament. . . .

No problema for a wise man. As Jefferson described the process in one of his letters:

We find in the writings of [Jesus's] biographers [i.e., the Evangelists] matter of two distinct descriptions. First, a groundwork of vulgar ignorance, of things impossible, of superstitions, fanaticisms and fabrications. Intermixed with these, again, are sublime ideas of the Supreme Being, aphorisms and precepts of the purest morality and benevolence, sanctioned by a life of humility, innocence and simplicity of manners, neglect of riches, absence of worldly ambition and honors, with an eloquence and persuasiveness which have not been surpassed. These could not be inventions of the groveling authors who related them. They are far beyond the powers of their feeble minds. They show that there was a character, the subject of their history, whose splendid conceptions were above all suspicion of being interpolations from their hands. Can we be at a loss in separating such materials, and ascribing each to its genuine author? The difference is obvious to the eye and to the understanding, and we may read as we run to each his part; and I will venture to affirm, that he who, as I have done, will undertake to winnow this grain from the chaff, will find it not to require a moment's consideration. The parts fall asunder of themselves, as would those of an image of metal and clay.

In another letter, Jefferson said "I separate . . . the gold from the dross; restore to [Jesus] the former, and leave the latter to the stupidity of some, and roguery of others of his disciples."

Well, the product of this exegesis is easy to imagine. It is a gospel fit for the Age of Reason—or indeed, for the wise of any age, including our own. I will satisfy your curiosity with examples from the beginning and the end. Jefferson's Bible does not begin with the betrothal of Joseph and Mary, the Annunciation by the angel Gabriel, the conception by the Holy Spirit. It begins with the decree from Caesar Augustus, the married couple Joseph and Mary going down to Bethlehem, and Jesus's birth in the stable. There are a few changes from the version you and I are familiar with. No shepherds in the fields, no multitude of the heavenly host, no wise men from the East, no slaughter of the innocents, no flight into Egypt. From Bethlehem, Joseph and Mary take the kid right back to Nazareth. As for the ending of the Jefferson Bible, I will read it to you:

> Now, in the place where he was crucified, there was a garden; and in the garden a new sepulchre, wherein was never man yet laid. There laid they Jesus, and rolled a great stone to the door of the sepulchre, and departed.

Cut. End of story. Run the crawl. As I told you earlier, the wise do not believe in resurrection of the dead (it is really quite absurd), just as they do not believe in virgin birth—so everything from Easter morning to the Ascension had to have been made up by those "groveling authors," those "rogues" Jefferson referred to, presumably part of their clever plan to get themselves crucified.

My point is not that reason and intellect must be laid aside where matters of religion are concerned. Assuredly not. A faith that has no rational basis is a false faith. That is why I am not a Branch Davidian. It is not irrational, however, to accept the testimony of eyewitnesses, who had nothing to gain by dissembling, about the resurrection of Jesus Christ, and about what Jesus taught them; or, for that matter, to accept the evidence of later miracles that establish the truth of the Church that Christ founded. What *is* irrational, it seems to me, is to reject a priori, with no investigation, the possibility of miracles in general, and of Jesus Christ's resurrection in particular—which is, of course, precisely what the worldly-wise do. They just will not have anything to do with miracles.

There was some excitement in the Washington area some years ago concerning a local priest who was said to have the stigmata, and in whose presence statues of the Virgin Mary and of the saints were said to weep. It didn't seem right. Stuff like that was supposed to happen in little villages in Italy or Portugal or Mexico—not inside the Beltway, for Pete's sake! (I felt sorry for our bishop, of course. Surely there can be nothing more difficult than having putative miracles occurring in your diocese. It's a no-win situation. In the histories of the great saints and visionaries, the local bishop, whose job is to be skeptical, is often the heavy—but never, as I recall, the hero.) Anyway, *The Washington Post* sent out a team of reporters, who produced a strange story about the phenomenon of these weeping statues: they obviously did not want to appear so unsophisticated as to believe this nonsense, but neither could they find any explanation for it. As far as they could tell, the young priest was not a charlatan, and puddles of water did indeed appear at the feet of the statues.

Well, I did not drive the few miles over to check it out; one more miracle is not going to make me believe any more than I already do. But the thought occurred to me: Why wasn't that church absolutely packed with nonbelievers, seeking to determine whether there might be something to this Catholic religion? Or why weren't *The Washington Post* reporters enthusiastic converts? Well, of course, the wisdom of the world does not operate that way. The wise do not investigate such silliness—and even if the miracle were performed under their nose, they would disbelieve. You may recall the parable of Dives, the rich man, and Lazarus the beggar who used to sit by his gate. When they die, Lazarus goes to heaven and Dives to hell. Dives prays to Abraham to send Lazarus to his brothers—to warn them, "lest they also come into this place of torment." But Abraham says, "They have Moses and the prophets; let them hear them," to which Dives replies "Nay, father Abraham: but if one went unto them from the dead, they will repent." And Abraham rejoins: "If they hear not Moses and prophets, neither will they be persuaded, though one rose from the dead." Quite so.

I have spoken to this lawyers' group (unflatteringly, sad to say) about one lawyer who was something of a universal man, Thomas Jefferson. To demonstrate what I mean about the intelligent Christian's appearing stupid to the world, let me say a few words about another lawyer and universal man: the patron saint of this organization, St. Thomas More. His life, or more precisely the ending of his life, is the prime example of the Christian as cretin.

More was, of course, one of the great men of his age: lawyer, scholar, humanist, philosopher, statesman—a towering figure not just in his own country of England but throughout Renaissance Europe. You will have missed the deep significance of More's martyrdom—and you will not understand why More is a particularly apt patron saint for lawyers, scholars, and intellectuals— unless you appreciate that the reason he died was, in the view of almost everyone at the time, a silly one. Many martyrs have died for refusing to deny Jesus Christ, or for spreading his gospel, or for adhering to his clear moral teachings. In going to their death, they have had the comfort of knowing that their Christian predecessors, contemporaries, and successors would praise and approve their obstinacy. Thomas More, on the other hand, went to his death to support the proposition that only the Bishop of Rome could bind or loose the marriage of Henry VIII. A papacy corrupt and politicized. A papacy that often granted or withheld divorce for reasons of diplomacy rather than doctrine—which may well have been the case with regard to the denial of Henry's divorce. More knew all that. More himself, like his humanist contemporaries such as Erasmus, had been a harsh critic of Rome.

Hillaire Belloc, in a lovely little essay on More entitled "The Witness to Abstract Truth," describes the situation like this:

> After four hundred years we have to-day forgotten how the matter looked to the men of the early sixteenth century. The average Englishman had little concern with the quarrel between the Crown and Rome. It did not touch his life. The Mass went on just the same and all the splendour of religion; the monasteries were still in being everywhere, there was no interruption whatsoever. Most of the great bodies—all the bishops except Fisher—had yielded. They had not yielded with great reluctance but as a matter of course. . . . To the ordinary man of that day, anyone, especially a highly placed official, who stood out against the King's policy *was a crank*. [Emphasis added.]

In what he did, More was unsupported by intelligent society, by his friends, even by his own wife. Robert Bolt's play *A Man for All Seasons* puts that point nicely. When More learns that the Convocation of Bishops has voted unanimously (except for John Fisher of Rochester) to adhere to the King's demands that they acknowledge his divorce despite the Pope, More decides that he must resign the chancellorship, and he asks his wife, Alice, to help him remove his chain of office. She says: "Sun and moon, Master More, you're taken for a wise man! Is this wisdom—to betray your ability, abandon practice, forget your station and your duty to your kin and behave like a printed book!" And later along the road, his friend the Duke of Norfolk says: "You're behaving like a fool. You're behaving like a crank. You're not behaving like a gentleman. . . . [I]t's disproportionate! . . . [W]e've all given in! Why must you stand out?" Foolish and disproportionate indeed. As one biographer put it, "More died for a Papacy that, as far as men could see, was little else than a small Italian princedom ruled by some of the least reputable of the Renaissance princes."

But of course More was seeing not with the eyes of men, but with the eyes of faith. He believed Christ's word that Peter was the Rock, and the Christian tradition that the Pope was the head of the Church. As low as the papacy had declined (one does not get much lower than Alexander VI, who reigned during More's lifetime), the Vicar of Christ alone—and not all the bishops of England—had the power to bind and to loose. I find it hard to understand the reasoning of those wise people who revere Thomas More as a saint rather than a world-class fool for dying to support the decision of Medici Pope Clement VII concerning King Henry's divorce of Catherine of Aragon, but who themselves ignore and indeed positively oppose the teachings of Pope John Paul II on much more traditional and less politically charged subjects. Go figure.

It is the hope of most speakers to impart wisdom. It has been my hope to impart, to those already wise in Christ, the courage to have their wisdom regarded as stupidity. Are we thought to be fools? No doubt. But, as St. Paul wrote to the Corinthians, "We are fools for Christ's sake." And are we thought to be "easily led" and childish? Well, Christ did constantly describe us as, of all things, his sheep, and said we would not get to heaven unless we became like little children. For the courage to suffer the contempt of the sophisticated world for these seeming failings of ours, we lawyers and intellectuals—who do not like to be regarded as unsophisticated—can have no greater model than the patron of this society, the great, intellectual, urbane, foolish, childish man that he was. St. Thomas More, pray for us.

BEING DIFFERENT

The Judicial Prayer Breakfast Group, first convened in 1972, is an informal gathering of judicial officers from the various ranks of the federal and D.C. governments. Open to any judge interested in its monthly meetings, it includes judges of diverse faiths. Justice Scalia presented this talk to the group in December 1992.

⸻

The announced topic for my talk today was "On Being Different." I am sure many of you come here today thinking to learn how or why in the world I can write these 8-to-l dissents, or not believe in substantive due process. In fact, however, I intend to speak not about being different in the law (a relatively unimportant subject), but rather about being different in life. More specifically, I want to speak about the expectation—the reality—that Christians will be different.

I and those Catholics in the room who are my age or older have had the great good fortune of growing up at a time when even in areas with large Catholic populations such as New York or Chicago, it was a little bit strange to be a Catholic. Catholic was not "mainstream." There were still some places where Catholics, like Jews, were not welcome. America had not yet had a Catholic president. John F. Kennedy had not yet appeared to express the hope that his fellow citizens would not vote against him "because," as he put it, "of my religious affiliation."

I have always hated that phrase, reducing the most profound commitment of a man's life to a mere membership preference. "Ah, yes, I am a Catholic. But I might be a Muslim or a Jew or even an Episcopalian tomorrow, if I should choose to change my 'religious affiliation.'" Perhaps there is an open season, like changing from Blue Cross to the Postal Worker's Plan. Surely the man should have said, "I hope no one will vote against me because of what I am." That is what my hero Popeye would have said. "I yam what I yam." But never mind.

My point, before I launched myself into this digression, is that when I was growing up to be Catholic was to be a bit different. It was a little bit beyond—in some parts of the country a lot beyond—what was respectable.

And the Church, I must say, far from seeking to eliminate that differentness, in some ways seemed to go out of its way to emphasize it. The Protestants here may remember that their Catholic friends used to have to eat fish on Fridays, when everyone else was having hot dogs. And at a Saturday night party the Catholics (or at least those who planned to receive Communion the next day) would no longer eat or drink anything after midnight. These dietary rules were not as strict, or as noticeable, as those observed by, for example, orthodox Jews. But they still served to increase rather than reduce our "apartness."

Now there were many bad aspects to that "apartness." It kept us Catholics, for example, from participating in the kind of fellowship with men and women of other Christian faiths we are enjoying here this morning. But there were some good aspects as well—and aspects that are sorely missed, I think, in modern Christianity. That "differentness" said to me in the field of religion what my parents repeatedly reminded me of in the field of social activity. Whenever I wanted to go to a certain movie, or a certain place, that my parents disapproved of, I would say, of course, as children always do, that *everybody else* was going. My parent's invariable and unanswerable response was: "You're not everybody else."

It is enormously important, I think, for Christians to learn early and remember long that lesson of "differentness"; to recognize that what is perfectly lawful, and perfectly permissible, for everyone else—even our very close non-Christian friends—is not necessarily lawful and permissible for us. That the ways of Christ and the ways of the world—even the world of Main Street America—are not the same, and we should not expect them to be. That possessing and expressing a worldview and a code of moral behavior that is comfortably in conformance with what prevails in the respectable secular circles in which we live and work is no assurance of goodness and virtue. That Christ makes some special demands upon us that occasionally require us to be out of step. It is only if one *has* that sense of differentness—not animosity toward others in any sense, but *differentness*—that one has a chance of being strong enough to obey the teachings of Christ on many matters much more significant than Friday abstinence and Communion-fast rules—for example, rules of sexual morality.

The divergence of Christian teaching from the morality of the general society seems especially obvious (and especially blatant) today. Just turn on the tube any night, or walk up to any newsstand. But it would be wrong to think that this divergence between the ways of the world and Christian teaching is new. To the contrary, it is as old as the faith itself. And it sets that Christian apart not only from utterly decadent societies such as Sodom and Gomorrah, but even from purportedly moral societies as Israel itself was when he was crucified. Christ said, "You will be hated by all men for my name's sake." He said at the Last Supper:

If the world hates you, know that it has hated me before you. If you were of the world, the world would love what is its own. But because you are not of the world, but I have chosen you out of the world, therefore the world hates you.

And again:

I have given them thy work; and the world has hated them, because they are not of the world, even as I am not of the world. I do not pray that thou take them out of the world, but that thou keep them from evil. They are not of the world, even as I am not of the world.

And he said to Pilate:

> My kingdom is not of this world. If my kingdom were of this
> world, my followers would have fought that I might not be de-
> livered to the Jews. But, as it is, my kingdom is not from here.

That thought pervades the Gospels. It is also in the early
church. Consider the following passage from a letter of one of the
early fathers in the late second century, describing the early Christians:

> Though residents at home in their own countries, their behav-
> ior is more like that of transients. They take their full part
> as citizens, but they also submit to everything as if they were
> aliens. For them, any foreign country is a homeland, and any
> homeland a foreign country.

And of course that same notion has come down faithfully to
modern Christianity. The most influential devotional work, in English, in Protestant Christianity was called *The Pilgrim's Progress*,
preserving the same ancient image of the Christian as an alien
citizen, a traveler just passing through these parts on the way to
the promised land.

It becomes quite obvious why the serious Christian must be a
pilgrim, an alien citizen, a bit "different" from the world around
him, when one considers how many Christian virtues make no
sense whatever to the world. Consider, for example, the first and
foremost Christian virtue, humility: awareness of the greatness of
God and hence the insignificance of self. That is a crazy idea to the
world, which values above all else self-esteem and self-assertion.

Or consider the Christian virtue (or practice) of self-denial. I
am not talking about self-denial in the sense of refraining from
what is sinful; but self-denial in the sense of deliberately depriving oneself of what is good and lawful, solely for the sake of doing
penance and asserting the dominance of the spirit over the flesh.
Self-denial in the sense of the serious fasting that the Gospels re-

peatedly describe Jesus as engaging in. Can the world possibly understand that? I had a teacher in high school, an elderly Jesuit, a saintly man, who was reputed to wear a hair shirt. My God, what a crazy thing! To wear this itchy thing just for the sake of being a little bit uncomfortable all day. It's almost—why, it's almost as crazy as John the Baptist. (I am not, let it be clear, recommending the hair shirt; personally, I can't even stand wearing synthetic blends. But my point is that only the Christian, and not the worldly person, can understand why one should not be deemed certifiably insane if he chooses to engage in such a practice.)

Or consider, finally, the Christian virtue of chastity. Except for divine command, it makes no sense. The world can find reasons for condemning dishonesty, deception, and manipulativeness in sexual relations. But if those secular evils are avoided—if the partners are really fond of each other, or are not *even* fond of each other, but both understand that they are just having a good time— what *possible* justification is there for chastity? Surely the worldly ideal is not chastity, but safe sex. And to preach the opposite is like—well, it's like talking about hair shirts.

When the values of Christ and of the world are so divergent—so inevitably divergent—we should not feel surprised if we find ourselves now and then "out of step." In fact, we should be worried if we are never that way. As Christ told us, we are *supposed* to be out of step. We must learn to accept it. Learn to take pride in it. For Jesus also said (and this is a scary thought):

> And I say to you, everyone who acknowledges me before men, him will the Son of Man also acknowledge before the angels of God. But whoever disowns me before men will be disowned before the angels of God.

I made remarks somewhat similar to these a few weeks ago, at a father-daughter Communion breakfast at Georgetown Visitation High School. The gospel for the day—I guess it was the second Sunday of Advent—happened to fit in beautifully with the subject and gave me a new insight into how much Christ values our willingness to be different, to stand by his side against the world. The gospel for the day was the story of the good thief Dismas, tradition tells us his name was. That story appears only in Luke, who sets the scene first, as follows:

> And the people stood looking on; and the rulers with them kept sneering at him, saying, "He saved others; let him save himself, if he is the Christ, the chosen one of god." And the soldiers also mocked him, coming to him and offering him common wine, and saying, "If thou art the King of the Jews, save thyself!"

So here is Christ, lifted up on the cross, looking down over the crowd, dying, and what he sees and hears is nothing but rejection, repudiation, and mockery. Luke continues:

> Now one of those robbers who were hanged was abusing him, saying, "If thou art the Christ, save thyself and us!" But the other in answer rebuked him and said, "Dost not even thou fear God, seeing that thou art under the same sentence? And we indeed justly, for we are receiving what our deeds deserved; but this man has done nothing wrong." And he said to Jesus, "Lord, remember me when thou comest into thy kingdom." And Jesus said to him, "Amen I say to thee, this day thou shalt be with me in paradise."

What an extraordinary thing. Dismas is the *only* saint canonized by Christ Himself. The only human being, including even Mary, that we know *from the Gospels*, indeed from the mouth of Christ Himself, to be in heaven. So much did Jesus value that man's standing beside Him when all the world had abandoned Him. And the same reward, for the same willingness to go against the world, awaits us.

Christmas is coming up soon. The world will celebrate that with us. The world likes to celebrate. It has not observed with us, of course, the penitential season of Advent that precedes Christmas—a sort of mini-Lent, when Christians have traditionally deprived themselves. The world does not like to deprive itself. Perhaps, in observing faithfully what remains of Advent, we can recapture some sense of our distinctiveness, our positive "weirdness," as the world judges. What can be more incomprehensible to the world than *intentionally* depriving oneself of pleasure or satisfaction—*not* in order to lose weight, or to retain one's health, nor even because the pleasure is in any way sinful, but *solely* in order to mortify the flesh (as we used to say) and thereby to affirm commitment to the truth that our only lasting pleasure and satisfaction is not here, where we are alien citizens, but hereafter.

CATHOLIC HIGHER EDUCATION

The Catholic University of America awards its James Cardinal Gibbons Medal annually "to honor any person who, in the opinion of the Alumni Association's Board of Governors, has rendered distinguished and meritorious service to the Roman Catholic Church, the United States of America, or the Catholic University of America." Its recipients are a diverse bunch: actress Helen Hayes, pro football Hall of Famer Darrell Green, Sister Mary Prejean, and in 1994, Justice Scalia. The justice used the occasion to discuss America's sociological development and to defend the importance of universities with a distinctively Catholic identity.

———

I am genuinely honored to be a recipient of the Cardinal Gibbons Medal. Surely there are few awards in the country that have such a distinguished list of recipients—from John Kennedy to Nancy Reagan, and including, to mention a few of those I admire particularly, Fulton Oursler, Fulton J. Sheen, Cardinal Baum, Archbishop Hannan, and Monsignor John Tracy Ellis. I am proud to be in such company.

It is always somewhat intimidating to receive an award from a Catholic organization. The Church has been wise, I think, not to pronounce its greatest heroes, that is to say, its saints, until after they are dead. Preferably not until long after they are dead, so that their entire life can be considered with some detachment—indeed, not merely with detachment but with a devil's advocate to point out all the warts. In honoring someone who may still go on to flub the dub, you take some risk. I am relieved to observe, however, that you are not honoring me for my saintliness; and doubtless the choirs of angels are pleased with that as well. Not to mention my loving but Hibernically frank wife, Maureen.

Besides not honoring me for having achieved sanctification, I am sure you also do not honor me for my position on what has become a defining issue for the Catholic Church in America, and indeed throughout the world: abortion. Or at least not for my position as a federal judge regarding the constitutionality of laws prohibiting that act. I accept no praise for that from Catholics, but only from lawyers; because I would hold otherwise, whatever my personal views on the practice, if I thought the law were different.

I am a natural object of your generosity, however, because my ties to Catholic University, though perhaps not unusually close, have been unusually long. I did my undergraduate studies, of course—in the mid-1950s—not at Catholic but at Georgetown. I was well familiar with CU, however—partly because I used to travel with some frequency to Little Rome, that part of the city occupied by CU and many other Catholic institutions, including the usual object of my visits, Trinity College. Many was the evening I recall standing on the island across from Peoples Drug Store on Dupont Circle, waiting for the transfer bus that would take me up North Capitol Street to your part of the city.

I was also painfully familiar with Catholic University as the object of my intense envy because of its drama program. I was president of the Mask & Bauble Society during my time at Georgetown, and we did our best—though with little hope of success—to match the highly professional productions staged by the fabled Father Hartke, who, I may note, is another of my predecessors as recipient of the Cardinal Gibbons Medal. I think it is fair to say that, in those days of the '50s, we thespians at Georgetown had the same feelings toward the Catholic U. theater group that the teams of the American League had toward the Damn Yankees. I am glad to see that the fine tradition of good theater at CU has held up better than the Yankees, and that Father Hartke was not succeeded by George Steinbrenner.

My later relations with CU were more sporadic. Of course I was reminded of it every year later in life—whether in Cambridge,

Cleveland, Charlottesville, Washington, Chicago, or Palo Alto—as the annual church collection would be taken for its support. And I would contribute or not, I must confess, depending upon whether one of its media theologians had rubbed me the wrong way that year. (That is one of the lesser reasons I am not up for sainthood.) During the 1970s I held, successively, several posts in the executive branch of the federal government. As one of them was coming to an end, I gave some thought to putting myself forward as a candidate for the deanship of your law school—and went so far as to interview with the search committee of the faculty. But I was wise enough, even at that young age, to conclude that being a law dean was indeed (as one of my former deans and mentors had described it) like running a zoo with the cages open. And since then, to bring my Catholic U. career down to date, I have spoken several times at the university and at the law school, and have come to be a friend, if not a confidant, of Father Byron and Brother Ellis.

I am, ladies and gentlemen, not a proponent of after-dinner speeches, particularly heavy ones. And so I shall make my substantive remarks this evening quite brief. I want to say a few words about Catholic education, and about its place in modern America. What a Catholic university must be depends upon the society in which that university functions. In Europe in the Middle Ages, when everything around was Catholic, I suppose the task of a Catholic university was simply to be a university; to preserve, expand, and pass on the body of human knowledge. It had no special or peculiar responsibility, except perhaps in its schools of theology, for nurturing or keeping alive the faith, and the manner of life that the faith entails. With the Reformation, that changed, as the great universities of Europe, and later of America, divided themselves on denominational lines. I did my third year of study at Georgetown in its junior-year-abroad program at the University of Fribourg, which was the only Catholic university in Switzerland. The others, at Geneva and Lausanne, for example, were officially Protestant. And in this country, the earliest colleges and universities were also denominational.

Even so, however, after the Reformation and until the great

upheaval of the Napoleonic Wars, Western society was still essentially Christian. It was still possible to speak of "Christendom." The sectarian universities, Catholic and Presbyterian, Lutheran, Congregationalist, Baptist and Methodist, espoused different dogmas, to be sure, but still taught, and existed in the midst of, a common, generally accepted Christian morality. That was true in the new United States no less than in Europe. While the magnificent Constitution we brought forth in 1787 banished sectarian religion from government, religion in general and Christianity in particular remained a prominent part of public life and manners. That lasted well into the nineteenth century, as the words to the "Battle Hymn of the Republic" well enough demonstrate.

That changed with the French Revolution, which ultimately spread throughout Europe a secularization of public life. The University of Paris, where Aquinas taught and Ignatius recruited Xavier to the Society of Jesus, became a secular state school. And that secularization eventually, though much later, came to these shores. Here it went through an intermediate stage, in which, acknowledging the identity and great contribution of our largest non-Christian religious minority, we became a nation that believed in, and celebrated, its Judeo-Christian character. That was not much of a stretch, after all, Christianity being—as the Romans recognized but we sometimes later forgot—a sect of Judaism. We were at that stage of development, the Judeo-Christian stage, when I was a boy—or at least we were at that stage in New York, where we acknowledged publicly our national beliefs in a personal God, and in certain common, revealed truths including the Decalogue, and agreed to differ respectfully about the rest.

One can trace the changes in America from the opinions of its Supreme Court—even (and indeed, especially) those opinions that were wrong about the law because they allowed it to be distorted by social beliefs. The prime example is one of my least favorite Supreme Court opinions, delivered without dissent in 1892, entitled *Church of the Holy Trinity v. United States*. The case involved a federal statute entitled "An Act to prohibit the importation and migration of foreigners and aliens under contract or agreement to perform labor in the United States, its Territories, and the District of Columbia." A church in the city of New York made such a contract with an English minister, whereby he was to come to New York and serve as the church's rector and pastor, which he did. The United States sued the church for the penalty provided by the statute, and the trial court upheld the sanction. The Supreme Court reversed. Even though the language of the statute was categorical, and made no exceptions for ministers (though it made exceptions for professional actors, artists, lecturers and singers), the Court simply refused to read it to mean what it said. "It is a familiar rule," the Court said, "that a thing may be within the letter of the statute and yet not within the statute, because not within its spirit, nor within the intention of its makers." I do not believe that. I think the text enacted by Congress is the law, and the duty of the Court is to apply it (unless it be unconstitutional), rather than to consult spirits. That awful case is frequently cited to us by counsel who want us to ignore what the statute says. But for present purposes I am interested in another mistake the Court made. The spirits it listened to caused it to go on for eight pages leading to the following conclusion:

> These, and many other matters which might be noticed, add a volume of unofficial declarations to the mass of organic utterances that this is a Christian nation. In the face of all these, shall it be believed that a Congress of the United States intended to make it a misdemeanor for a church of this country to contract for the services of a Christian minister residing in another nation?

To be fair to the Court, its opinion made clear that it was just as unthinkable that the statute would prohibit a Jewish synagogue's importation of an "eminent rabbi." But the official recognition that we were a "Christian nation" surely had no place in the *United States Reports*. Legally it was false. But sociologically I have no doubt it was (in 1892) true—which is why the opinion was unanimous and so readily accepted.

For the next stage of our national development, the Judeo-Christian stage, we can jump forward about half a century in the *United States Reports*, to a case called *Zorach v. Clauson*, decided in 1952. It involved a program which I myself had been involved in in the New York City public schools—the so-called "released time" program, in which public-school children of all faiths whose parents made the request could be released from school an hour early one day a week, to attend religious instruction or devotional exercises. New York City taxpayers challenged the practice as unconstitutional. The Court upheld it. The opinion for the Court by Justice Douglas, hardly one of the more conservative justices, spoke of Catholics, Protestants, and Jews, and included the following passage:

> We are a religious people whose institutions presuppose a Supreme Being. . . . When the state encourages religious instruction or cooperates with religious authorities by adjusting the schedule of public events to sectarian needs, it follows the best of our traditions. For it then respects the religious nature of our people and accommodates the public service to their spiritual needs.

That description of our national character reflects, I think, stage two of our national sociological development: the Judeo-Christian stage, in which monotheistic religion in general was favored, though no particular denomination.

The last and most recent stage, the secularization of our national character, came quickly and is reflected most clearly in the language of a 1968 Supreme Court case called *Epperson v. Arkansas*. There you will find no more talk about a "religious people," and about "accommodating the public service to [the people's] spiritual needs." "The First Amendment," the Court says in *Epperson*, "mandates governmental neutrality"—not merely between the various religious sects, but "between religion and nonreligion."

My point in this discussion is not to criticize the holdings of these cases, but to point out the progression that they demonstrate in the perception of our national character: from a Christian nation, to a religious nation, to a nation that has no preference between religion and irreligion. I think that perception is by and large accurate, at least insofar as concerns what might be called the "governing classes" of society. The signs of the passing of the old religiousness are everywhere. In our laws, for example, which now approve many practices formerly forbidden because of a national aversion rooted primarily in religious beliefs. In our body of common knowledge, which used to include *The Pilgrim's Progress*, and now seemingly does not include the Bible. A recent survey found that only about half of the American people could name the first book of the Old Testament; only about a third could say who gave the Sermon on the Mount; and only about a fifth could name a single Old Testament prophet. A nation that used to abound with names like Ezekiel and Zebadiah now presumably thinks that the Beatitudes are a female singing group, and that the Apocrypha is a building in Greece. I read in a national newspaper recently a piece about some war-torn country, describing how anxious women went to church to "light a candle and make a prayer." "Make" a prayer! Our information media have begun to lose even the vocabulary of religion.

As one who believes in God, and who believes that those nations who love or at least fear Him, and do His will, will by and large prosper, I regret this secularization of our country, or at least of our intellectual classes. My object here, however, is not to bemoan or even criticize it, but to point out that it has a bearing upon what the nature and the mission of the modern American Catholic university must be. If you are serious about your Catholicism, you are operating in a more hostile environment, or at any rate in a less supportive environment, than used to be the case. That has several consequences which you must be prepared to accept—or else be prepared to lose your institutional soul.

First, you cannot expect to be as attractive a place for many faculty members and students as a secular institution that shares their beliefs and values (or the lack of them). If the place is indeed infused with Catholicism, it will be uncongenial. In the days when I was a law professor at the University of Chicago, I served for a term as a member of the Board of Visitors of the J. Reuben Clark Law School of Brigham Young University in Provo, Utah. Rex Lee, who is now the president of Brigham Young, and was then the dean of the law school, had been a colleague of mine at the Department of Justice. The J. Reuben Clark Law School was a place that had not lost its religious character—and for that reason would in some respects have been a difficult place for even me to teach. Oh, sure, it would have been sort of nice to stay in a place where dinner conversation does not stop and forks pause midway to the mouth when you mention that you have nine children. But I would have had to take on my entire daily ration of caffeine before I left home in the morning and would have had to sneak cigarettes in the men's room. In a Catholic university, there are, or ought to be, similar constraints concerning an expected lifestyle that is increasingly different from that of the surrounding world.

Indeed, I will go further than that. Part of the task of a Catholic university, at least at the undergraduate level, must be precisely moral formation. Not long ago, all colleges, even nondenominational ones, used to consider that their task: to teach young men and women (and college freshmen are indeed still young and impressionable) not merely to think well but to live virtuously. Perhaps because our society no longer has firm beliefs about what is virtuous, there are few if any nondenominational schools that even pretend to pursue that task—unless it is the service academies, which still seek to inculcate the values of honor, duty, and country. Catholic universities, however, cannot avoid that task, and indeed betray the expectations of tuition-paying Catholic parents if they shirk it. Demands for a moral and virtuous lifestyle that is different from much of the world about us will lose you faculty members; and it will lose you students. I think the alternative is to lose your Catholic character.

Besides constraints upon lifestyle, there are, yes, constraints upon what is taught. The only justification for a Catholic university, it seems to me, is that there is some distinctive approach to human knowledge that is peculiar to Catholic, or at least

Christian, belief. Otherwise, devote the money to Newman Clubs on secular campuses, or give it to the missions.

There are some things that must be taught at Catholic universities, and some things that must not: How to use human fetuses for useful scientific research, for example. Or how Mary was in fact not a virgin and Jesus had two brothers and a sister. Or how artificial birth control and abortion are morally okay. Is this a restriction on free intellectual inquiry? I think not. It is simply a restriction on where it shall be done and who shall pay. If one does not believe in such restrictions, one does not believe in Catholic dogma, and one should not believe in Catholic universities. Catholic universities do not exist, I suggest, simply to make it easier for the press to locate a Catholic theologian who disagrees with the Pope.

The American academic landscape is strewn with colleges and universities—many of them the finest, academically, in the land—that were once denominational but in principle or practice no longer are. Antioch University, for example, was founded by the Christian Church and was later Unitarian. Bucknell and the University of Chicago were Baptist. Dartmouth and Yale were Congregational. Duke, Northwestern, and Vanderbilt were Methodist. Lehigh was Episcopalian; Princeton, Presbyterian. I used to marvel, when I was a young man, at how institutions founded out of religious enthusiasm, and once imbued with religious zeal, could have so far changed. With foolish sectarian pride, I thought that could never happen to Catholic institutions. Of course I was wrong. We started later, but we are on the same road.

Catholic University has a heightened immunity against that development, because of its pontifical charter, because of its board of directors (the American bishops), and indeed because of its very name. But by the same token it has a heightened responsibility. To demand that any Catholic university be more Catholic than this school is to demand, so to speak, that it be more Catholic than the Pope. By and large the school has lived up to that responsibility. I do not mean to minimize the difficulty that entails—in reducing the size of the pool of brilliant faculty and students that the university can draw upon; in producing diminished esteem from a generally secularized national academic establishment; and in diverting financial and emotional resources toward difficult and unpleasant administrative tasks and even, sometimes, litigation. But as the parson says in the *Canterbury Tales*, if gold should rust, then what would iron do? All Catholic parents who aspire to send their children to Catholic universities—and not merely those who send them here—owe the directors, the administrators, and the faculty of this institution a debt of gratitude for the hard task they have undertaken.

CHURCH AND STATE

In December 1989, Justice Scalia discussed the American tradition of separation of church and state before an audience of American Catholics at the Pontifical North American College, the seminary of the American Catholic bishops in Rome. Just a few years later, his son Paul would study for the priesthood there.

————

I want to speak to you this evening about a subject that has been of particular interest to Americans and that Americans have been particularly good at—the relationship between church and state. And I want to look at that subject from each of the particular viewpoints that you and I share: first (and just briefly), from the point of view of citizens of the United States; and, second, from the point of view of Roman Catholics.

No principle of American democracy is more fundamental than what has come to be known as the separation of church and state. Unlike many constitutional prescriptions that bear upon individual liberties, this one is reflected not only in the Bill of Rights adopted in 1791—which says that "Congress shall make no law respecting an establishment of religion or prohibiting the free exercise thereof"—but also in the *original* Constitution, which forbids a religious test for federal office.

A separation of church and state was more politically needful in the American republic than elsewhere, because of the sheer diversity of religious views. (A prominent French judge once explained to me the essential difference between France and the

United States as follows: France has two religions and three hundred cheeses; the United States has two cheeses and three hundred religions.) But perhaps more than any other principle of American government, that one—the separation of church and state—has swept the Western world. I hope you will excuse my cynicism if I believe that the single most significant cause of that healthy development has been, quite probably, a decline in the vigor of religious belief. Keeping the state out of matters of religion is a much easier political principle for the agnostic than it is for the "true believer" (to use Eric Hoffer's term) of any faith. If one is a skeptic, or not entirely convinced of the truth of one's own religious beliefs, it is quite easy to agree that those beliefs should not be imposed, and indeed should not even be fostered, by the state. After all, they might be wrong. But for the Ayatollah Khomeini—or, for that matter, for devout Christians of the sort who managed the Inquisition—the doctrine is more difficult. If one truly believes that the *hereafter* is all-important, that the pleasures and griefs of our eighty years or so in this world are insignificant except as a means of entering the next, then the temptation is to take whatever action is necessary, including coercive action by the state, to save people—for their own good, whether they know it or not.

In any case, our American political tradition has happily removed this temptation from the path of even the zealous religious believer. It would be wrong to think, however, that the separation of church and state means that the political views of men and women must remain unaffected and uninformed by their religious beliefs. That would be quite impossible to achieve and is assuredly not part of our political tradition. The Declaration of Independence begins by invoking "the Laws of Nature and of Nature's God," and concludes "with a firm reliance on the Protection of Divine Providence." The philosophy expressed in that document, that "all men are endowed *by their Creator* with certain unalienable Rights," underlay the Bill of Rights. Belief in God, leading to that belief in human freedom, had much to do with the greatest war in our national history, as the words of "The Battle Hymn of the

Republic" make plain. From abolition to prohibition, the secular arrangements that Americans have voted for, or indeed fought for, have often been related to their religious beliefs.

It has become fashionable to speak of the American constitutional system as though it contained within itself the philosophy of John Stuart Mill—that everything must be permitted, and nothing can be forbidden, unless it physically harms another human being. That is simply not so. Consider, for example, laws against bigamy, which the Supreme Court has held to be constitutional. Or laws against public nudity. Or laws against cruelty to animals. It cannot be said that any of these prevents physical harm to another human being—or even aesthetic harm of much significance. (If the nudity bothers you, avert your eyes.) It seems to me that society's desire for laws of this sort—and all societies have them—is traceable to some common ethos, either religiously based or indistinguishable from religious prescription, which the old writers used to call *bonos mores*—"good morals." The most difficult task of constitutional adjudication in modern times, when these shared values are less uniform than they once were, is to decide how far the state can go in preserving a common fabric of morality.

Though its commands may be vague at the margins, however, our American tradition of separation of church and state is in its essentials firm and clear. I intend to address most of my remarks this evening to the subject of church and state looked at from the other perspective that you and I share, the perspective of a Roman Catholic. There the outlines are not as clear—but I think they ought to be. It seems to me (and I think I am not impressing my American notions upon the matter) that our faith's message on the subject is essentially the same as that of the Constitution: church and state are separate. One can reason at least partway to the conclusion, I suppose, theologically: state coercion of religious belief is wrong because it suppresses the free will that is precisely the respect in which man is made, as we say, "in the image of God." It is not possible to save someone "in spite of himself." But I think the revealed word of God, the Gospels, go much further than this modest point and display a vision of the separate sphere of operation of church and state that is similar to what the Founding Fathers produced.

The strongest evidence—and Christ's only explicit statement on the subject—is the well-known exchange with the Pharisees on the subject of taxes. Knowing the Jews' hatred of Roman rule, and the religious scruples of many of them against paying taxes to a heathen emperor who styled himself a god, the Pharisees asked Christ whether it was lawful—that is, lawful under the Jewish religious law—to pay tribute to Caesar. A question, it seemed, which had no answer that would not be damaging to Jesus's cause in one way or another: either by alienating devout Jews, or by making himself an enemy of the Roman state. As you recall, he asked the Pharisee to show him a coin and inquired whose image was on it. When the answer came back "Caesar's," he delivered that devastating line, "Render unto God the things that are God's and unto Caesar the things that are Caesar's." It was, in modern terms, a stopper. As St. Luke records it, "marvelling at his answer, they kept silence."

But it was, of course, more than just a snappy comeback. Christ said it not only because it was a hard point to answer, but because it was true. The business of the state, he was saying, is not God's business. Not that the state is in any way inherently evil; or that there are not good governments and bad governments insofar as pursuing the proper ends of government are concerned; or that some governments are not more conducive to their citizens' service of God than others. But in the last analysis the most important objectives of human existence—goodness, virtue, godliness, salvation—are not achieved through the state; and those who seek them there are doomed to disappointment.

The Gospels are so full of that message that it is surprising it can be so readily ignored. St. John records, for example, that after Jesus fed the five thousand with five barley loaves and two fishes, the crowd was so impressed that they wanted to make him king. Not a bad post, one would think, if the state were particularly useful for achieving the most important things Christ was after. John records Christ's reaction to that prospect as follows: "When Jesus perceived that they would come to take him by force and make him king, he fled again to the mountain, himself alone."

Or, of course, the memorable interview with the Roman procurator Pilate—almost a personification of confrontation between religion and government, displaying so succinctly how little the latter understands the former. Pilate asks Jesus whether it's true that he's a king. Jesus replies—I have always thought it a very playful reply under the circumstances—Did you come to this conclusion on your own, or did somebody tell you? And Pilate bristles. "Am I a Jew?" Jesus then goes on to talk about his kingdom. "My kingdom is not of this world. If my kingdom were of this world, my followers would have fought that I might not be delivered. . . . But, as it is, my kingdom is not from here." Pilate replies, in effect, "So you admit you're a king," and Jesus answers: "Thou sayest it; I am a king. This is why I was born, and why I have come into the world, to bear witness to the truth." And Pilate ends the interview with that sad line—so expressive of the cynicism that comes with power, then as now—"What is truth?"

It could not be clearer from all of this that the state is not the Christian's source of power, nor his means of salvation. The fundamental reason, I suggest, is also clear from the Gospels: that the focus of concern of the two kingdoms is fundamentally different. A good government should not, to be sure, impede the religious practices of its people; it ought indeed, as many of the decisions of our Supreme Court have said, accommodate those practices where possible. But its main function is not the hereafter but the here: assuring a safe, just, and prosperous society. Contrast that with the main function of the kingdom Christ was referring to. I mentioned a little earlier the feeding of the five thousand. The Gospels mention a similar incident in which Christ fed four thousand. How significant, I have always thought, that they mention no others. From all indications, there was plenty of poverty in Judea in those days—yet Christ chooses to alleviate it by miraculous means only twice, in circumstances in which the object of the exercise is to show his compassion and his power rather than to end once and for all the hardship of a poor country. How different from the way

Caesar would—and should—have acted if he possessed the same power. The central concerns of their kingdoms were, you see, quite different. Caesar would never have said—*should* never have said—the following:

> [D]o not be anxious for your life, what you shall eat; nor yet for your body, what you shall put on. The life is a greater thing than the food, and the body than the clothing. . . .
>
> Consider how the lilies grow; they neither toil nor spin, yet I say to you that not even Solomon in all his glory was arrayed like one of these. But if God so clothes the grass which flourishes in the field today but tomorrow is thrown into the oven, how much more you, O you of little faith! . . .
>
> [D]o not seek what you shall eat, or what you shall drink. . . . But seek the kingdom of God, and all these things shall be given you besides.

I suggest that, coming from a temporal ruler, that would be a perfect recipe for national disaster. It is assuredly the business of the state to be concerned about precisely those things.

I hope you will not mistake what I am saying. My point is not that the Christian has no concern for how government operates, or what it achieves. Of course he does. In everything he performs, from baseball to government, the Christian is supposed to put on the mind of Christ, which includes a concern for all his fellow men. So a government that serves the interests of the few at the expense of the many is to that extent an un-Christian government. But to fix upon good government as the objective, or even the principal manifestation, of Christianity is to give the business I am in more credit than it deserves—and to miss the point of the faith. Rulers who do not follow Christian principles—of justice, of unselfishness, and of charity—have *personally* much to account for; but they do not necessarily rule over a less Christian society. And vice versa: rulers who follow Christian principles may well store up merit for *themselves* in the next world; but they do not necessarily bring the Kingdom of God to their subjects.

I may digress momentarily to make the related observation that Christian principles in the context of government do not coincide with Christian principles in the context of personal morality. For when government acts, it does not act merely as one of God's creatures dealing with another of God's creatures of equal worth and dignity; rather, if it is a lawful government, it acts (as I shall discuss at greater length later) pursuant to God's authority and indeed on His behalf. What is Christian morality in person-to-person dealings, therefore, is not necessarily Christian morality in dealings between the government and those lawfully subject to its power. Christ says, of person-to-person dealings, that if a person should steal your cloak, give him your tunic as well. Could a state possibly operate on such a principle? He says, of person-to-person dealings, that we should forgive him who wrongs us seven times seventy times. Could a criminal-law system possibly heed this advice? The epitome of personal Christian perfection is to distribute all one's worldly goods to the poor; but that does not translate to the proposition that the epitome of Christian government is communism (with or without official atheism)—any more than the personal Christian virtue of poverty translates to a governmental Christian virtue of poverty.

But to return to my principal thesis: preoccupation with government misses the point—which is not the material salvation of the society, but the spiritual welfare of individual souls. To acquire a theological fixation upon the former is ultimately to distort the gospel message. That is, by the way, the sort of distortion that has probably always occurred. We tend to remember how ideas about religion have influenced government, but to forget how ideas about government have influenced religion. A single example will suffice: In the last century, when individualistic capitalism was the governmental ideal, the churches stressed the Christian virtues of honesty, hard work, and self-denial. Charity, compassion, and love of the poor were acknowledged to be Christian virtues as well—but they were not emphasized. In the twentieth century, the century in which socialism rather than capitalism dominated governmental theory, the priorities were reversed: charity, compassion, and love of the poor were stressed; and the more Calvinistic values of honesty, hard work, and self-denial were seldom heard. Those theologians who think we have corrected the errors of the past are mistaken. We are just repeating, in this century as in the last, the error of accommodating the gospel to the secular ideology of the time.

In sum, our American tradition that church and state are separate is in my view an authentically Christian tradition as well. There are good religious reasons for it as well as good political reasons; the confusion of the two hurts *both*. Sectarian struggles for control can destroy the state; and religious preoccupation with government—with material welfare, with power, with coercion—can destroy the church.

The second point I want to make, in looking at the church-state relationship from the standpoint of our religion, is that the Christian bears a moral obligation toward the just state. It is popular in some revisionist histories to portray Jesus as (literally) a Zealot—one of a band of Jewish rebels against Roman rule. Of course his remark about rendering to Caesar contradicts that—as does his remark to the Roman procurator after the scourging: "You could have no power at all over me, unless it had been given you from above." Far from being a revolutionary, Christ seems to have been more deferential to lawful authority than most Christian Americans I know these days. Nor were the apostles contemptuous of government, even pagan Roman government. Consider Paul's letter to the Romans:

Let everyone be subject to the higher authorities, for there exists no authority except from God, and those who exist have been appointed by God. Therefore he who resists the authority resists the ordinance of God; and they that resist bring on themselves condemnation. For rulers are a terror not to the good work but to the evil. Dost thou wish, then, not to fear the authority? Do what is good and thou wilt have praise from it. For it is God's minister to thee for good. But if thou dost what is evil, fear, for not without reason does it carry the sword. For it is God's minister, an avenger to execute wrath on him who does evil. Wherefore you must needs be subject, not only because of the wrath, but also for conscience' sake. For this is also why you pay tribute, for they are the ministers of God, serving unto this very end. Render to all men whatever is their due; tribute to whom tribute is due; taxes to whom taxes are due; fear to whom fear is due; honor to whom honor is due.

The passage must be read to refer to lawful authority, of course—and there is plenty of room to argue that some authorities that are de facto in place are not lawful ones, either because of how they got there, or because of what they did when they arrived. It is not those details to which I wish to direct your attention, however, but rather to the central proposition that, for the Christian, lawful civil authority must be obeyed not merely out of fear but, as St. Paul says, for conscience' sake.

That proposition was once widely accepted. I recall reading, a few years ago, an essay of C. S. Lewis that simply assumed, without significant discussion, that a good Christian who had been guilty of a serious criminal offense would turn himself in. Lewis used the now-quaint expression "pay his just debt to society." That attitude is long gone—mostly, I think, because we have lost the perception, expressed in that passage from St. Paul, that the laws have a moral claim to our obedience.

That truth is greatly obscured in an age of democratic government. It was once easy, perhaps, to regard God as the ultimate source of the authority of a hereditary king, whose bloodline reached back to the mists of history—where, for all one knew, God did anoint his forebear. It is even easy to see the hand of God in the accession of a new ruler through the fury of battle, whose awesomeness and unpredictability seem to display the working of the Lord of Hosts. It is more difficult to regard God as making His will known through PACs, thirty-second spots, Gallup polls, and voting machines. And even apart from the less-than-Jehovian process of election, the fundamental principle of *vox populi, vox dei* has never been a very persuasive proposition. How hard it is to accept the notion that those knaves and fools whom we voted against, but who succeeded in hoodwinking a majority of the electorate, will enact and promulgate laws and directives that, unless they contravene moral precepts, divine law enjoins us to obey.

It is particularly hard for someone in the American democratic tradition to have the proper Christian attitude toward lawful civil authority. We are a nation largely settled by those fleeing from oppressive regimes, and there is in our political tradition a deep strain of the notion that government is, at best, a necessary evil. But no society, least of all a democracy, can long survive on that philosophy. It is fine to believe that good government is limited government, but it is disabling—and, I suggest, contrary to long and sound Christian teaching—to believe that all government is bad. It is true, of course, that those who hold high office are, in their human nature and dignity, no better than the least of those whom they govern; that government by men and women is, of necessity, an imperfect enterprise; that power tends to corrupt; that a free society must be ever vigilant against abuse of governmental authority; and that institutional checks and balances against unbridled power are essential to preserve democracy. But it is also true that just government has a *moral* claim—that is, a divinely prescribed claim—to our obedience. It is not an easy truth, because as Eden showed, obedience is not an easy virtue.

Religious Retreats

Antonin Scalia graduated summa cum laude from Georgetown University in 1957 and was the valedictorian of his class. In April 1998, he spoke at Georgetown to students who had taken part in a retreat program and offered some very personal reflections on what life had taught him in the intervening four decades.

Father Paul Scalia recalls one occasion on which his father "spoke to me quite excitedly about the retreat he had just attended. His time away had clearly served its purpose—bringing him to reflect more upon his faith and to deepen his devotion."

———

The little instruction sheet I got after I agreed to give this talk said that I should not talk about values in the abstract but should relate a few instances from my own life in which my values bore upon my decisions. I will do my best—though the fact is that I am not very good at such anecdotal discourse. I also detest the term "values," which suggests to me a greater degree of interchangeability than ought to exist—as though the principles that guide a man's life are something like monetary exchange rates, subject to change with the times. (As in: "The value of the yen has fallen.") I prefer the view of things expressed by Sir Thomas More in the play *A Man for All Seasons*, when his friend the Duke of Norfolk urged him to sign the damned accession to the divorce, even if he doesn't really agree with it:

> Some men think the Earth is round, others think it flat; it is
> a matter capable of question. But if it is flat, will the King's

command make it round? And if it is round, will the King's command flatten it? No, I will not sign.

You have just returned from a retreat. Any person who believes in the transcendental has to go on a retreat periodically. Because the world believes in the pragmatic rather than the transcendental, and you will lose your soul (that is to say, forget what and who you are) if you do not get away from the noise now and then to think about the First Things. In the Gospels, of course, Jesus is constantly going off all by himself; and he doubtless needed it less than we do.

The most memorable retreat of my life was the one that I made at the end of my senior year in high school—a Jesuit high school, St. Francis Xavier in New York. It was so memorable because it was the year in which the big decision had to be made: whether to go on to college or (as many of my classmates did) to go on to St. Andrew's on Hudson, the Jesuit seminary for the New York Province. I might have made a heck of a Jesuit—though perhaps somewhat out of step these days. But I concluded I had certain talents that might do more good out in the world. And I am not referring exclusively to my capacity to procreate, though it is true that I have nine children. I was affected, I might add, by the fact that I was the end of my family—the only descendant of a previous generation that consisted on both sides, of nine brothers and sisters. Anyway, a retreat was a good occasion to think that through; and, of course, to pray for guidance.

I somehow got out of the habit of making retreats. The world crept in—which is what those of us who do not enter the seminary or the convent (and perhaps many of those who do) have to worry about. I have gotten back into the habit in the last ten years, and I recommend it to you. If you don't have a weekend to spare once a year to think exclusively about the things that really matter— well, you haven't planned your life correctly.

Another thing I can tell you—with an anecdote or two to back it up—is that things do not work out the way you want, but the way God wants. And sometimes what seems to you a crushing disappointment may in fact be a great blessing. I won a Naval ROTC fellowship when I graduated from high school. It was very hard to get in those days. All I had to do to cash in on the fellowship was to be accepted at a college that had Naval ROTC. As it happened, the only college that did which I was interested in attending—very interested in attending—was Princeton. And Princeton turned me down. A major disappointment. So I came to Georgetown instead, and I am sure I am a different person (and a better person) than I would have been if *my* will had been done.

The next biggest disappointment in my life was the morning in Palo Alto, California (I was teaching at Stanford Law School), when I received a phone call from the attorney general informing me that of the two finalists whom he had interviewed for the post of solicitor general, I had *not* been chosen. A really bad call on his part, I thought; and a bitter and unexpected disappointment for me. But had I become SG, I have little doubt that I would not be on the Supreme Court today. So pray for things, but accept what you are given; He knows better than you what is for your own good.

If you have transcendental principles—which for Catholics means if you believe in Jesus Christ and His Church—they have to shape your entire worldview. Perhaps the best lesson I ever learned here at Georgetown occurred during my oral comprehensive examination in my major (history) at the end of my senior year. My history professor was Dr. Wilkinson, a prince of a man. He was the chairman of the three-professor panel that examined me. And I did, if I may say so myself, a smashingly good job. As the time for the examination was almost at hand, Dr. Wilkinson asked me one last question, which seemed to me a softball. Of all the historical events you have studied, he said, which one in your opinion had the most impact upon the world? How could I possibly get this wrong? There was obviously no single correct answer. The only issue was what *good* answer I should choose. The French Revolution perhaps? Or the Battle of Thermopylae—or of Lepanto? Or the American Revolution? I forget what I picked, because it was all driven out of my mind when Dr. Wilkinson informed me of the *right* answer—or at least the right answer if I really believed what he and I thought

I believed. Of course it was the Incarnation. Point taken. You must keep everything in perspective, and not run your spiritual life and your worldly life as though they are two separate operations.

And finally I want to tell you something my father told me that I have never forgotten. You are all here at Georgetown, devoted to the life of the mind, admiring your brilliant professors and envying, perhaps, your brilliant classmates. My father was also committed to the life of the mind—much more of an intellectual than I ever was or can be. He taught Romance languages at Brooklyn College, and of course once you have mastered the grammar of a language there is nothing to do but read all the great literature and philosophy that has been written in that language. Which is what my father did. As my mother described it, he always had a book in front of his face. So this was not a man who spurned the life of the mind. But on one occasion he told me this (I have never forgotten it, and if you take away nothing else from this talk, I hope this will be it): "Son, brains are like muscles. You can rent them by the hour. The only thing that is not for sale is character."

Keep things in perspective, including the value of this education you are getting. At the end of the day, it is not that which will make you a good or a bad person.

FAITH AND JUDGING

When Monsignor Frank Maniscalco invited Justice Scalia to speak on faith and judging at the thirtieth-anniversary celebration of the Long Island Catholic *newspaper in October 1992, Scalia jokingly insisted on one condition: that he not be given another plaque. To Scalia's surprise and delight, Monsignor Maniscalco instead presented him a first-class relic of his patron saint, Saint Antoninus, a fifteenth-century Dominican friar and archbishop of Florence known for his great learning. Scalia kept the reliquary in a place of honor in his study.*

———

I am happy to join you this evening in celebration of the thirtieth anniversary of the *Long Island Catholic*. I am an appropriate speaker for the occasion, I suppose, since I am myself a Long Island Catholic. I grew up in Elmhurst, and as a child used to spend the major part of my vacations at a little summer cottage my grandfather had built a stone's throw from here—in the days when Woodbury was still the country. At that time, of course, the *Long Island Catholic* did not exist; our paper was the *Brooklyn Tablet*. It is always good to come back.

When Monsignor Maniscalco invited me to give this talk, he specified the subject that you have printed on the program before you—"Personal Conscience, Public Person"—but he described at some greater length just what he meant that subject to embrace. I quote from his letter:

How one's faith and one's judicial obligations either reinforce one another or create a degree of tension or both; whether, indeed, someone who holds high office in a pluralistic society is able to fulfill the Church's vision of the laity bringing Christian values to the world of which they are a part.

I always try to stick fairly closely to the text I have been assigned. This is a tricky one, but I will give it a try.

How one's faith affects the practice of one's vocation depends primarily upon what one's vocation is. No matter how good a Catholic a short-order chef may be, for example, there is no such thing as a Catholic hamburger. Unless, of course, it is a perfectly made and perfectly cooked hamburger. That is, I suppose, one way in which the faith affects all vocations: when Christ said, "Be ye perfect, as your heavenly Father is perfect," I think he meant perfect in all things, including that very important thing, the practice of one's life work. A good Catholic cannot be an intentionally sloppy worker—or to the extent that he is a sloppy worker, he is a less satisfactory Catholic. Jesus of Nazareth the twenty-nine-year-old carpenter had never put together a poorly made cabinet. *Laborare est orare*, the old monastic motto goes. To work is to pray. And to work badly is to pray badly.

But beyond this aspect of Catholic belief that affects *all* professions and occupations, how and whether one's faith affects one's work depends entirely upon what one's work happens to be. In some occupations, certain connections are clear: A Catholic doctor cannot, consistently with his faith, perform an abortion or assist a suicide. A Catholic publisher cannot, consistently with his faith, market obscenity, libel, or pornography. But what about the area of "public life"—that is, the profession of government service—which is my assigned topic for this evening?

Let me talk first about the legislative and executive branches—I will discuss judges last. There are those who believe that it is wrong for an executive or a legislative official to pursue a policy that he deems desirable solely because of his religious beliefs. Indeed, there is at least one Supreme Court opinion suggesting that legislative action which is religiously motivated is unconstitutional. That seems to me quite wrong. The Free Exercise Clause of the

First Amendment is violated when legislative or executive action is directed against others' religious beliefs; but neither the Free Exercise Clause nor the Establishment Clause is violated simply because legislative or executive action pursues a policy that the lawmaker or executive considers desirable because of his own religious belief. It would be quite impossible to apply such a principle. The religious person—the truly religious person—cannot divide all of his policy preferences into those that are theologically motivated and those that proceed from purely naturalistic inclinations. Can any of us say whether he would be the sort of moral creature he is without a belief in a Supreme Lawgiver, and hence in a Supreme Law? I am reminded of G. K. Chesterton's humorous poem entitled "The Song of the Strange Ascetic," in which the narrator describes the sort of self-indulgent, lustful, power-seeking life he would lead if he were a heathen—ending each stanza, however, with the observation that Higgins is a heathen, and Higgins does none of those things! Higgins is a Scrooge-like, nose-to-the-grindstone, abstemious, teetotaling, utterly dull banker. The poem ends:

> *Now who that runs can read it,*
> *The riddle that I write,*
> *Of why this poor old sinner*
> *Should sin without delight—*
> *But I, I cannot read it*
> *(Although I run and run),*
> *Of them that do not have the faith,*
> *And will not have the fun.*

Besides the practical impossibility of distinguishing all religiously motivated social policies from those that would exist even without religious motivation, adopting the principle that religiously motivated government policies are un-American would require the rewriting of a good deal of American history. The primary impetus for the drive to abolish slavery was a religious one. Recall the words of "The Battle Hymn of the Republic," which ends "As He died to make men holy, let us die to make men free, While God is marching on." The same is true of government laws prohibiting the manufacture and sale of strong drink, up to and including the constitutional amendment instituting Prohibition: mandated temperance was a religious cause. Religious motivation underlies many traditional laws still on the books, such as those against bigamy, or those proscribing public nudity. Societies with different religious beliefs manage well enough without them. Far from being a nation that has excluded religious-based policies from the sphere of government, official public expression of belief in God, and the adoption of policies thought by the people to be in accord with God's law, have distinguished us from most Western democracies, at least in the current century.

Of course, to acknowledge that religiously based social policies are not ipso facto unconstitutional is not to affirm the opposite: that they are ipso facto constitutional (though there is no question, I think, of the constitutionality of laws regulating traditional areas of public morality—laws preserving *bonos mores*, to use the common-law expression). Moreover, to say that a religiously motivated law would be constitutional is not to say that it would necessarily be wise. Laws severely restricting civil divorce, for example, are constitutional, but surely it is a matter of prudence whether they will achieve more good than harm in a society with a large plurality that no longer shares the moral premises on which they were based. Of course at some point the moral imperatives are so overwhelming that there is no room for prudential compromise. One does not argue about whether it will do more harm than good to oppose laws permitting genocide. That is in essence the Church's position regarding laws permitting abortion.

Mentioning the Big A (that is what the abortion issue is called on Capitol Hill) leads me quite naturally into the next part of this talk. Up until now I have been speaking about the relationship between religious belief and "public life" insofar as the legislative and executive branches are concerned. You will recall that I said at the outset, however, that how one's faith affects one's work depends upon what one's work happens to be. The work of the judicial branch is fundamentally different from that of the legislative and executive—or at least it is fundamentally different as I view things. Unlike presidents, cabinet secretaries, senators, and representatives, federal judges do not (or are not supposed to) *make* policy, but rather are to discern accurately and apply honestly the policies adopted by the people's representatives in the text of statutes—except to the extent that those statutes conflict with the text, the underlying traditions, or valid Supreme Court interpretation of the United States Constitution. Just as there is no Catholic way to cook a hamburger, so also there is no Catholic way to interpret a text, analyze a historical tradition, or discern the meaning and legitimacy of prior judicial decisions—except, of course, to do those things *honestly* and *perfectly*.

I find myself somewhat embarrassed, therefore, when Catholics, or other opponents of abortion, come forward to thank me earnestly for my position concerning *Roe v. Wade*. I must tell them that I deserve no thanks; that that position is not a virtuous affirmation of my religious belief, or even a sagacious policy choice, but simply the product of lawyerly analysis of constitutional text and tradition; and that if legal analysis had produced the opposite conclusion I would have come out the other way, regardless of their or my views concerning abortion. My religious faith can give me a personal view on the right or wrong of abortion; but it cannot make a text say yes where it in fact says no, or a tradition say "we permit" where it in fact has said "we forbid." If my position on *Roe v. Wade* were a reflection of Catholic beliefs and policy preferences, then I would say that the Constitution not only *permits* the banning of abortion, but *requires* it. Imaginative judges have derived results much more implausible than that from the provision of the Constitution that says no person shall be deprived of life, liberty, or property without due process of law. In fact, however, the Constitution does not *ban* abortion any more than it confers a right to abortion, and no amount of religious faith or zealous enthusiasm can change that.

These remarks reflect, of course, a view of the Constitution as a document containing a fixed and limited number of specific guarantees that do not expand and contract from age to age (though of course they must be applied to new phenomena). That is the traditional view. In recent years, however, the American people seem to have become persuaded that the Constitution is not a fixed and limited text, but rather an all-purpose, shorthand embodiment of *whatever they care deeply about.* Do we abhor the burning of the flag? Why, then, it must be constitutional to criminalize it. Do we favor homosexual rights? Why, then, it *must* be unconstitutional to deny them. And so forth, through a whole list of passionately felt issues, down to and including both sides of the abortion issue. Never mind the constitutional text; never mind the tradition that underlies that text. We know what we want, and if we want it passionately enough, it must be guaranteed (or if we hate it passionately enough, it must be prohibited) by the Constitution! We cannot leave such issues to be decided by the democratic process; only *un*important issues belong there. The really significant, heartfelt issues are *all* resolved in the Constitution, whether the text says anything about them or not. And we will assure that the Constitution means what we want it to mean by interrogating nominees to the Supreme Court concerning all the "unenumerated" rights that we care about, one after another—conducting a plebiscite on the Constitution, in effect, each time a new nominee is put forward.

How different this is from the traditional American notion of what the Constitution means—from the notion that prevailed until very recently—is evident from considering the Nineteenth Amendment, adopted in 1920, which provides that "[t]he right of citizens of the United States to vote shall not be denied or abridged by the United States or by any State on account of sex." No one doubted that a constitutional amendment was necessary for that purpose, even though, in 1920 as today, the Constitution forbade denial of "equal protection of the laws." What could be more obviously a denial of equal protection than denial of the vote? But the Americans of 1920 understood, as the Americans of 1992 seemingly do not, that the vague provisions of the Constitution, such as the Equal Protection Clause and the Due Process Clause, are not invitations to constitutionalize our current desires from age to age, but rather bear a constant meaning that accords with the understanding of those terms when they were adopted. Standing by itself, the phrase "equal protection" can mean almost anything. As applied to distinctions between the sexes, it *could* be thought to require unisex public toilets and dormitories. Of course it does not mean that, because no one ever thought it meant that. So also (the Americans of 1920 understood) with respect to the right to vote.

The problem with making the Constitution an all-purpose embodiment of our current preferences—pro-abortion, anti-abortion, or anything else—is that it deprives the Constitution of its essential character as an *obstacle* to majority self-will and converts it (ironically) into a mechanism for placing the majority's current will beyond further democratic debate. The danger of that development—and the consequent need to restrain yourselves from asserting that all your deeply held beliefs are constitutional imperatives—is the only moral I hope to leave you with this evening. It is a moral rooted in law rather than theology, so if you have awarded me for my theological skill you have been greatly deceived.

ON LAW

---

*"A freedom-loving people respectful of the
rule of law may be expected to let lawyers decide
what a constitutional text means; but they cannot
be expected to let lawyers decide what a constitution
ought to say. That is not a job for lawyers,
but for the people."*

The Idea of the Constitution

How and why has our Constitution endured over the centuries? Justice Scalia explored this topic during and after the Constitution's bicentennial in 1987, including in this Alexander Meiklejohn Lecture at Brown University in April 1991. For all that we celebrate the Bill of Rights, it is, he argued, the "humdrum" structural and mechanistic provisions of the Constitution that deserve the lion's share of credit for its durability.

———

I want to share a few thoughts with you this evening concerning the Constitution of the United States.

If you have ever been to a formal dinner—a dinner of this sort—in England, you will recall that after dessert and coffee, and before it is permitted to light a cigarette, a toast is customarily presented: "Ladies and gentlemen, the Queen." And if you have ever been to a diplomatic function involving participants from England and the United States, you will recall that it is the custom to reply to that toast with a toast "To the president of the United States."

Every time I hear that progression it strikes me that the comparison does not really work. The president is, to be sure, both our chief executive and our head of state, our prime minister and queen combined. But if one wishes to evoke the deep and enduring symbol of our nationhood and our unity as a people, it seems to me the toast ought to be "Ladies and gentlemen, the Constitution of the United States." For that is the equivalent of the royal armies that brought forth one nation out of a diversity of states; and not only the token but indeed the substance of what continues to bind us together as a people.

The constitutional scholar and political philosopher Walter Berns recently published a book entitled *Taking the Constitution Seriously*, in which he makes the striking observation—striking to me, at least, because it is obviously true but I had never thought of it— that the word *un-American* has no equivalent in any other nation. It would mean nothing in French or German political debate to call a particular idea (let us say the abolition of the rights of free speech) "un-French" or "un-German." Unlike any other nation in the world, we consider ourselves bound together, not by genealogy or residence but by belief in certain principles; and the most important of those principles are set forth in the Constitution of the United States.

The wondrous durability of the Constitution is attributable to a whole series of irreplicable circumstances—incredibly lucky, if you will, or, as many of the Founders thought, providential. When else has a government been established, not by conquerors dividing up the spoils, or even by political parties parceling out the power, but by a four-month seminar consisting of many of the most erudite *and politically experienced* individuals in the nation? The historian Clinton Rossiter has described the prominence of the fifty-five delegates as follows:

> The Republic had two men of world-wide fame, and both were on the list. [He was referring to Washington and Franklin, of course.] It had perhaps ten who were well-known within the bounds of the old [British] empire, and at least five of that description (Johnson, Livingston, Robert Morris, Dickinson, and Rutledge) were on it, too. Gorham, Gerry, Sherman, Ellsworth, Hamilton, Mifflin, Wilson, Madison, Wythe, Williamson, Charles Pinckney, and the untraveled Mason had won themselves—as best one could in those days of poor communications—continental reputations; Langdon, Read, Randolph, Alexander Martin, Jenifer, and C. C. Pinckney were major figures in their states; and almost every other delegate was someone whose standing was unchallenged in his part of the country.

As for governmental experience: "All but two or three Framers had served as public officials of [a] colony or state." A remarkable forty-two of the fifty-five had served in the Congress of the United States. As for education: "In an age when few," even from the richest families, "went to college," the fifty-five members of the Convention included nine graduates of the College of New Jersey (Princeton), four graduates of Yale, four from William and Mary, three from Harvard, two from King's College (Columbia), two from the College of Philadelphia (University of Pennsylvania), and one each from Oxford and St. Andrews. Several others had studied law at the Inns of Court. A number of those mentioned earlier had done graduate work—and six held professorships or tutorships. (All per Rossiter.)

These extraordinary individuals—much of the cream of the society at the time—did not meet a couple of times to vote on reports prepared by their staff. They met personally five or six hours a day, six days a week—from mid-May to mid-September—almost an entire baseball season! And after, the plenary sessions often filled their evenings with committee work or informal discussion. Imagine getting individuals of that prominence in our national life to make that kind of a time commitment today.

Yale University Press has recently come out with a paperback edition of Farrand's *Records of the Convention*—consisting principally, of course, of the notes that Madison meticulously kept. I urge you, some rainy weekend, to read them. They are full of the spirit of the Age of Reason—the belief, which seems almost naive to many of us cynical moderns, that the application of logic and experience to any problem will produce, if not perfection, at least improvement. They were engaged in the enterprise of applying what Madison called "the new science of government." The records are also full of the spirit of honest, open discussion and persuasion. What must impress the reader is how often views expressed by particular participants at the beginning of the summer are different from the views those same participants express in the fall—their minds having been changed by the intervening discussion. I might interject that that openness to persuasion is as essential to the continuation of our republic as it was to its formation. So also is the spirit of humility, and of generous acceptance of the majority's judgment, expressed in the famous concluding speech of Benjamin Franklin, when he urged all the delegates, on the last day of the Convention, to come forward and sign the final document. We have that speech in its original form since Franklin, who was eighty-one and in poor health, was unable to stand long enough to deliver it and gave the written text to James Wilson to read, and later to Madison to copy. It went in part as follows:

> I confess that there are several parts of this constitution which I do not at present approve, but I am not sure I shall never approve them: For having lived long, I have experienced many instances of being obliged by better information or fuller consideration, to change opinions even on important subjects, which I once thought right, but found to be otherwise. It is therefore that the older I grow, the more apt I am to doubt my own judgment, and to pay more respect to the judgment of others. . . .
>
> In these sentiments, Sir, I agree to this Constitution with all its faults, if they are such; because I think a general Government necessary for us, and there is no form of Government but what may be a blessing to the people if well administered, and believe farther that this is likely to be well administered for a course of years. . . . I doubt too whether any other Convention we can obtain may be able to make a better Constitution. For when you assemble a number of men to have the advantage of their joint wisdom, you inevitably assemble with those men, all their prejudices, their passions, their errors of opinion, their local interests, and their selfish views. From such an Assembly can a perfect production be expected? It therefore astonishes me, Sir, to find this system approaching so near to perfection as it does; and I think it will astonish our enemies. . . . Thus I consent, Sir, to this Constitution because I expect no better, and because I am not sure, that it is not the best. The opinions I have had of its errors, I sacrifice to the public good—I

have never whispered a syllable of them abroad—Within these walls they were born, and here they shall die.

Having said a lot about the process of the Grand Convention, let me say just a little about its product. That product did not include the portion of the Constitution that Americans most often invoke, the Bill of Rights. That was added on the proposal of the First Congress, as the first ten amendments—though the understanding that something of the sort would be added was almost a condition of its ratification by many of the states. It is paradoxical that what was an afterthought should have become its most celebrated feature. In the commemorations of the bicentennial that are currently being held, the specific provisions that are normally given the most extensive (if not indeed the exclusive) praise are not the bicamerality of the legislature, or the separate election of the president, or the presidential veto power, or life tenure for judges, or the brief, two-year terms for members of the House, or the six-year terms for members of the Senate, or any of the other expertly crafted provisions that pertain to the structure, the "constitution," of our government; but rather, freedom of speech, freedom of religion, and freedom of the press—provisions of the subsequently adopted Bill of Rights. So completely does that portion of the document attract the affection and the devotion of the people.

If the virtue of a constitution is to be assessed primarily on the basis of this popular feature, one must admit that the Constitution of the United States fares rather badly. Take, for example, protections against governmental intrusion upon privacy. The United States Bill of Rights contains no more explicit protection than the following:

The right of the people to be secure in their persons, houses, papers, and effects, against unreasonable searches and seizures, shall not be violated, and no Warrants shall issue, but upon probable cause, supported by Oath or affirmation, and particularly describing the place to be searched, and the persons or things to be seized.

Compare that to the much more explicit and extensive guarantees of a prominent modern constitution:

> Citizens are guaranteed inviolability of the person. No one may be arrested except by a court decision or on the warrant of a procurator.

> Citizens are guaranteed inviolability of the home. No one may, without lawful grounds, enter a home against the will of those residing in it.

> The privacy of citizens, and of their correspondence, telephone conversations, and telegraphic communications is protected by law.

Or consider freedom of religion. Our First Amendment says no more than the following:

> Congress shall make no law respecting an establishment of religion, or prohibiting the free exercise thereof.

Compare that with a prominent modern constitution, which says:

> Citizens are guaranteed freedom of conscience, that is, the right to profess or not to profess any religion, and to conduct religious worship or atheistic propaganda. Incitement of hostility or hatred on religious grounds is prohibited.

Or freedom of speech and assembly, as to which the United States Constitution says only:

> Congress shall make no law ... abridging the freedom of speech, or of the press, or the right of the people peaceably to assemble, and to petition the Government for a redress of grievances.

Compare that paltry guarantee with the modern constitution I have been describing, which says:

Citizens are guaranteed freedom of speech, of the press, and of assembly, meetings, street processions and demonstrations.

Citizens have the right to associate in public organizations that promote their political activity and initiative.

Persecution for criticism [of state bodies and public organizations] is prohibited. Persons guilty of such persecution shall be called to account.

You will see the point I have been driving toward when I tell you that the modern constitution I have been describing is that of the Union of Soviet Socialist Republics. I would not trade our old Constitution for that in a million years. And if I had to pick a country other than my own in which I thought my individual rights would be most secure, I would very likely choose England or Australia, both of which are among the significant holdouts in the universal movement toward bills of rights.

The reason, of course, is that a bill of rights has value only if the other part of the constitution—the part that really "constitutes" the organs of government—establishes a structure that is likely to preserve, against the ineradicable human lust for power, the liberties that the bill of rights expresses. If the people value those liberties, the proper constitutional structure will likely result in their preservation even in the absence of a bill of rights; and where that structure does not exist, the mere recitation of the liberties will certainly not preserve them. So while it is entirely appropriate for us Americans to celebrate our wonderful Bill of Rights, we realize (or should realize) that it represents the fruit, and not the roots, of our constitutional tree. The rights it expresses are the *reasons* that the other provisions exist. But it is those other humdrum provisions—the structural, mechanistic portions of the Constitution that pit, in James Madison's words, "ambition against ambition," and make it impossible for any element of government to obtain unchecked power—that convert the Bill of Rights from a paper assurance to a living guarantee. A crowd is much more likely to form behind a banner that reads "Freedom of Speech or

Death" than behind one that says "Bicameralism or Fight"; but the latter in fact goes much more to the root of the matter.

Besides the importance of structure, there is another characteristic of a constitution, or at least of a written constitution, that I think you ought to bear in mind. Like any written document, it says some things (which it means); and it does *not* say other things (which it therefore does not mean). As lavishly as I have praised our Constitution, I do not mean to suggest that it contains, not only what it contains, but *all* that is good and true. Indeed, I do not even mean to suggest that every single thing it *does* contain is necessarily good and true for modern society, or indeed was even necessarily good and true when it was adopted. Nor did the Founders think so—which is why they specifically included a provision for amendment.

The notion has somehow gained currency, however, that if something is intensely bad, it must be prohibited by the Constitution; or if intensely desirable, it must be required by the Constitution. How can one possibly think that of a document that determined the apportionment of representatives among the various states on the basis of population consisting of "the whole Number of free Persons" and "three fifths of all other Persons"—a not-so-subtle reference to slavery, which was then and there *known* to be an evil, recognized as such even by some Convention delegates from the southern states that supported it. The Constitution was not perfect when crafted, in other words—just the best that could be done if the Union was to be achieved. We fought our bloodiest war, and adopted our most important amendment, to get rid of that particular defect.

It is plainly unhistorical, therefore, to regard the Constitution as simply a shorthand embodiment of all that is perfect—to think that whatever element of perfection does not appear there explicitly *must* be contained within more vague guarantees, such as the guarantee of due process, or freedom from unreasonable searches, or equal protection. But who cares if it is unhistorical; we have never been a nation that cared much about history. More important is the fact that the practical consequences of such an attitude will, in the long run—indeed, in the not so long run—destroy the ability of the Constitution to preserve the guarantees that it *does* contain. If the Constitution does not mean what it objectively *says*, but rather what it *ought to say*; if "due process," for example, does not mean what it originally meant, but rather what it *ought to mean* today; then someone will have to decide the normative question of what it *ought to mean*. And in a democratic society that someone will ultimately be the majority. The individual guarantees of the Constitution will thereby have been placed under the supervision of the very entity it was their purpose to restrain: the majority.

But, you may object, that normative question will *not* be decided by the majority; it will be decided by the Supreme Court. And the Supreme Court is an anti-majoritarian institution if there ever was one. That is true enough, or at least has been. But the Supreme Court has, throughout most of our history, been able to get away with pronouncing decisions against majority sentiment only because our society has accepted it to be the Court's job, not to say what the Constitution *ought to provide*, but what it *did* provide: what its text meant in light of the traditions within which that text was adopted. To be sure, now and then—perhaps even more often than now and then—the justices might shade a point, and distort text or history a bit in order to produce what they considered a more desirable result. But they at least had the decency to lie about it; they purported to be applying the Constitution as it was enacted, and not a constitution that they themselves adjusted to accord with modern times. Only in the past few decades has that changed, so that modern justices, with full support of the academy, feel authorized to revise original meaning in order to accord with "the evolving standards of decency that mark the progress of a maturing society." That is a new ball game, and we are only beginning to see how it will be played.

Initially, perhaps, the justices who adopted the new vision of their role could find the "evolving standards" to be those of an intellectual elite from which judges are drawn. But in the nature of things, that could not last. Once the cat was out of the bag—once the society at large accepted the version of the Court's role that the Court set for itself: conformance with modern standards—it was inevitable that the majority would assert itself, and the text of the Constitution could no longer defend against it. If the criterion of constitutionality is desirability; if judges (or at least justices) are not to be men and women "learned in the law," skilled in techniques of textual construction familiar to lawyers and faithful to traditions set forth in old and musty cases; if they are instead barometers of "evolving standards of decency" and arbiters of what the modern American Constitution *ought to be*—why, then, the method of selecting this Supreme Court ought to be much different from what it has been in the past. We should look not for learning and lawyerly skills, but for attunement to what the "evolving standards of decency" are, to what the current society's vision of a good constitution happens to be—we should look, in other words, for people who agree with the majority. Thus, under this new regime, we can expect to have confirmation hearings in which exchanges with the senators (representatives of the majority) might be expected to go something like this:

Q: Judge Jones, do you think there is a right to bear arms [or a right to homosexual conduct, or a right to burn the flag—or whatever—fill in your favorite or least favorite right]? Do you think there is such a right in the Constitution?

A: No, Senator, I do not.

Q: You don't? Well, I think it's there; and my constituents think it's there. [Or, if the answer has been that the right does exist, "Well, I don't think it's there, and neither do my constituents."] And we certainly don't want somebody with your views, with your lack of sensitivity [or, if the opposite, "your radical philosophy"] sitting on the Supreme Court.

Never mind that neither the senator nor his constituents have intensively studied the constitutional text, and the tradition that lies behind it. That doesn't matter. That is no longer relevant. We, the majority, want the Constitution that we want, and we want it now.

One of the fallacies of the theory of the evolving Constitution is that it always evolves in the direction of greater personal liberty—so there is no harm done. That is demonstrably false. The swift highway of a Constitution that means what it ought to mean leads in both directions: to more individual freedom, or to less. Take, for example, the reduction, in Supreme Court jurisprudence, of the protections afforded to property rights, a development that has not in all respects been faithful to text and tradition. We (the majority) all agree with that development—it is more in accord with our twentieth-century notions that value property rights less than the Founders did. (When Canada recently adopted a bill of rights, modeled in some respects on ours, its Due Process Clause was worded to protect, not "life, liberty and property," as ours does, but "life, liberty and security.") So hooray, that is all well and good. But let us not pretend that that development has not been a *reduction* of individual liberty. Economic rights are liberties: entitlements of individuals against the majority. When they are eliminated, no matter how desirable that elimination may be, liberty has been reduced.

Finally, let me make one last point about the idea of a constitution, which is perhaps already implicit in what I have already said. No part of the Constitution—neither the structural portions nor the individual guarantees—can be preserved for the people by the Supreme Court alone. A Supreme Court fiercely dedicated to preserving that document cannot exist in the midst of a society that does not understand it. The Court is at best a safety net. The first, and ultimately the most influential, interpreters of the document are the people's elected representatives—who in turn reflect the understanding of the people. The Court can stand against the distortion of original understanding produced by the temporary excess of one brief era—the era of McCarthyism, for example. But in the nature of things the Court cannot stand against a departure from our traditional attitudes—toward the Commerce Clause, toward the reasonableness of searches, toward any constitutional guarantee—that is deep and sustained. The reason is quite simple: the justices of the Court are not dispatched from Mars but are drawn from the same society that shares those new understandings. So if the understanding persists long enough among the people, it will prevail.

In the last analysis, in other words, the Court cannot save the society from itself—because in the last analysis the Court is no more than the society itself. The compromises of principle, the misperceptions of liberty, that are believed in the homes, learned in the schools, and taught in the universities will ultimately be the body of knowledge and belief that new justices bring with them to the bench. The Constitution will endure, in other words, only to the extent that it endures in your understanding and affection. That is why I used to find it so upsetting, when I taught constitutional law, to learn how many law students in major universities— the best, and the brightest, and presumably those most interested in the law—had never read, cover to cover, such a basic part of our constitutional tradition as the *Federalist Papers*. And it is why I thought it worth the time to speak to you about the idea of the Constitution tonight.

THE VOCATION OF A JUDGE

In May 2007, Justice Scalia became the first U.S. Supreme Court justice to visit Peru. Helping to celebrate the University of Applied Sciences' tenth anniversary of its Faculty of Law, he reflected on the qualities that make a good judge.

During his spare time in Peru, Scalia enjoyed drinking pisco sours, playing the maracas, and traveling to Machu Picchu. He found the visit so delightful that he would return six years later.

———

*B*uenas tardes. You have asked me to say a few words about "The Vocation of a Judge." It is an interesting subject, and one largely unaddressed by the laws of my country. There are, in both the states and at the federal level, laws concerning judicial ethics—when a judge must recuse himself from a case, what public appearances he must avoid, what gifts he can accept, what involvement in political matters is permissible. But these are all negatives and say nothing about what makes a *good* judge. On that subject, there are really no prescribed criteria.

In fact, the Constitution of the United States does not even require that justices of the Supreme Court (or any other federal judges) be lawyers. Moreover, in the federal court system of which I am a part, and in all of the fifty states so far as I am aware, a person becomes a judge not through any sort of formal training or apprenticeship. There is no Judge School from which one must earn a certificate of authenticity establishing that the holder is in fact possessed of those qualities conducive to the art (or science, if it is that) of good judging. Instead, as the old saying goes, a judge is a lawyer who knows the governor.

Which reminds me of the story that is told about the lawyer who visited the governor's mansion in the wee hours of the night. "I need to talk to the governor," pleaded the lawyer, "it's an emergency!" The governor's aide finally relented and roused the governor, who came down in his bathrobe. "What is so important that it can't wait until the morning?" the governor grumbled. "It is Judge Jones," the breathless lawyer exclaimed. "He has just died and I want to take his place." To this the governor replied: "Well, it's okay with me if it's okay with the undertaker."

I want to spend my time discussing two related topics: first, the qualities that I believe make for a good judge, and next, how in the United States the public perception of the "good" judge has become distorted. Let me begin with the qualities of a good judge. I preface this discussion with the disclaimer that these are qualities to which I aspire, not necessarily ones that I claim to have achieved. What are the qualities of a good judge? Chief Justice Taft, who served on my court many years ago and who prior to that appointment had actually served as president of the United States, said the following: "I love judges and I love courts. They are my ideals that typify on Earth what we shall meet hereafter in heaven under a just God." I am not sure that judicial qualities are so celestial—and I am sure that the thought of spending eternity with judges and courts is much less attractive than the seventy-two virgins promised to the faithful Muslim. With all due respect to Taft, and with earthly limitations in mind, I would propose three qualities that one would presume in a good judge.

First, a judge must be, above all else, a servant of the law—and not an enforcer of his personal predilections—about the issues that come before him. The good judge must suppress his personal views and must decide each case as the law dictates, not as he would have resolved the matter if he had drafted the law or the constitutional provision at issue. Let me give an obvious example, which is capital punishment. Capital punishment in the United States is a very controversial issue. Some states have it, some do not. By a recent calculation, twelve states have no death penalty whatsoever. The remaining states have it in some form or another, imposing it for somewhat different crimes, and choosing to carry it out with varying degrees of regularity. The arguments on both sides of the capital punishment debate are understandable ones. Proponents think that it promotes deterrence, or that justice demands retribution from those who have so grievously wronged the innocent. Opponents of capital punishment believe that the death penalty serves no real deterrent function, and that the very idea of government-initiated execution is inhuman. Think what you may of these arguments. But if you are a judge in the United States, deciding whether capital punishment is unconstitutional, it is not your job to resolve the debate. The Constitution allows a person to be deprived not only of liberty or property, but also *of life*, provided the deprivation is made with due process of law.

Some years ago, a justice on my court announced that the death penalty in the United States was unconstitutional, citing his personal and moral views on the subject, and writing (quite famously, I might add) "[t]hat from this day forward, I no longer shall tinker with the machinery of death." He was, in my view, quite wrong. While the words that I have just quoted from his opinion are quite poetic, they do not reflect my ideal view of the judge who sets to the side his personal preferences in favor of the law. If he has moral objections to what the law requires him to do, his proper course is to resign from the bench, and perhaps lead a revolution.

So adherence to the law, even over personal objection—that is the first quality. Before moving to the second quality, however, I want to add a very important footnote to the preceding discussion. In the example I have just given, capital punishment, the judge who finds the death penalty unconstitutional could be said to be aiding the downtrodden, the poor condemned criminal. But that would not *normally* be the result if judges preferred their own opinions over the law. Take a tour through the Constitution of the United States. The individual rights it accords are of greatest importance to those in the minority: those who wish to express controversial views (the First Amendment, "Congress shall make no law . . . abridging the freedom of speech"); those who wish to be members of an unpopular religious faith (again the First Amendment, "Congress shall make no law . . . prohibiting the free exercise" of religion); criminal defendants, who are accorded a variety of protections, such as the right to a jury trial and the right to confront adverse witnesses, both found in the Sixth Amendment. If we assume (as is surely correct) that a judge's personal predilections will usually be those of the *majority* (he was, after all, elected by the majority, or appointed by officials who were elected), his nonadherence to the law will more often *disadvantage* the minority members and the downtrodden.

My preceding discussion has focused on "the law." Whatever "the law" is, judges should follow it, and they should follow it at the expense of their own private views. But what is "the law"? How does a judge figure out what "the law" requires? My example of capital punishment was an easy one, because it is so clearly permitted by the Constitution. But what about the harder cases? How can a judge be sure that he is, in fact, rendering a judgment based on objective, nonbiased principles, and not one that is the product of a latent, subconscious personal preference?

This brings me to the second quality that I would wish in a judge, a quality that I shall refer to as "scholarship." By this I mean that in resolving cases according to law, the judge must be led to his answer by following the framework for neutral, objective decision-making that is dictated by the traditions of the legal system in which he operates. The good judge carefully ensures that the methods of interpretation he employs are the traditional ones, and not those which direct him to the result he would prefer. He asks himself whether the outcome he reaches is independent of, rather than driven by, his natural inclinations. The process must be a studious one, with careful attention given to the relevant legal authorities. And of course, the question of which legal authorities are relevant must also be answered without a thumb on the scales. In sum, the good judge consistently applies interpretive theories of general applicability that shield him against the misuse of judicial power, whether intentional or unintentional.

The third quality that I would wish in a judge is an appropriate demeanor that projects to the parties and to the public fairness and impartiality. This does not mean that judges cannot have strong views, nor need they keep those views hidden. But it does mean that when a litigant comes before a court, he knows that he will be playing on an even field, and that his legal arguments will be carefully considered. A judge who possesses my second quality—scholarship—will be less of a credit to his profession if he is unable to communicate his studious approach to those who receive his judgments. This does not mean that a judge must convince the public to like him. To the contrary, the honest judge who is applying constitutional protections that protect the minority against the majority can expect to be disliked by the majority. Rather, the judge must conduct himself and his court in a way that inspires public confidence in the *process* by which the decision was reached.

So those are my three ideal qualities for a judge—adherence to the law, scholarship, and an even-handed demeanor. But is that the public perception of the good judge in the United States? The answer is: not really. The public perception of the good judge, both outside of the American legal community but more importantly within it, is the judge as moral representative, the all-powerful expositor and selector of the *best* law. Adherence to "the law"—where the meaning of "the law" is arrived upon through traditional modes of legal reasoning—has been discarded in favor of adherence to "the law" as an elite group of like-minded lawyers and judges would wish it to be. Is it a good idea to punish homosexual sodomy between two consenting adults? No, a majority of American lawyers might think, and so therefore a judge who finds a constitutional right to same-sex sexual intercourse is a very, very conscientious judge. And a judge who refuses to recognize such a right—even though it is nowhere in the Constitution and even though sodomy had been criminally sanctioned for centuries—is a very, very bad judge, entirely out of touch with "the law." Same thing with abortion, capital punishment, and the right to die. Same thing when the legislature has passed a clear and unambiguous law, but the law results in consequences that are unfair or absurd.

This is a very untraditional view of the judge. Where did it come from? Like so many unfortunate trends, it comes from American law schools. The first year in an American law school is a life-changing experience. It's all so very exciting, really. After wasting away in a liberal arts education, American law students get to actually do something semi-tangible. But even though courts in the United States spend most of their time interpreting statutory law—law formally enacted by a legislature that is written into a statutory code—American law schools treat this as a mere afterthought. Instead, they devote most of the first year of law school to that great body of law known as the common law, which my country inherited from England. The subjects of the common law include, primarily, contracts, torts, and property law. They are the bread and butter of the first-year law student experience.

But the nature of the common law, and the fact that American law students become experts in it, have much to say about the prevailing perception of the good judge. For if the common law was ever just the simple embodiment of customary local practices—the law's reflection, say, on the prevailing yet unspoken rules that governed local business transactions—it is no longer. The common law is *judge-made* law, crafted and refined *by judges* over time to fit the needs of a changing and developing society. This is not to say that it is illegitimate. The common law is a venerable legal tradition, and jurisdictions may of course choose to retain it. But this *is to say* that when American law students are first exposed to the common law, the idea of the judge who fashions *the best rule* is indelibly imprinted into their minds as the shining example of what judges ought to do.

Let me give you a classic example of a case that is taught in American law schools, perhaps a case that is even taught here in Peru. The year was 1928, and the case was *Palsgraf v. The Long Island Railroad Company*. Many of the great American cases involved railroads. Our engineers apparently hadn't quite figured out how to make these machines safe, because death or injury by railroad-inflicted wound was a fairly common occurrence, if the numerous cases involving railroads as defendants are any evidence. The *Palsgraf* case involved a situation that wasn't really the railroad's fault. Or was it? That was the entire question.

The facts are unusual. Helen Palsgraf, the plaintiff, was standing on a New York railroad platform waiting for her train. A train soon pulled up at the station, although it was bound for a different destination than her own. Two men raced to catch this train, which had already started to roll away from the station. One of these two men made it onto the moving train safely. The second man, who was carrying a package, jumped aboard the train car, but seemed unsteady, perhaps about to fall off. A train guard inside the moving train lent him a hand, while another guard on the platform gave him a little push from behind. It is assumed that the actions of these guards were negligently performed, that the guards should have exercised greater care given the situation. And here is where it gets very interesting. Recall that the second man was carrying a package. In the process of getting this man onto the train, the package fell from his arms, and landed on the rails. This package was just over a foot long and was wrapped in newspaper. Nothing gave any indication of its contents, although the package in fact contained . . . fireworks! And when the package landed on the rails, there resulted a rather large pyrotechnic explosion, which caused a set of scales a considerable distance away on the far end of the platform to fall over and to land on top of poor Mrs. Palsgraf, who was injured.

She brought suit against the railroad, alleging that the railroad's guards had negligently assisted the man onto the train, thereby causing the package to fall, thus leading to the explosion, which in turn created the falling of the scales, which itself produced plaintiff's injury. But could the railroad really be held liable for an injury that seemed so remote from the negligence of its employees? There was no doubt that the railroad conductor's negligence was the "but for" cause of the injury, in the sense that without the negligence, the plaintiff would not have been injured. The question was instead one of proximate cause—an elusive concept to be sure, but it essentially means legal causation, those causes of an injury that the law recognizes as direct enough to warrant the imposition of liability on the defendant.

That question produced in the *Palsgraf* case a classic debate between Judge Cardozo, for the majority, and Judge Andrews in dissent. Judge Cardozo said that the railroad could not be held liable: "The conduct of the defendant's guard, if a wrong in its relation to the holder of the package, was not a wrong in its relation to the plaintiff, standing far away. Relatively to her it was not negligence at all. Nothing in the situation gave notice that the falling package had in it the potency of peril to persons thus removed." Judge Andrews would have held that the railroad was liable for the injury: "[W]hen injuries do result from our unlawful act we are liable for the consequences. It does not matter that they are unusual, unexpected, unforeseen and unforeseeable. . . . What we do mean by the word 'proximate' is that, because of convenience, of public policy, of a rough sense of justice, the law arbitrarily declines to trace a series of events beyond a certain point. This is not logic. It is practical politics." In this case, Judge Andrews believed, the negligence of the train guards "was a substantial factor in producing the result—there was here a natural and continuous sequence—[a] direct connection."

Don't you see how much fun all of this is? You're all enthralled! What is the right answer? Law students across America have nothing better to think about! Maybe Judge Cardozo was right—the liability has to end somewhere. If the railroad is liable here, it will be liable for every manner of injury suffered on its premises, and even beyond. And who ends up footing the bill? The passengers of course, in the form of higher ticket prices. But wait. Maybe Judge Andrews was right. Surely there was some connection between the negligence of the railroad and the injury sustained by Mrs. Palsgraf. If the plaintiff is not allowed to recover, the railroad gets off without paying a penny. Everyone seemed to agree that the railroad's employees had performed negligently in helping the man onto the moving train. What incentive will the railroad have to alter its course of conduct if it isn't punished here?

And so on. You get the idea. As Judge Andrews remarked in dissent in *Palsgraf*, "[t]here is in truth little to guide us other than common sense." And this is how young American lawyers are taught to reason, by taking part in the great debates of the common law. The question in every case becomes *which rule is the best*. And judges are measured in the public eye on the basis of whether they select *the best rule*. Naturally, which judge you think best and which rule you think superior depends in large part upon your personal intuitions about how the world works, or at least how you think it should work.

This is all fine and good for the common law, because that entire system of law was concededly *judge-made*. But that is decidedly not the system of law with which most judges in the United States must grapple, especially those judges who sit on my court. Rather, we deal primarily with laws enacted by Congress, and much less frequently, questions concerning the interpretation of our Constitution, which is of course written down and is *not* the product of judicial creation. In the United States, however, the image of judge as lawmaker—the judge to whom law students are first introduced—persists *outside* the common law and has come to be viewed as the appropriate role for judges deciding questions in every case, including questions of statutory and constitutional law.

This, as I hope my discussion has made clear, is in significant tension with my own view of the proper vocation of a judge. For to simply decide each case by providing the "best answer" is to reduce the law to whatever the judge happens to think makes the most sense. Judge Cardozo didn't think the railroad should be liable. Judge Andrews thought it should. It's difficult to say who is right without resorting to ideas that are fairly external to the law as I understand it. And when the law simply becomes the best answer as a judge would see it, what does it mean to follow the law above and to the exclusion of the judge's own personal preferences? The two are simply collapsed. The judge as servant of the law is replaced by the judge as servant to himself, a self-serving prophecy if there ever was one. And what is more, the entire process of careful legal reasoning that I think emblematic of a good judge becomes reduced to considerations that are disturbingly difficult to separate from the personal or the moral. Ours is a government of laws, not of men. The common-law-judge-for-all-occasions is not compatible with that principle.

The consequences of this phenomenon in the United States have not been good, either for judging or for democracy. As for judging: to get confirmed to a federal court in the United States, one must be nominated by the president and confirmed by the Senate. This used to be, for the most part, a fairly routine process. But it has become a major battleground for the political parties and the interest groups, a major issue in every presidential campaign. When an individual is nominated for a federal judgeship, few Americans care whether the nominee will approach each case with an independence of mind, or a reasoned process of decision-making. Americans care instead about results. Will the nominee, for example, uphold the right to abortion on demand? This trend is an unfortunate one, but it is entirely understandable. Once the vocation of a judge is conceived of as the vocation of the common-law judge, why shouldn't Americans care what that judge thinks about the moral issues of the day? The result is a nomination process that politicizes the judiciary.

The judge as legislator has also not been good for democracy. When the vocation of a judge is reduced to simply selecting the best rule, remarkable power is placed in the hands of a few persons who are barely accountable for their decisions. In my country, most judges are given life tenure, and it is almost impossible to get a judge impeached. This was originally designed to give judges some insulation from the public indignation that often accompanies unpopular decisions. But when the vocation of a judge is more akin to that of a lawmaker, such insulation seems remarkably inapt. Moreover, there is no reason to suspect that the justices on my court, for example, are particularly good representatives of the views that a majority of Americans hold. We all live in Washington, D.C., for goodness' sake—we are totally out of touch with America! And we are all lawyers. Since when would a majority of Americans think that a group of nine lawyers from elite law schools should be entrusted with deciding the "best rules" for all of our countrymen to live by?

The vocation of a judge is a proud one, but in the United States, it is undergoing a serious transformation. Perhaps we are qualified to decide whether railroads should be liable for fireworks explosions. But when that mode of reasoning supplants every other, I wouldn't trust us much more than that.

ORIGINAL MEANING

Antonin Scalia was a judge on the U.S. Court of Appeals for the D.C. Circuit when he accepted Attorney General Edwin Meese's invitation to speak at the Attorney General's Conference on Economic Liberties on Saturday, June 14, 1986. On June 13, the speaking engagement suddenly took on added drama: Meese called Scalia to invite him to meet with President Reagan at the White House the following Monday. What wasn't yet known publicly was that Chief Justice Warren E. Burger had informed Reagan that he would be retiring.

Scalia's speech might well have turned into a sort of audition. If so, it was a successful one: during their interview on Monday, June 16, Reagan offered to nominate Scalia and on June 18 he announced his plan to elevate Associate Justice William H. Rehnquist to chief justice and to have Scalia fill Rehnquist's seat. In September, the Senate confirmed Scalia's nomination by a 98–0 vote.

Scalia's proposal to rebrand "original intent" as "original meaning" is significant in the intellectual history of originalism, the school of interpretation that holds that a legal text bears the meaning that it had when adopted. The "original meaning" approach, which aims to discover the original public meaning of the Constitution's provisions rather than the subjective intentions of the Framers, soon became the dominant school of originalism—thanks in large part to Scalia's continued advocacy and to the powerful example of his opinions as a justice.

———

When I was in law teaching, I was fond of doing what is called "teaching against the class"—that is, taking positions that the students were almost certain to disagree with, in order to generate some discussion, if not productive thought. I have tended to take a similar contrary approach in public talks; it is neither any fun nor any use preaching to the choir. Thus, when Prof. [Richard] Epstein and I last appeared on the same program in Washington it was at the Cato Institute, where I took the position that we should not extend (or re-extend) the concept of substantive due process to economic rights. I did not have the feeling that I was the home team. This endearing quality of saying the right thing at the wrong time is the secret of my popularity.

When I was invited to give this luncheon address, I was initially at a loss to think of a subject that would be sufficiently obnoxious. On the expansion of substantive due process, for example, I figured this audience would be split about 50-50. I could whine about why judges should be paid more money, even though attorneys general and assistant attorneys general should not—but that subject has such an air of unreality about it that if it raised any hackles they would be make-believe hackles. As I was musing in my chambers over this perplexing problem, the room was filled with the sound of a voice—loud, though it was in a whisper—which seemed to be coming from the picture of Mount Sinai that we have hanging in the D.C. Circuit's conference room. It said: CRITICIZE THE DOCTRINE OF ORIGINAL INTENT. The voice, I must admit, sounded a little like David Bazelon.* Then again, it sounded a bit like Robert Bork.† In any case, since I am rarely given these revelations, I thought that was what I should do.

There is also a less supernatural urging that led me to the same conclusion—and that is, public reaction to what is referred to in my chambers as the Speech. You may recall that when President Reagan ran in 1980, he had a set talk that he would give around the country, with minor alterations as the circumstances warranted. Well, I have found that to be a pretty useful format for at least some of those events at which federal judges are invited to speak. Each year I have picked out one particular subject that

---

*   Longtime liberal judge on the D.C. Circuit.

†   Scalia's originalist colleague on the D.C. Circuit.

interests me and have addressed it in a number of talks—the text gradually expanding over the course of the year as I have time for new research, or as new ideas occur to me.

The Speech for this year has been about judicial use of legislative history in the interpretation of statutes. My general attitude toward it can be summed up (I don't want to give the entire Speech here) by saying that I regard it as the greatest surviving legal fiction. If you can believe that a committee report (to take the most respected form of legislative history) in fact expresses what all the members of Congress (or at least a majority of them) "intended" on the obscure issues that it addresses; if you can believe that a majority of them even *read* the committee report; indeed, if you can believe that a majority of them was even *aware* of the *existence* of the obscure issue; then you would have had no trouble, several hundred years ago, in permitting all tort actions to be squeezed into the writ of assumpsit by the patently phony allegation that the defendant had *undertaken* (assumpsit) to be careful. Even beyond the unreliability of almost all legislative history (most of which is now cooked-up legislative history) as an indication of intent, it seems to me that asking what the legislators *intended* rather than what they *enacted* is quite the wrong question.

Nero, it is said, used to have his edicts posted high up on the pillars of the Forum, thus rendering them more difficult to read and more easy to transgress unknowingly. The secrets of legislative history are the twentieth-century equivalent of high-posting. Statutes should be interpreted, it seems to me, not on the basis of the unpromulgated intentions of those who enact them (assuming— quite unrealistically as to most points of interpretation—that such unpromulgated intentions actually existed on the part of more than a few legislators) but rather on the basis of what is the most probable meaning of the *words* of the enactment, in the context of the whole body of public law with which they must be reconciled.

But to return to the point: On most occasions on which I delivered the Speech, I would receive a Pharisaic question from the floor (modeled after the question "Master, is it lawful to pay tribute to Caesar?"), which would go something like this: "From what you say, Judge Scalia, I presume you disagree with Attorney General Meese concerning original intent as the correct criterion for interpreting the Constitution." Of course there is a lot less to that question than meets the ear. The debate regarding the doctrine of original intent—which has, after many years, finally been elevated to a public level—focuses upon the first, rather than the second, word of the doctrine. The fighting issue is not whether "intent" should govern, but rather whether *original* intent should govern, as opposed to some manner of interpretation that permits application of the provision to evolve over time.

So much of the attention has been focused on the first word, however, that I am not sure whether even the main participants in the debate (whoever they are) are clear about what they mean by the second. The burden of my brief remarks today is that it seems to me they should mean not "original intent of the Framers" but "original intent of the Constitution." What was the most plausible meaning of the words of the Constitution to the society that adopted it—regardless of what the Framers might secretly have intended?

This does not mean, of course, that the expressions of the Framers are irrelevant. To the contrary, they are strong indication of what the most knowledgeable people of the time understood the words to mean. When the proponents of original intent invoke the Founding Fathers, I in fact understand them to invoke them *for that reason*. It is not that "the Constitution must mean this because Alexander Hamilton thought it meant this, and he wrote it"; but rather that "the Constitution must mean this because Alexander Hamilton, who for Pete's sake must have understood the thing, thought it meant this."

How else to explain, for example, reliance on those five numbers of the *Federalist Papers* written by John Jay, who was not a delegate to the Constitutional Convention? Or, come to think of it, reliance upon Thomas Jefferson, who also was not there? Indeed, how to explain greater reliance upon those knowledgeable national figures who were present at the Convention than upon the remarks in the state ratifying debates—since it was ultimately the *states* (or the *people*) who were the parties to this contract, and whose innermost "intent" (if anyone's) is relevant?

But really the trump card to establish that "original intent" would more accurately be expressed "original meaning" is this: Even if you believe in original intent in the literal sense, you must end up believing in original meaning, because it is perfectly clear that the original intent was that the Constitution would be interpreted according to its original meaning. If you had asked the participants at the Constitutional Convention whether their debates could be an *authoritative* source for construing the Constitution, there is no doubt that the answer would have been no. This is apparent not only from the fact that the use of legislative history was in those days anathema—as it remains today in England—but also from many extrinsic indications. The *Journal of the Convention*, for example (which was taken in fairly slipshod form and never reviewed by the whole body), was not immediately published but was turned over to George Washington, subject to disposition by the future Congress under the new Constitution. It remained under seal in the Department of State until it was published by resolution of Congress (after editing by Secretary of State John Quincy Adams) in 1818.

This presents an interesting quandary, by the way. If original intent in the narrow sense is the touchstone, then we have got it all wrong in believing that judicial decisions that date closest to the Constitution are the most reliable. To the contrary, the benighted judges writing before 1818 did not have the *Journal of the Convention* to guide them. Those writing before 1840 did not have Madison's extensive notes; and before 1845, *Elliot's Debates*, which included debates in the ratifying conventions. And only in 1911 did Farrand undertake a comprehensive compilation of all the records pertaining to the adoption of the Constitution. More documentation has of course come to light since. So, logically, Chief Justice Burger should know more about what the Constitution originally prescribed than Chief Justice Marshall.

Beyond the decision not to publish the *Journal* as an indication that the original intent was to use the original meaning, there are quite explicit statements on the point by some of the most prominent Framers. In his 1791 "Opinion to President Washington on the Constitutionality of an Act to Establish a Bank," Alexander Hamilton wrote:

> [W]hatever may have been the intention of the framers of a constitution, or of a law, that intention is to be sought for in the instrument itself, according to the usual and established rules of construction. Nothing is more common than for laws to *express* and *effect*, more or less than was intended. . . . [A]rguments drawn from extrinsic circumstances, regarding the intention of the convention, must be rejected. [Emphasis in original.]

In one of his letters, James Madison drew a sharp distinction between the "true meaning" of the Constitution and "whatever might have been the opinions entertained in forming the Constitution." The reason Madison gave for not publishing his notes of the Convention until his death was that he wished to wait until

> the Constitution should be well settled by practice, and till a knowledge of the controversial part of the proceedings of its framers could be turned to no improper account. . . . As a guide in expounding and applying the provisions of the Constitution, the debates and incidental decisions of the Convention can have no authoritative character.

In yet another letter, Madison wrote:

> [W]hatever respect may be thought due to the intention of the Convention, which prepared and proposed the Constitution, *as a presumptive evidence of the general understanding at the time of the language used*, it must be kept in mind that the only authoritative intentions were those of the people of the States, as expressed through the Conventions which ratified the Constitution. [Emphasis in original.]

Of course it was true in the eighteenth century, as it remains true now, that there is one very good (if unprincipled) reason for using legislative history: it sometimes supports the position one wishes to establish. As it turns out, even George Washington was not immune to the blandishment of this reality. In 1796, when the House was debating whether certain treaties had to be concurred in by the lower house, President Washington sent the House a message opposing that position. It included the following:

> If other proofs than these, and the plain letter of the Constitution itself, be necessary to ascertain the point under consideration, they may be found in the journals of the Great Convention, which I have deposited in the office of the Department of State. In those journals it will appear, that a proposition was made, "that no Treaty should be binding on the United States which was not ratified by a law," and that the proposition was explicitly rejected.

(Although George Washington did write a wonderful letter to the Jewish Community of Newport, Rhode Island, it is not recorded that he was familiar with the word *chutzpah*. The above quoted message, however, relying upon documentation that only he and his administration knew about, since it was under seal in the State Department, suggests that he had some grasp of the substance of the thing.) The reaction by the House was outrage. Madison objected to use of the *Journal* as "a clue to the meaning of the Constitution," and said he "did not believe a single instance could be cited in which the sense of the Convention had been required or admitted as material in any Constitutional question" in Congress or the Supreme Court.

As I have said, therefore, it seems to me a no-win situation: even if you believe in original intent, you must believe in original meaning. I suppose it is tolerable to use the one term to mean the other—Alexander Hamilton did just that in his "Opinion on the Constitutionality of an Act to Establish a Bank," which I quoted from earlier. He used the term "intent of the Convention" to mean the "true meaning" as it was determined by the "obvious & popular sense" of the constitutional provision in question (the Necessary and Proper Clause) and the "whole turn of the clause containing it." And as far as I know, Attorney General Meese and Justice Brennan use the term in the same sense.

In the interests of precision, however, I suppose I ought to campaign to change the label from the Doctrine of Original Intent to the Doctrine of Original Meaning. As I often tell my law clerks, terminology is destiny.

INTERPRETING THE CONSTITUTION

On what must have been hundreds of occasions, large and small, over the decades, Justice Scalia delivered his stump speech in favor of originalism and of an enduring Constitution—and against the "living Constitution" approach to revising the meaning of the Constitution. He typically relied only on a single-page outline consisting of about fifty typed words and various scribbled accretions. But when he spoke in Parliament House in Sydney, Australia, in August 1994, he presented a fully prepared version.

———

I want to speak to you this evening about principles of constitutional interpretation in the United States.

I am aware that United States law is often looked to in this country as a useful model of what to do, or a useful model of what to avoid. Indeed, insofar as constitutional interpretation is concerned, my court seems to be the model for (and the envy of) many supreme courts around the world. In my view it is emulated and envied for all the wrong reasons—and that is what I propose to talk about.

I am one of a small but hardy group of judges and academics in the United States who subscribe to the principle of constitutional interpretation known as originalism. Originalists believe that the provisions of the Constitution have a fixed meaning, which does not change: they mean today what they meant when they were adopted, nothing more and nothing less. This is not to say, of course, that there are not new applications of old constitutional rules. The Court must determine, for example, how the First Amendment guarantee of "the freedom of speech" applies to new technologies that did not exist when the guarantee was created—to sound trucks, for example, or to government-licensed over-the-air television. In such new fields the Court must follow the trajectory of the First Amendment, so to speak, to determine what it requires—and assuredly that enterprise is not entirely cut and dried, but requires the exercise of judgment. But acknowledging the need for projection of old constitutional principles upon new physical realities is a far cry from saying what the non-originalists say: that the Constitution *changes*; that the very act which it once prohibited it now permits, and which it once permitted it now forbids.

The notion has somehow gained currency—to some extent in the United States itself, but particularly abroad—that American courts and the American people have always regarded the Constitution as a so-called "living" document, which changes from age to age as social necessity and convenience demand. John Marshall himself is invoked as supporting this view—his famous statement in *McCulloch v. Maryland* that "we must never forget that it is a constitution we are expounding" is taken to mean that constitutions, unlike other enacted laws, must grow and change and expand. Of course the statement meant (or rather *assumed*) just the opposite. Marshall's point in *McCulloch* was that since a constitution must govern for ages to come, in circumstances and under conditions we cannot yet envision, the powers it accords to the government must be broadly construed. That is to say, since the Constitution cannot be thought to mean different things from age to age, its *permanent* meaning must be broad enough to give the government the tools it will need both now and in the future.

Originalism was constitutional orthodoxy in the United States until, in historical terms, very recent times—the post–World War II era of the Warren Court. I do not mean to suggest that prior to then the Supreme Court was always faithful to the original meaning, and never departed from it in order to produce what it considered a more desirable result. Assuredly it did so. Willful judges who bend a text to their wishes have always been with us, and always will. But in earlier times they at least had the decency to lie about it, to pretend that they were saying what the unchanging Constitution required. That is no longer necessary. Under the "living Constitution" philosophy that now dominates American jurisprudence, it no longer matters what the Constitution meant. The only relevant question is "What ought it to mean today?"

Examples abound of the changes that have been forced upon American society by this philosophy—not state by state, but instantaneously, on a national basis, from New York City to the smallest hamlet, from Maine to the Rio Grande and New Jersey to Oregon. So that you may appreciate the vast extent of the phenomenon, I will give you a few examples:

The First Amendment to our Constitution provides that "Congress shall make no law . . . abridging the freedom of speech, or of the press." It had never been thought that "the freedom of speech" included the freedom to libel. But in 1964 the Supreme Court held, without benefit of any historical precedent, that neither federal law nor state law could permit a public figure to recover damages for libel, so long as the libel was not (in effect) intentional. Arguably a good rule that the states and the federal government should democratically adopt by legislation; but assuredly *not* what the People adopted when they ratified the First Amendment.

Also in the realm of freedom of speech, the Supreme Court held, in 1957, that pornography could not be prohibited. Only *obscenity* can be prohibited, which we have later described as consisting not of pandering to an interest in sex, but of pandering to something other than a good, healthy interest in sex, whatever that means. There was no historical precedent for this restriction upon a democratic society's ability to use its police powers to regulate matters of sexual morality. The First Amendment had never meant that the sexual permissiveness of Akron, Ohio, had to match that of Reno, Nevada. Once again, that is arguably a good idea, which the voters of Akron or of Ohio might wish to embrace (if you will forgive the pun). But it is assuredly *not* an idea that the People of the United States gave the Supreme Court the power to impose when they adopted the First Amendment.

The First Amendment to our Constitution also provides that "Congress shall make no law respecting an establishment of religion." It had never been thought that this prohibited, not merely the official favoring of one religious sect over another, but even a government policy of favoritism toward religious practice in general. All our presidents since George Washington had issued Thanksgiving proclamations, proclaiming a national holiday in gratitude to God for his blessings upon our nation. All the states had exempted property used for religious services from real-estate taxes. The military had always provided chaplains at government expense, even in an all-volunteer army. The Senate and House had had their own publicly paid chaplains. The Supreme Court itself had opened each of its sittings (and still does) with the invocation "God save the United States and this Honorable Court." Nonetheless, the Supreme Court proclaimed, in 1973, in contradiction of our entire national history and several prior Supreme Court cases, that the government could not show favoritism toward religion. This is called the "principle of neutrality." In the most recent manifestation of this doctrine, two terms ago, the Court held that it was unconstitutional for a public high school to begin its graduation ceremonies with a nondenominational benediction read by a rabbi.

The Fourth Amendment to our Constitution prohibits unreasonable searches and seizures. The Court held in 1961—without any basis in national tradition, and indeed contrary to a prior Supreme Court case—that when an unreasonable search or seizure *does* occur, the sanction must be exclusion of the evidence from the criminal trial. The policeman will be punished by setting the criminal free. Arguably a good rule, to deter unlawful police conduct. But not one that had ever been democratically prescribed in the Fourth Amendment.

The Fifth Amendment provides that no person shall be compelled in any criminal case to be a witness against himself. The Supreme Court held in 1966—with no basis in historical practice—that this requires the exclusion of seemingly voluntary confessions if they have been given by a prisoner in custody, *unless* the prisoner has formally been advised of his right to remain silent and to have an attorney—the so-called *Miranda* warning that you hear read on all the American cop shows.

The Fourteenth Amendment assures all citizens the equal

protection of the laws. The Supreme Court has held in the past few years that this means what it never before meant: that parties in civil and even criminal cases cannot exercise peremptory challenges on the basis of race or sex. A black defendant accused of raping a white woman cannot, for example, peremptorily strike whites or women from the jury.

But perhaps the area of our jurisprudence that most clearly reflects the "living Constitution" philosophy is that which pertains to the Eighth Amendment, the provision of our Bill of Rights that proscribes "cruel and unusual punishments." Our court has used that provision in recent years to place restrictions upon both the substance and procedure of capital punishment that never existed before and were not conceivably embodied in the amendment as originally enacted. We have prohibited, for example, the imposition of that penalty for any crime except murder—though the death penalty was until recently sometimes imposed for rape, and at the time the Eighth Amendment was adopted was even imposed for horse-thieving. We have also held that the death penalty cannot be automatic (if you are convicted of first-degree murder, you die); the sentencer must always be required to consider all mitigating circumstances and must be given the option of imposing a lesser sentence.

Once again, all this may be very sensible; but it was never in the Eighth Amendment. Our cases acknowledge that, but they say that the content of the Eighth Amendment changes from age to age, to reflect (and I quote) "the evolving standards of decency that mark the progress of a maturing society." You will note the wide-eyed, youthful meliorism in this sentiment: every day, in every way, we get better and better. Societies always *mature*; they never *rot*. This despite the twentieth century's evidence of concentration camps and gas ovens in one of the most advanced and civilized nations of the world. Of course the whole *premise* of a constitution in general, and of a bill of rights in particular, is the very opposite of this. Certain rights are sought to be "locked in"—placed beyond the normal legislative process—out of fear that they will be disregarded by a *less enlightened* or *less virtuous* future generation.

The proponents of the living Constitution indulge the optimistic assumption that whatever changes are made in original meaning will always be in the direction of according greater individual freedom—which to their way of thinking is always *good*. Only the anarchist, of course, would agree that it is always good. Any system of government involves a balancing of individual freedom of action against community needs, and it seems to me quite foolish to assume that every further tilt in the direction of greater freedom of action is necessarily good. But assuming that to be true, I cannot for the life of me understand why the proponents of a living Constitution expect it to be a one-way street. The "evolving standards" approach can take away old rights as well as create new ones. That has happened during my time on the Court.

Our Sixth Amendment provides that "[i]n all criminal prosecutions, the accused shall enjoy the right . . . to be confronted with the witnesses against him." We nonetheless held, in 1990, that in a prosecution for sexual abuse of a young child, the child could be permitted to testify out of the presence of the defendant, with the defendant observing the proceedings over closed-circuit television from another room. This procedure is acceptable, we said, where the child would be too nervous or frightened to testify in the defendant's presence.

Well, that may be a very reasonable disposition—but it is certainly not the disposition established by the Sixth Amendment. There is no doubt about what it means "to be confronted with the witnesses against [you]." It means (at a minimum) that they give their damning testimony *in your presence*. The reason for that disposition is that there is something in the human psyche which makes it difficult to tell a lie in the very presence of the person being condemned. Difficult for adults, and difficult for little children, too. Now perhaps, in the case of little children, the truth-finding benefit of this protection is outweighed by the truth-finding detriment of childish fear. That is, I suspect, how modern America, which is much more sensitive to "psychic trauma" than our hardy forebears, would evaluate it. But it is certainly not how the Sixth Amendment evaluated it. They had sexual abuse then; they had child witnesses then; they did not, to be sure, have closed-circuit television but they had other devices that would have achieved the same end of permitting the defendant to see the witness but preventing the witness from seeing the defendant—for example, a simple screen placed in front of the defense table. They did not permit these evasions in the case of children, but required, *in all criminal prosecutions*, the right to be confronted.

In other words, our 1990 decision eliminated a right that used to exist. Perhaps it is, as I have suggested, a right that (at least in the case of child witnesses) the majority no longer cares for. But a right consists precisely of entitlement *against the wishes of the majority*. There is no blinking the fact that we have eliminated a freedom that used to exist—that the "evolving Constitution" can evolve toward less freedom as well as toward more.

The most frequently pressed argument of the "living constitutionalists" is that their philosophy is absolutely essential in order to provide the necessary "flexibility" that a changing society requires. They would have you believe that the American Constitution would have snapped if it had not been permitted to bend and grow. This would be a persuasive argument if most of the "growing" that the living constitutionalists have brought upon us in the past, and are determined to bring upon us in the future, were the *elimination* of restrictions upon the governmental process. But just the opposite is true. Most living constitutionalists want to create *new* restrictions upon the legislative process, not to *eliminate* old ones. They favor, in other words, *less* flexibility in government, not *more*. As things now stand, the state and federal governments in the United States may either apply capital punishment or eliminate it, permit suicide or forbid it, permit homosexual conduct or forbid it—all as the changing times and the changing sentiments of society may demand. But when capital punishment is held to violate the Eighth Amendment, and when suicide and homosexual conduct are held to be protected by the Fourteenth Amendment, all flexibility is gone. There is no flexibility anymore, for example, with regard to abortion: the living constitutionalists have created a regime in which it *must* be permitted, regardless of the changing needs and desires of American society. No, the reality of the matter is that living constitutionalists are not seeking to facilitate social change but to *prevent* it, by enshrining their views of morality or of natural law in the Constitution.

Besides supposed inflexibility, the other principal defect attributed to originalism is the difficulty of figuring out, at a distance of two hundred years, or in the case of Australia one hundred years, what the original understanding of a particular provision was. Modern deconstructionists, who abound in law as in literature, insist that words have no *inherent* meaning, and it is folly to pretend otherwise. Well, of course they have enough inherent meaning for all practical purposes, which is why these deconstructionists tend to make their arguments in learned articles composed of words, rather than in music or dance. It is true, however, that what the meaning was two hundred years ago is often difficult to discern, and originalists will sometimes disagree among themselves as to what it was.

Originalists' response to this particular argument against originalism sometimes reminds me of market economists' response to the argument that "market failure" makes government regulation imperative. They used to spend enormous time and energy denying that, except in the rarest of circumstances, market failure could exist. Then University of Chicago economist (and Nobel laureate) George Stigler came along and pointed out that the proper question was not whether the market was *perfect*, but rather whether it was better than a government-managed economy. He then applied to government actors the same rigorous assumptions of self-interested action that the critics of market economy applied to commercial actors in order to demonstrate market failure—and lo and behold, it turns out that even in a market that is not perfectly competitive, government regulation is likely to perform even worse. Well, originalists would do well to apply the same approach to the charge that originalism does not always produce clear answers. Granted. But the relevant question is whether any other system produces clearer ones.

And that question is not at all difficult to answer. For the originalist, most constitutional questions pose no difficulty at all. Whether the Confrontation Clause requires confrontation, for example, is, in the current jargon, a no-brainer. For the constitutional evolutionist, however, every question is an open question, and every day is a new day. Three of the justices with whom I have sat—Justice William Brennan, Justice Thurgood Marshall, and Justice Harry Blackmun—have held that the death penalty is unconstitutional, even though it is specifically acknowledged *twice* in the Constitution: in the provisions of the Fifth Amendment that prevent the deprivation of "*life*, liberty or property without due process of law," and that require grand jury indictment for prosecution of a "*capital*, or otherwise infamous crime." Notwithstanding the clarity of these provisions, the non-originalist must ask himself, decade after decade (or is it year after year?), "Is capital punishment constitutional?"

One of the interesting features of the massive modern attack upon originalism is that, while its many opponents are unified in the view that that mode of interpretation is wrong, they display no agreement whatever upon what is right—that is to say, no agreement upon what criterion of constitutional meaning should replace it. For of course "non-originalism" or "evolutionism" is not itself a theory of constitutional construction. It is simply an *anti*-theory—opposition to an original, fixed meaning. There is a saying in American electoral politics (invoked when an incumbent's popularity polls are very low, but the other party has no credible candidate to oppose him): "You can't beat somebody with nobody." The same is true in constitutional theory. If originalism is to be supplanted, it must be supplanted with *something*. If the judge is not to look to the original understanding of the text, what is he to look to? Here, of course, the academics explode into a hundred different groups, or indeed into as many groups as there are academics. Some would use the philosophy of John Locke; others, the philosophy of John Rawls; others, simply the "natural law," as though that defines an identifiable body of knowledge. The fact is that *no* principle of interpretation other than originalism has even the shadow of a chance of attracting general adherence. As a practical matter, there is no alternative to originalism but standardless judicial constitution-making.

And that, of course, is the very *appeal* of non-originalism for the judges: once they are liberated from the original meaning, they are liberated from any other governing principle as well. Nothing constrains their action except perhaps their estimation of how much judicial social engineering the society will tolerate. Consider, for example, how the learned legal discussion must proceed in a conference that is to determine whether there is a constitutional right to die. Well, of course the text of the Constitution says absolutely nothing about such a right. And our states have always had laws against suicide. Yes-yes-yes. But all of that is lawyerly analysis about the past, which is quite irrelevant. The question is not whether the Constitution *originally* established a right to die, but whether there is a right to die *today*. Do you think there is a right to die, Justice X? I don't. What about you, Justice Y? Let's have a show of hands. Well, that's five in favor of a right to die. Now on to the next case.

I would be more hopeful of recalling my country to the sound mode of constitutional construction that it followed for most of its history, if the problem were merely one of reconverting judges and scholars to the old ways of thought. I fear, however, that the infection has spread further than that. We now face a problem, not merely of judicial and academic analysis, but of *public belief*— and that is a lot harder to change. When the proposition that the Constitution means whatever it ought to mean was first put forward, knowledge of it was restricted to the cognoscenti—to the judges and scholars who could be trusted with such a powerful secret. In public speeches, orators, even judges, continued to refer to the anchor, the rock, of our unchanging constitutional principles. But inevitably, the secret trickled out, and now, thirty years or so after the Warren Court, the man in the street knows it. *The Constitution means whatever it ought to mean.* The American citizen now believes that whatever he feels intensely about—whether it be abortion rights, or homosexual rights, or the right to die—must be *required* by the Constitution. Insignificant matters may be left to

the ordinary democratic processes of legislation, but really important matters, that is to say matters on which I feel intensely, are
resolved by the Constitution, whether it mentions them or not.

When I was a child, Americans used to say, to express their
deep frustration about a certain state of affairs: "There oughta
be a law." In fact there was a comic strip with that title. Well, I
haven't heard that expression in years. It has been replaced with a
phrase that now comes readily to the lips of every American: "It's
unconstitutional."

The depth of the change in our national attitudes, as we went
from a Constitution that meant what it originally meant to a Constitution that means whatever it ought to mean, can readily be
seen by considering the Nineteenth Amendment to our Constitution, adopted in 1920, the amendment that guaranteed women the
right to vote. It is hard for the modern American to understand
why that amendment was needed. We had an explicit constitutional guarantee of equal protection of the laws in 1920; and as an
abstract matter, what could possibly be a greater denial of equal
protection than deprivation of the franchise? If we thought then as
we think now, surely we would not have gone through the national
upheaval of the women's suffrage movement that led to the Nineteenth Amendment. The Supreme Court would simply have pronounced that—even though it had never previously been thought
unconstitutional to deny various classes of citizens the vote,
whether it be women, or non-property-holders, or non-English-
speaking citizens—it now *was* unconstitutional. That course would
not have occurred to people in 1920. To be sure, in the abstract
the Equal Protection Clause could be given such a meaning. But
in the abstract it could also be thought to mean that public buildings must have unisex toilets. Did it mean that? Of course it didn't
mean that. It never meant that. Words in the Constitution were
not to be interpreted in the abstract, but rather according to the
understandings that existed when they were adopted. And if new
protections were desired, then new protections would have to be
enacted democratically—as the Nineteenth Amendment was.

That was how Americans thought in 1920. It is not how we

think today. Our attitude today is that if something *ought* to be so, why then the Constitution, that embodiment of all that is good and true and beautiful, *requires* it. And we fight out these battles about what ought to be—whether women's suffrage or abortion or homosexual rights or the right to die—not in the democratic forum but in the law courts. The major issues that shape our society are to be decided for the whole nation by a committee of nine lawyers: Justice Scalia and his colleagues. There is a certain irony in the fact that the society which takes all these issues out of the democratic process, and requires them to be decided as constitutional absolutes, prides itself upon (of all things) its *toleration*. It is willing to tolerate anything, apparently, except disagreement and divergence and hence the need for continuing democratic debate and democratic decision-making, on an ever-increasing list of social issues.

What foreigners would be well advised to understand about the "living Constitution" system I have described is that it is new and it is inherently unstable. Do not suppose that it has endured for two hundred years. It is, as I have said, essentially forty years old; and its ultimate consequences are only now becoming apparent. In the days when interpreting the Constitution was regarded by the people as an essentially *scholarly* task—determining the original meaning of text—they were content to leave that task to judges selected principally because of their qualifications as eminent lawyers. To be sure, some nonsubstantive political factors would often intrude—for example, a Supreme Court seat vacated by a New Englander would presumptively be filled by another New Englander. And occasionally, even a single "hot-button" *substantive* issue might influence the selection. Andrew Jackson, for example, wanted to nominate a justice who would reject the constitutionality of a Bank of the United States; and Teddy Roosevelt a justice who would uphold his trust-busting legislation. But the kind of selection process we have today was unheard of. I mean a process in which each nominee to the Court is asked a series of questions by a series of senators (representatives of the people) regarding the existence of one right after another in the Constitution: "Judge so-and-so, do you believe that there is a right to X in the Constitution? [Fill in for X whatever your most favorite constitutional claim happens to be.] You *don't?* Well, *I* do; and my constituents do; and I certainly won't vote to put someone on the Court who has such a radical [or, depending on the answer, uncompassionate] view of the Constitution. Now what about a right to Y? Do you think that exists in the Constitution? You *do?* Well, I don't, and my constituents don't, and I certainly won't vote etc. etc."

Our appointment and confirmation process has, in other words, evolved into a mini-plebiscite on the meaning of the Constitution whenever a new justice is to be seated. The important point to grasp is that that evolution was inevitable. A freedom-loving people respectful of the rule of law may be expected to let lawyers decide what a constitutional text means; but they cannot be expected to let lawyers decide what a constitution *ought* to say. That is not a job for lawyers, but for the people. One way or another, in a well-functioning democracy, if the task of saying what the Constitution *ought* to provide is to be done, it will be done by the people themselves. Once the secret is out that the judges are evolving a new constitution rather than applying an old one, the people will see to it that judges are selected who will evolve it the way *they* want it to evolve. Then, of course, the whole value of a constitution will have been destroyed, by placing its content within the hands of the very body it is meant to protect against: the majority.

I entertain some small hope that my country may someday return to the mode of constitutional construction that brought it almost two centuries down the road. I have a somewhat greater hope that other countries will not attribute the durability of my country's constitution, and the lasting prominence of my country's Supreme Court, to a novel and corrosive principle of constitutional interpretation that is, even as we watch, in the process of undoing the Court and the Constitution alike.

THE FREEDOM OF SPEECH

Wesleyan University president Michael Roth warmly remembers the "playful intellectual openness" that Justice Scalia displayed during his visit to campus in March 2012. In addition to presenting the Hugo L. Black Lecture on Freedom of Expression, Scalia enjoyed the discussion and debate with undergraduates in a constitutional-law course and "spent much more time with them than we could have expected."

———

I plan to discuss the originalist approach to constitutional interpretation in general, the application of that approach to the free-speech provision of the First Amendment—and, because this is, after all, the Hugo L. Black Lecture, to say a little bit about how an originalist approach differs from the views of Justice Black.

Let me begin by telling you what originalism is. The Constitution, as you know, contains a number of broad provisions, which are necessarily vague in their application: due process of law, equal protection of the laws, cruel and unusual punishments, the freedom of speech, to name a few. Originalism gives to those terms the meaning they were understood to have when the people adopted them. Is the death penalty cruel and unusual punishment? A hard question, perhaps, for the non-originalist. I have sat with four colleagues who thought it was. But for the originalist the answer is easy: at the time the people ratified the Eighth Amendment— the Cruel and Unusual Punishments Clause—no one thought it forbade the death penalty. The death penalty was at the time, and remained for some years later, the only penalty for a felony.

Originalism is not a novel approach to textual interpretation.

In fact, it remains the approach that virtually everyone uses for statutes. Nobody thinks that a statute's meaning changes from decade to decade. And originalism was, for most of our history, the orthodox manner of interpreting the Constitution as well. Justice Story and Chief Justice Marshall would have been astounded at the notion that the Constitution changes to mean whatever each successive generation would like it to mean. It would be not much use to have a First Amendment, for example, if the freedom of speech included only what some future generation wanted it to include. That would guarantee nothing at all.

To be sure, the Constitution has to be applied to new and emerging phenomena. The First Amendment, for example, had to be applied to radio in the 1920s and must be applied to the Internet today. But under an originalist interpretation, its application to *pre-existing phenomena* does not change: libelous face-to-face oral communication that was unprotected by the First Amendment at the time of the Framing remains unprotected today. Moreover, those pre-existing applications are the data that determine the First Amendment's application to new phenomena. Thus, libel over the radio or on the Internet is unprotected as well.

Let me proceed, now, to apply originalist methodology to the speech guarantee of the First Amendment. I start where originalists always start: with the text. "Congress shall make no law . . . abridging the freedom of speech, or of the press." A good example of how originalist and non-originalist interpretations differ can be seen by applying this text to laws providing causes of action for libel. There is no doubt that at the time it was adopted in 1791 no one thought that this provision invalidated laws against libel—which existed then and have continued to exist ever since. The issue is an easy one for originalists: libel laws are constitutional. The famous case of *New York Times v. Sullivan* (1964), much beloved by the press, is a classic example of non-originalist interpretation. That case held that suit would not lie for libel of a public figure, unless the libel was in bad faith—that is, with knowledge, or reason to know, that it was false. There is no doubt that libel of a public figure was unprotected by the First Amendment in 1791 (and it remains unprotected speech, by the way, in England). But the Warren Court determined, as the Framers had not, that allowing good-faith libel of public figures would be good for democracy, and so the First Amendment was revised accordingly.

Justice Black voted along with the majority in that case, though he would have gone even further to say that *no* libel, not even bad-faith libel, was outside the scope of "the freedom of speech." Here are a few excerpts from his opinion:

> I vote to reverse exclusively on the ground that the *Times* and the individual defendants had an absolute, unconditional constitutional right to publish in the *Times* advertisement their criticisms of the Montgomery agencies and officials. . . . [S]tate libel laws threaten the very existence of an American press virile enough to publish unpopular views on public affairs and bold enough to criticize the conduct of public officials. . . . In my opinion, the Federal Constitution has dealt with this deadly danger to the press in the only way possible without leaving the press open to destruction—by granting the press an absolute immunity for criticism of the way public officials do their public duty.

How Justice Black arrived at this view is summed up in an interview he gave in 1962:

> I am for the First Amendment from the first word to the last. I believe it means what it says, and it says to me, "Government shall keep its hands off religion. Government shall not attempt to control the ideas a man has. Government shall not attempt to establish a religion of any kind. Government shall not abridge freedom of the press or speech. It shall let anybody talk in this country."

As I said earlier, originalists are textualists—they begin with the text. So you might expect me to agree with Justice Black. But the flaw in his reasoning is that the First Amendment does *not* say that government shall not abridge freedom of speech. It says that government shall not abridge "THE freedom of speech"—that is, that freedom of speech which was the understood right of Englishmen. Thus, there are several types of speech or categories of speech unprotected by the First Amendment because the Framing generation never understood them to fall within "the freedom of speech." Libel is one of them. Another is obscenity. Justice Black would not acknowledge that exception either. He wrote in one dissenting opinion:

> In my view the First Amendment denies Congress the power to act as censor and determine what books our citizens may read and what pictures they may watch. . . . [But] for the foreseeable future this Court must sit as a Board of Supreme Censors, sifting through books and magazines and watching movies because some official fears they deal too explicitly with sex. I can imagine no more distasteful, useless, and time-consuming task for the members of this Court than perusing this material to determine whether it has "redeeming social value." This absurd spectacle could be avoided if we would adhere to the literal command of the First Amendment that "Congress shall make no law . . . abridging the freedom of speech, or of the press. . . ."

Now I agree with Justice Black that it is "distasteful, useless, and time-consuming" for the Court to sort through obscene materials deciding what should and should not be allowed. But it is non-originalist jurisprudence that has made this a difficult chore, by adding to the requirement that the material appeal to a prurient interest in sex the requirements that it do so "as a whole," that it "portray sexual conduct in a patently offensive way," and that "taken as a whole, it . . . not have serious literary, artistic, political, or scientific value." In any case, it is only Justice Black's "literal" reading of the First Amendment (which as I have said is not really very literal) that enables him to avoid the difficulty.

One outspoken critic of originalism has called Justice Black "by far the most successful originalist of the last century." Both the adjective and the noun are wrong. As for successful, only Justice William O. Douglas ever joined Justice Black in his "absolutist" views of the First Amendment, and no one on the current Court has taken up their banner. And as for originalist, as we have seen, with respect to the First Amendment Justice Black did not take an originalist approach. His opinion in *New York Times v. Sullivan,* for example, spent a great deal of time explaining why libel laws were a bad idea, and then, for support in the original understanding, offered up a footnote with a single citation, telling the reader to "See, e.g.," an 1803 commentary from a law professor that did not even support his claims.

There are other examples of speech that is unprotected by the First Amendment because "the freedom of speech" was not understood to cover it. Incitement to violence and fighting words, for example. Other speech, such as criminal conspiracy and solicitation or fraud, has not yet come before my court in a First Amendment case, but since these forms of speech have long been criminalized without serious First Amendment challenge, I doubt we would find that the First Amendment was understood to protect them. I have no idea how Justice Black would have handled them. Would he really say that laws prohibiting false advertising are unconstitutional?

Under an originalist approach, not only is speech unprotected at the Founding unprotected today, but speech *protected* at the Founding *remains* protected today. Exemplifying that point is a recent Supreme Court case, *Brown v. Entertainment Merchants Association,* which involved a California law restricting the sale or rental of violent video games to minors. First, the Court (in an opinion I wrote) reaffirmed the principle I mentioned earlier, that "the basic principles of freedom of speech ... do not vary" with a new and different communication medium. Next it noted that the First Amendment excludes from its protection certain limited categories of historically unprotected speech, such as obscenity, incitement, and fighting words. But speech about violence was not among those historically unprotected categories. The California legislature was not free to create its own new category of unprotected speech—speech about violence—by weighing the value of such speech against its social costs. That balance was already struck by the founding generation, and we are not free to reweigh it on a continual basis. The California statute was invalid.

Thus far, I have spoken mostly about the original meaning of "the freedom of speech," but even in free-speech cases, that is not the only part of the First Amendment that the originalist approach helps elucidate. In some of those cases, it may be fairly easy to determine that the speech at issue is protected by the First Amendment but much harder to tell whether the government has "abridg[ed]" that freedom. In *National Endowment for the Arts v. Finley*, a majority of my court made things very difficult for itself in upholding as constitutional a federal statute that allowed government subsidies only for art that was determined to be decent and in line with American values. The Court engaged in what I considered extreme mental and linguistic gymnastics to conclude that the law did not discriminate against artists based on the viewpoint expressed in their art. For me, that vote was much easier. Of course the law discriminated based on the views expressed by the artist! And if the National Endowment for the Arts had been deciding whether to fine or punish the artists, the law would certainly have been unconstitutional. But instead, the NEA was deciding only whether the artists should receive *government subsidies* for their work. When the Bill of Rights was passed, as now, *to abridge* meant "to contract, to diminish; to deprive of." Simply put, when the government decides not to pay you for your speech, it is not "abridging" the freedom of speech within the meaning of the First Amendment.

Now that you have seen examples of the application of originalist methodology, let me address some of the principal criticisms lodged against it—not just in the First Amendment area but generally. Some claim that it is just camouflage for the imposition of conservative views. That is patently false. The best proof I can give is another free-speech case, *Texas v. Johnson* (1989). There the Supreme Court held that it was a violation of the First Amendment to make unlawful the burning of an American flag. I consider that action a form of speech—which shows, by the way, that

I am not a "strict constructionist." Texts should be construed neither strictly nor sloppily, but reasonably. And if you think the First Amendment covers only "speech" and "press" in the *literal* sense (which is what Justice Black said he believed), you must believe that Congress can censor handwritten mail. Of course "speech" and "press" are stand-ins for *the expression of ideas*—and that expression can be made through symbols and symbolic acts as well as through words. Semaphore and Morse code are covered, and so is the burning of a flag, a classic expression of disapproval or contempt for the government that it represents. The Court held in *Johnson* that it was unconstitutional to ban the burning of a flag. It was a 5–4 decision, and I made the fifth vote.

You should be in no doubt that, patriotic conservative that I am, I detest the burning of the nation's flag—and if I were king I would make it a crime. But as I understand the First Amendment, it guarantees the right to express contempt for the government, the Congress, the Supreme Court, even the nation and the nation's flag. And I could give you many other examples of opinions that I have joined and written that reach decidedly unconservative results. In the criminal-law field in particular I have insisted upon protections for the accused that a law-and-order conservative ought not to like. Far from facilitating conservative opinions, originalism prevents judges, conservatives and liberals alike, from judging according to their desires.

Another criticism of originalism—perhaps the most common one—is that it petrifies the law. Thus, the approach set up in opposition to originalism is sometimes called the approach of the "living Constitution"—a constitution that evolves as the needs of society require. Seems very attractive. But if you think that the proponents of a living Constitution are trying to bring you flexibility and the power to change, you should think again. A constitution is designed to provide not flexibility but rigidity—and that is precisely what the proponents of a living Constitution use it for. The originalists' Constitution permits expansive change when the people desire it. Do you want the death penalty? Elect those who will impose it. Do you abhor the death penalty? Elect those who will abolish it.

And you can change your mind. If you find that the murder rate goes up after the abolition of the death penalty, elect those who will reinstitute it. If, however, the living constitutionalists have their way and declare the death penalty unconstitutional, the people's power to choose is eliminated. No death penalty, period.

That is what has happened, of course, with abortion. The Constitution says nothing about the subject. It neither forbids (as the pro-choice people claim) nor requires (as the pro-life people claim) restrictions upon it. For two centuries, laws in every state prohibited it, but now, under a living-Constitution theory, it cannot be prohibited. No use trying to persuade your fellow citizens one way or the other about the subject. It has been taken off the democratic stage. And that is, of course, precisely what those who argued for *Roe v. Wade* desired to achieve. So don't love the living Constitution because it will bring you flexibility and choice; it will bring you rigidity, which is precisely what it is designed for.

A third criticism of originalism is that judges are incompetent historians. History, after all, is a science unto itself, and a science different from the science of law. Judges are trained as lawyers. What possible reason is there to believe that they can function effectively as historians? To begin with, I deny the premise that law has nothing to do with historical inquiry. Utterly central to the law is the meaning of words, and the meaning of a word often changes over time, as any reputable dictionary will show by its use of a parenthetical description such as "obs." (obsolete). Thus, the assertion that inquiry into the past has nothing to do with the law begs the question: historical inquiry has nothing to do with law only if original meaning is irrelevant—only if the law means not what it meant when adopted, but what it ought to mean today. To tell the truth, even the most thoroughgoing non-originalist will often have to resort to historical inquiry. Otherwise, what possible meaning could he assign to such phrases in the Constitution as "[t]he Privilege of the Writ of Habeas Corpus," "Bill of Attainder," "Letters of Marque and Reprisal," "Cases of admiralty and maritime Jurisdiction," "Corruption of Blood"?

It would not be accurate, however, to suggest that the only

historical inquiry demanded of originalists is a sort of lexicographer's investigation into the verbal usage of an earlier time. That is part of the enterprise, to be sure. Let me use a fairly recent Second Amendment case, *District of Columbia v. Heller*, as an example. There the petitioners contended that the term "bear arms" in the Second Amendment had an exclusively military connotation. It was necessary—and easy enough—for the Court's originalist opinion to show that this was not so, by citing many examples of usage prior to and contemporaneous with adoption of the Second Amendment. This is, as I say, almost lexicographer's work. But other historical inquiry was demanded as well. One of the significant aspects of the Second Amendment was that it did not purport to *confer* a right to keep and bear arms. It did not say that "the people shall have the right to keep and bear arms," or even that "the government shall not prevent the people from keeping and bearing arms," but rather that "the right of the people to keep and bear arms" (as though it were a pre-existing right) "shall not be infringed." (The First Amendment is not so different in prescribing that "Congress shall make no law . . . abridging the [pre-existing] freedom of speech.")

In *Heller*, this reference to a pre-existing right engendered historical inquiry which showed that, indeed, the right to have arms for personal use (including self-defense) was regarded at the time of the Framing as one of the fundamental rights of Englishmen, described as such by Blackstone, and found in the explicit guarantee of the English Bill of Rights of 1689. Once that historical pedigree was understood, it was difficult to regard the guarantee of the Second Amendment as no more than a guarantee of the right to join a militia. Moreover, the prologue of the Second Amendment ("A well regulated militia being necessary for the defense of a free state") could not be logically connected with a personal right to keep and bear arms without the historical knowledge (possessed by the Framing generation) that the Stuart kings had destroyed the people's militia, not by disbanding it, but by disarming those of its members whom they disfavored. Here the opinion was surely dealing with history in a broader sense than mere lexicography.

I must concede, therefore, that in some cases historical inquiry into the original meaning may be difficult. An example from the free-speech field is the 1995 case of *McIntyre v. Ohio Elections Commission*, which involved a First Amendment challenge to state requirements that all election campaign literature must identify the person or organization promulgating it. ("Printed by Citizens for Schwartz.") All the states had had such requirements and had had them for over a century. The plaintiff in the suit claimed that they were unconstitutional, since she had a right to anonymous political speech. It was quite difficult to determine what the people who ratified the First Amendment would have thought of such a claim, since the election process was so radically different before we adopted, toward the end of the nineteenth century, the Australian ballot—that is, the secret ballot.

While I cannot determine what the Framers thought, I am disinclined to think that, for over a century, all the states—with no registered protest—misunderstood the First Amendment. And so I rejected the challenge. Justice Thomas, another originalist, accepted it, and wrote the opinion for the Court holding such identification requirements unconstitutional. He relied for that conclusion upon the fact that the *Federalist Papers*—the most famous political tracts of the time—were published anonymously, under the name of Publius. Pseudonymous political speech was common at the time and, Justice Thomas concluded, must have been valued by the Framing generation. A not unreasonable conclusion—as, I also think, was mine. (For those keeping score, Justice Black shared Justice Thomas's view that the First Amendment protects a right to anonymous speech, but we know by now that Justice Black thought *all* speech was protected by the First Amendment.)

So the originalist methodology does not always yield a clear and easy answer. But the question before the house is not whether originalism is perfect. I will stipulate that it is not. The question is whether it is better than anything else. My burden is not to show that originalism is perfect, but merely to show that it beats the other available alternatives. And that is not difficult. In the vast majority of cases—and especially the most controversial ones—the historical inquiry will be easy. Is libel of public figures prohibited by the First Amendment? Is the death penalty prohibited? Are laws against abortion, homosexual sodomy, and assisted suicide prohibited? It is a piece of cake to determine that no one in the founding generation thought so. And for the more difficult questions, judges have the assistance of a growing number of legal historians—on law faculties and history faculties—to provide expert assistance on historical questions, just as engineers provide expert assistance on patent questions, and economists on antitrust questions.

By contrast, how are the living constitutionalists going to arrive at their decisions? To tell the truth, I don't know—and neither do they. How are they to decide what are "the evolving standards of decency that mark the progress of a maturing society"—the criterion of constitutional evolution that our Eighth Amendment opinions set forth? What would an elite group of the country's best lawyers, isolated in a marble palace, know about that? Earlier Supreme Court cases looked to the consensus of state laws. That is a dubious criterion of "evolved standards" to begin with. If it were true (which it is not) that a majority of the states have abolished the death penalty, that would not show that the people of those states consider that penalty unconstitutional, rather than just a bad idea—any more than the fact that a majority of states forbid the union shop would show that they consider the union shop unconstitutional. In any case, the Supreme Court has abandoned this approach, and has explicitly said that what the living Constitution prescribes does not depend on any consensus of state laws, but on the judgment of the justices. Do you think that judges (that is to say, lawyers) are better at the science of What Ought to Be than at the science of history?

The reality is that originalism is the only game in town—the only real, verifiable criterion that can prevent judges from making the Constitution say whatever they think it should say. Show Scalia the original meaning, and he is prevented from imposing his nasty, conservative views upon the people. He is handcuffed.

And if he tries to dissemble, he will be caught out. The source material is accessible to all; convenient omissions of inconvenient evidence can easily be identified; suspect conclusions can be effectively challenged. But if original meaning is not the criterion, what other criterion can there be that prevents judges from imposing their ideological preferences on society? Think about it. There is none. The living constitutionalist is a happy fella, because it turns out that the Constitution always means precisely what he thinks it ought to mean. That is indeed much of the attraction of the living Constitution. And it is an attraction not just to judges, but to the people at large. How wonderful to think that whatever you care passionately about—from abortion to the death penalty—is resolved precisely the way you think it should be *by the Constitution.* Never mind whether the people ever voted to put that in the Constitution and thus to remove it from the realm of democratic choice—only originalists care about that. It is there if it *ought* to be there. I urge you not to yield to that seductive and extremely undemocratic falsehood.

The American republic is a democracy. And the background rule of democracy is that the majority rules. We discuss matters, try to persuade one another, and then put it to a vote—directly, or through our representatives. And the majority rules. But in a liberal democracy (which we are) the majority does not always rule. It does not rule with regard to the freedom of speech, or freedom of religion, or the right to bear arms, or the right to trial by jury, and so forth—the provisions of the Bill of Rights. But who adopted those limitations on democracy? The people themselves, not some committee of judges. And it is only the people themselves who can add to or subtract from those limitations, through the amendment provision of the Constitution. If you believe in democracy, you are an originalist, because it is only the limitations that the people voted for—which means the limitations that the people understood they were imposing—that can frustrate the will of the people.

CONGRESSIONAL POWER

*When Justice Scalia initially agreed to speak at a January 2011 event orga-
nized by the Tea Party Caucus of the House of Representatives, ill-informed
critics faulted him for supposedly making a political alliance with House
conservatives. Never mind that his topic was the separation of powers and
that the event was open to all members of Congress. In the end, liberal members of the House who attended the speech praised it as a nonpartisan legal
discussion "at a very high level."*

Y ou should be warned that I will probably be telling you some
stuff you do not want to hear. That is part of my charm. I find
it not very helpful to tell people things they want to hear, and thus
probably already believe.

Since you will find some of my remarks uncongenial, I want to
point out that I am no enemy of the First Branch. To the contrary,
I think the legislative branch is the core of democracy, the most
immediate voice of the people, all of one House and one-third of
the other being elected every two years. And in the jurisprudence
I have applied on the Court, I have been hostile to what seemed
to me unjustified judicial limitations upon the legislative power. I
do not favor, for example, making the constitutionality of legislation depend upon the procedures Congress has followed, beyond
the requisite constitutional procedures of enactment of the law
by both Houses, with the approval of the president or an override
of his veto. I have refused to join opinions that make the constitutionality of legislation depend upon the nature of the hearings
conducted by Congress, and the adequacy of those hearings to

support the findings set forth in the prologue to the statute. I have referred to that process as reviewing the Congress's homework, a function inappropriate for our court.

I am, moreover, no fan of the so-called doctrine of unconstitutional delegation—or, more precisely, no fan of the doctrine that it is up to the Court to decide whether Congress has given the executive too much power. The factors that go into that determination are in my view nonjusticiable—whether, for example, that broad delegation is necessary to prosecute an ongoing war, or to solve an economic crisis. So, while there is undoubtedly a constitutional imperative that the principal federal decisions for the society are to be made by Congress, where that line falls is for Congress itself to determine. The check against excessive delegation is precisely that jealousy between the branches fostered by the separation of powers, a doctrine I will have something to say about today. If the separation of powers is working properly, Congress will not want to give the president more power than he needs.

Another respect in which I favor congressional power is this: I do not believe that the Constitution makes the Supreme Court in all respects the ultimate and dispositive arbiter of the meaning of the Constitution. Like Abraham Lincoln, I believe it makes us the ultimate and dispositive arbiter of the application of the Constitution to the case before us; Congress cannot overturn our judgment. But also like Abraham Lincoln, I do not believe that Congress is constitutionally *required* to accept the constitutional analysis that underlay our judgment. Dred Scott had to be handed over; but Congress did not have to accept the proposition that slavery had to be acknowledged in all the states. It could legislate on the basis of its differing view. The Supreme Court gets into the business of construing the Constitution not because the Constitution explicitly says it is our job (as do the constitutions of some European countries) but simply because we take an oath (prescribed by the Constitution) to support the Constitution, and must honor that oath when we decide a case. But you take the very same oath, and it is no less your responsibility than ours to make sure that your governmental acts comply with that document.

That said, it is certainly our tradition, and a good one, that Congress will ordinarily accept not just the judgment but also the constitutional reasoning of the Supreme Court. That is so for several reasons. For one thing, justices are, or ought to be, experts on the subject. It is lawyers' work—or at least it is lawyers' work if you believe, as I do, that the Constitution is a binding text whose meaning does not change. For another, the Third Branch is, as the Framers recognized, the least dangerous branch; it has power only to the extent that the other branches acknowledge its power. It cannot compel the appropriation of federal funds, initiate federal prosecutions, or imprison the federal defendants that it convicts. And finally, even if Congress ignores the constitutional principles that its opinions set forth, the Court itself usually does not. The doctrine of *stare decisis* (adherence to precedent) assures in most cases that laws enacted against its jurisprudence will not be able to be applied to our citizens.

But the important point here is that you have a responsibility, no less solemn than ours, to ensure that your actions comply with the Constitution. And since that is so, the Court ordinarily defers to your judgment. Every piece of legislation comes to us with a presumption of constitutionality. Which means that you are in a real sense more important expositors of the Constitution than we are. There are (you will be unsurprised to learn) many gray areas of constitutional law, where a particular disposition could reasonably be thought legitimate but could also reasonably be thought illegitimate. If you conclude the latter and for that reason do not enact the disposition, that is an end of the matter. We cannot (or should not) indulge such fine-tuning at our end.

Now some of the bad part. Once upon a time, Congress took its responsibility of constitutional interpretation very seriously. In the very first Congress, for example, when the proposed bill creating the Department of State was under debate in the House, James Madison objected to the provision authorizing the president to dismiss the secretary of state, because it implied that without such authorization the president would have no such power. Madison's view prevailed, and the provision was deleted.

Debate over constitutionality was fairly common, particularly in the Senate, right through the first half of the twentieth century. But things have changed. Congress now seems to have the attitude—and I have seen it expressed in some floor debate—that it is, after all, the Supreme Court's job to determine the constitutional limits on what Congress can do, so let's run it up the flagpole and see if anyone salutes. Only that attitude can explain some of the extravagant assertions of congressional power that have come before me during my years on the bench. That attitude has caused me to speculate, in one of my separate opinions, whether it makes sense anymore to give deference to a congressional assessment of constitutionality that probably never occurred. I will describe only a few of the cases involving legislation that seems to me to go over the edge. Most such cases involve efforts to eliminate or control powers belonging to one of the other two branches; some, the assertion of a general police power that has never been given to the federal government and belongs only to the states.

But before I get into the cases, let me tell you something that you will really find unpalatable, but which ought to make you approach this task of applying the Constitution with fear and trembling: within the structure of our Constitution, you, ladies and gentlemen, are the most dangerous branch. That is not my opinion; it is the opinion of the men who designed that structure. Let me read you a famous passage from number 48 of the *Federalist Papers*:

> [I]n a representative republic, where the executive magistracy is carefully limited, both in the extent and the duration of its power; and where the legislative power is exercised by an assembly, which is inspired, by a supposed influence over the people, with an intrepid confidence in its own strength; which is sufficiently numerous to feel all the passions which actuate a multitude, yet not so numerous as to be incapable of pursuing the objects of its passions, by means which reason prescribes; it is against the enterprising ambition of this department that the people ought to indulge all their jealousy and exhaust all

their precautions. The legislative department derives a superiority in our governments from other circumstances. Its constitutional powers being at once more extensive, and less susceptible of precise limits, it can, with the greater facility, mask, under complicated and indirect measures, the encroachments which it makes on the co-ordinate departments.

To be sure, it is fashionable to speak of the imperial presidency—but most of the extensive powers a modern president has, he has only because Congress has conferred them. And Congress can take them away. The reality is that Congress is the nine-hundred-pound gorilla in this town. And that is entirely as it should be. (As I have said, the legislature is the core of democratic government.)

To moderate the overwhelming power of the legislative branch, the Framers included in our Constitution a number of features that do not appear in the constitutional structure of most countries of the world. If the question were put to them, most Americans would say that what makes our country the most free country in the world is the Bill of Rights—the guarantees of freedom of speech, freedom of the press, freedom of religion, right to trial by jury, etc. That is demonstrably not so. Every tinhorn dictator in the world, every banana republic, every president for life operates under a bill of rights. I will not trouble to quote it for you, but the bill of rights of the former Evil Empire, the Union of Soviet Socialist Republics, contained guarantees much more expansive than ours. They were nothing but words on paper—what our Framers would call a parchment barrier.

Consider the word *constitution*. What does it mean? It does not mean a bill of rights. To say that a person has a sound constitution means that his physical structure is sound. The real constitution of the Soviet Union, the structure of its government, did not prevent the consolidation of all power in one person or one party. Once that happens, the most admirable bill of rights can be ignored. The structure of our Constitution prevents that consolidation of power—and does so in a more thoroughgoing fashion than any other country of the world.

Very few countries of the world have a genuine bicameral legislature—two equally powerful houses, elected in a different fashion. England's House of Lords, for example, has very little power: it can require the Commons to pass its legislation a second time. Italy and France have senates that are largely honorific. As those of you who have already served in Congress know, and those who are new will soon find out, it is terribly difficult to get the same language of a bill through two houses with different leaders, different agendas, sometimes under the control of different parties. And not many countries of the world have a separately elected chief executive. In the parliamentary system, the prime minister is the creature of the parliament. There is never any serious disagreement between the two. When that happens, there is a vote of no confidence, and a new prime minister is appointed who agrees with the parliament. And in the parliamentary systems, of course, the prime minister and all the cabinet secretaries must have been elected members of parliament. That is why the principal parties in the U.K. make sure that their candidate for prime minister runs for election in a safe district. In our system of course, not only is our president separately elected, but it is not only not required, but absolutely forbidden, that the cabinet secretaries or any other officer of the executive branch remain a member of Congress. Oh, and I almost forgot: to further protect the president against the nine-hundred-pound gorilla, the Framers gave him the veto power. Any legislation he disapproves must be passed by a two-thirds vote of each House.

The Europeans, and most other countries of the world, look at our system with something approaching disbelief. One House passes a bill, and the other House, which may be controlled by the other party, disapproves it. Or they both approve it, but the president exercises a veto. This is, they solemnly pronounce, a recipe for gridlock. It is indeed, and our Framers would say hooray. It is precisely that dispersal of power that they believed would be the primary bulwark of minorities against the tyranny of the majority. It does not take much to stop legislation that grievously injures a determined minority. It is easy to throw a monkey wrench into the works. By and large, only legislation with broad support will emerge from the complex system.

It is too much for me to expect that you will learn to love these many impediments to your working your will. But I hope that you will accept them, and indeed respect them, as core elements of our great democratic republic.

Because my time is short, I will mention just a few cases where Congress ignored the Constitution. Sometimes it is by accident. When I was the head of the Office of Legal Counsel in the executive branch, during the Ford administration, Congress created the Consumer Product Safety Commission. The law provided that the general counsel of that agency would be appointed by the head of the agency, with the advice and consent of the Senate. The problem was that that is not a mode of appointment available under the clear text of the Constitution, which says that officers of the executive branch must be appointed by the president, with the advice and consent of the Senate, or else, if Congress so provides, by the president alone, the heads of departments, or the courts of law. There is simply no provision for appointment by the head of the department with the advice and consent of the Senate. I suspect that what happened is that the Senate version of the bill provided for appointment by the president with the advice and consent of the Senate, the House version for appointment by the head of the agency alone—and they compromised.

But sometimes the ignoring (or evasion) of the Constitution is intentional. One of the cases I sat on in my earlier years on the Court involved a beautiful example of congressional encroachment upon the executive masked, as the *Federalist Papers* predicted, "under complicated and indirect measures." Congress decided to create a regional airport authority, which would have jurisdiction over National Airport and Dulles, which previously had been run by the federal government. That would be achieved through a compact between the District of Columbia and the Commonwealth of Virginia, establishing a board of directors for the Metropolitan Washington Airports Authority that would manage the airports. Congress did not wish, however, to yield its control over (especially) National Airport, fearing that the Authority would re-route a lot of traffic from convenient National Airport to much less convenient Dulles (which in those days was underused). So some of the proposals envisioned a congressional board of review that could disapprove decisions of the Authority's board of directors. The Justice Department advised that that would constitute legislative action, requiring action by both Houses and submission to the president. So what Congress did was to create a board of review composed of key committee members of both Houses, who were to serve "in their individual capacities as representatives of users of the Airports." This perhaps solved the problem of legislative action without the formalities required by Article I, section 7. But if one disregarded, as one should, the transparent fiction that these committee chairmen were acting purely in the individual capacities, it ran squarely into the constitutional prohibition against Congress or its members exercising executive powers. The Court held it unconstitutional.

Well, I have talked a lot about the importance of Congress's making a genuine, good-faith determination of constitutionality. But what is the criterion of constitutionality? There's the rub. Once upon a time, the answer was clear. The Constitution did not change. What the people universally understood it to mean when it was adopted, it continues to mean today. Did they think it forbade the death penalty, or forbade restrictions upon abortion? If not, it does not do so today. Both of those things may be very bad ideas, and if the people think so, they may enact laws abolishing them; but the Constitution does not invalidate them.

In relatively recent years, however, a new theory has emerged—the theory of the so-called "living Constitution," a document whose meaning changes according to the needs of modern society. I can hardly say that this is an unthinkable theory for you to embrace, since it is embraced by a majority of my court. In fact, it is in a way a much more reasonable theory for you to embrace than it is for the Supreme Court to do so. For while the Supreme Court speaks, in some of its "living Constitution" opinions, about "the evolving standards of decency that mark the progress of a maturing society," the reality is that you are much more likely to know what *are* the evolving standards of decency of American society than we are. You represent American society, and you rub elbows with American society at all levels—as we do not. So if the "living Constitution" theory were true, if the meaning of the document depended upon current social perceptions rather than upon the meaning of words that lawyers can debate about, *Marbury v. Madison* was wrong and the Supreme Court has no business second-guessing the determinations of Congress. Constitutional interpretation is no longer lawyers' work, and hence no longer judges' work. We should have a system like that in England, whose constitution is what the Parliament says it is.

But I urge you not to embrace the living Constitution—for a number of reasons. The most important one is that only the traditional view that the meaning of the Constitution does not change places any real constraints upon the decisions of future members of Congress or future judges. Since I accept that view, I am handcuffed. Show me what the original understanding was, and you got me. I cannot do the nasty, conservative things I would like to impose upon the country (if you believe the press). I would have to vote, for example, to hold unconstitutional a statute forbidding the burning of the American flag. But if you abandon that criterion of original meaning, what other possible criterion is there to control your judges or, for that matter, your members of Congress? Think about it. There is no other criterion that is not infinitely manipulable. Unless you conduct a national opinion poll, the "evolving standards of decency . . . of a maturing society" tend to be whatever you (or I) care passionately about, whether it be abortion or homosexual sodomy, or the death penalty. To leave that visceral call to the unelected Supreme Court is to frustrate democratic self-government; and to leave it to the current Congress is to make the Constitution superfluous. We do not need a Constitution to change according to the desires of current society; all we need is a legislature and a ballot box. The whole function of a Constitution is to prevent future majorities from doing certain things, and if you turn over the identification of those things to the future majorities themselves, you have accomplished nothing.

I have already gone on for longer than I should, and the only reason to continue is to avoid answering questions. But let me say one final thing. Why listen to me? Read the *Federalist Papers*, the explication of the proposed Constitution authored by Madison, Hamilton, and Jay and published in newspapers of New York State during the period when the proposed Constitution was under consideration by the people. Buy a hardcover copy, which should be dog-eared on your desks. That, more than anything else, can give you a real appreciation for the meaning of the Constitution, the reasons for its finely wrought provisions, and the brilliance of the Founders who created it. It used to be taught in our schools, but alas is unknown nowadays to most Americans.

THE CRISIS IN JUDICIAL
APPOINTMENTS

This speech at Doshisha Law School in Kyoto was one of several that Justice Scalia delivered during a February 2003 trip to Japan. His youngest child, Meg, accompanied him on a return visit to Kyoto the next year and recalls "how tireless he was in his love for travel":

> *He had a very busy schedule, yet he never groaned at another temple, another garden, or another breakfast of pickled everything. He immersed himself in the culture and loved the history, the tradition, the nature, and of course the food. At one formal meal, raw beef was placed in front of him. Having become accustomed to raw fish, he started to take a bite, only to have his previously very quiet dinner hosts suddenly yell "No, no, no!" at him. They explained that they were waiting for pots of boiling water to cook the* shabu shabu. *He was quick to laugh at himself.*

In this speech, the justice examines the causes of the political heat that now inflames judicial nominations.

The principle of separation of powers is central to the American system of government. The Framers of the American Constitution believed that that principle—as popularized by Montesquieu—was the single most important guarantee of freedom. "No political truth," wrote James Madison in the *Federalist Papers*, "is certainly of greater intrinsic value, or is stamped with the authority of more enlightened patrons of liberty." The separation of powers is infinitely more important to the American system than to the civil-law systems of Europe and the companion common-law system of Great Britain—which seek to separate only the judicial power from the legislative and executive, and not (as we do) to separate the legislative and executive powers themselves.

In their separation of the judicial from the political branches, however, the civil-law and British systems may be thought to be more absolute. The appointment of their judges is by competitive examination, without political input; and the promotion of their judges to higher courts is generally decided upon by the judiciary (or, in the case of England, the bar) itself. In the United States, by contrast, all federal judges are appointed by the president and confirmed by the Senate. As one might expect, politics have always entered into the appointment process. It is rare that a president will appoint a judge from the other political party: Republicans will appoint Republicans, and Democrats will appoint Democrats.

Europeans and the British have sometimes been very critical of this feature of the American judiciary. It is inconceivable to an Englishman that considerations of political affiliation should enter into the decision to appoint a high-court judge. There is, however, good reason for the difference between the two systems: in the American system, it is within the power of the ordinary judge to frustrate the will of the legislature. All federal judges (and not just those appointed to some special constitutional court) can refuse to enforce legislation that they believe to be unconstitutional. With such a degree of political power in the hands of the judiciary, it is unsurprising that the Founding Fathers felt the need for some political check—and that political check is applied at the most harmless time: in the appointment process. Once appointed, the judge cannot be harmed in his work by the political branches. He can only be removed by impeachment, for misconduct in office; and his salary cannot be reduced.

I may note parenthetically that when the Europeans, in the years following World War II, adopted the American system of judicial review of legislative action, they entrusted that review not to the ordinary courts that were totally removed from political influence but to constitutional courts whose members are appointed by the political branches. Indeed, in the case of Germany's Bundes-verfassungsgericht, appointments are made *by the political parties.*

In the past, involving the political branches in the appointment of judges had (I think it is fair to say) relatively little effect upon the development of American law. With rare exceptions, political appointment has had less to do with furthering the political programs of the president's party than with rewarding those lawyers who had worked to get the president's party elected. (As I said earlier, a Republican president would almost never nominate a Democrat, and a Democratic president would almost never nominate a Republican.) And rejection of an appointee by the Senate has had less to do with the political program of the party controlling the Senate than with some personal antagonism to the nominee on the part of one or more senators.

The most prominent exception to this proposition that the appointment power had little effect upon federal law was President Franklin Roosevelt's use of the appointment power to achieve a reversal of the Court's traditionally narrow interpretation of the powers of the federal government under the Commerce Clause of the Constitution. Both Roosevelt and the largely Democratic Congress favored expansive federal powers, and the Court did an about-face to approve that view after Roosevelt threatened to seek legislation expanding the number of justices on the Court from nine to as many as fifteen, so that he could appoint new justices that would form a majority favoring his view. (There is an English saying that "a stitch in time saves nine." The Court's abrupt change of course was humorously called "the switch in time that saved nine.")

But successful use of the appointment power—or even attempted use of the appointment power—to affect the holdings of the Court has been relatively rare. Moreover, in the past all of them—like the Roosevelt "court-packing" incident—tended to involve a single issue. The court-packing incident itself involved the scope of the federal government's Commerce Clause powers. In the nineteenth century, President Andrew Jackson sought a nominee who would sustain his views on the particular issue of the constitutionality of a Bank of the United States. And in the early twentieth century, President Theodore Roosevelt appointed Oliver Wendell Holmes to the Supreme Court in the expectation that he would support the expansive federal antitrust powers that Roosevelt desired. Even these single-issue appointments have not always been successful. Holmes, for example, did precisely the opposite of what Theodore Roosevelt expected—evoking from the voluble Roosevelt the remark that Justice Holmes had all the spine of a banana. President Dwight Eisenhower was said to have remarked that he had made two mistakes during his presidency, and both of them were sitting on the Supreme Court.

In recent years, however, the use or attempted use of the appointment power to affect judicial opinions has become commonplace—and it has *not* been limited to a single, temporarily prominent, issue. Indeed, ever since the presidential candidacy of Richard Nixon, use of the judicial appointment power has been a prominent *election* issue. Nixon and subsequent Republican presidential candidates have promised to appoint so-called non-activist judges to the Supreme Court, and their Democratic opponents have promised to appoint justices who will uphold *Roe v. Wade*, which is synonymous with judicial activism. Senate confirmation of Supreme Court nominees has become the focus of extensive lobbying by various political groups, and the confirmation process has produced extraordinarily bitter and controversial hearings—as the hearings on the nominations of Robert Bork and Clarence Thomas demonstrated. It is reported that interest groups favoring a wide variety of political causes—from abortion to racial preferences to environmental protection to women's rights—have already conducted extensive investigations into the backgrounds of a number of candidates rumored to be on the "short list" for President Bush's next Supreme Court nomination—gathering ammunition to use against those nominees in the Senate confirmation hearings.

The contentiousness of judicial appointments, and the degree of prominence that this issue has come to possess in American politics, are reflected in the following fact: in the last presidential campaign, more than a few informed observers expressed the view that *the single most important issue* was who would get to fill upcoming vacancies on the Supreme Court and the courts of appeals. What an extraordinary phenomenon! How can it possibly be that in a functioning democracy anyone should think that *the* most important issue in a national election was the composition of the unelected judiciary? A body of men and women so individually obscure that polling data regularly finds the majority of citizens unable to name two members of the Supreme Court. And the branch of government that the Framers of the Constitution thought to be the least dangerous because the most impotent—having (as a famous passage in the *Federalist Papers* described it) "neither FORCE nor WILL but merely judgment."

The explanation is this: the appointment of judges has become a significant political issue in national elections, and Senate confirmation of judges has become a politically charged enterprise, because courts have taken upon themselves the making of a vast number (indeed, an infinite number) of decisions that are properly of a political rather than a juridical nature. I will describe briefly how that has occurred.

The most significant function of the federal courts, of course, is interpretation of the federal Constitution and application of its requirements to executive and legislative action of both the state and national governments. Until about the 1960s, there was general agreement in the legal culture—and among the citizenry at large—that the Constitution had a fixed and permanent meaning. It was a rock of unchanging principles to which the society was safely moored. The guarantees that it contained were limited to those expressed in its text; and the meaning of that text (which did not vary over time) could be discerned by legally trained experts (judges) on the basis of the words used, manifestations of society's understanding of the text at the time it was adopted, and subsequent constitutional traditions bearing upon the text. There were of course some disagreements about what the Constitution meant, but there was consensus on the proposition that that meaning—whatever it was—did not change. What was constitutional in 1789, when the Constitution was adopted (or, in the case of the Bill of Rights, in 1791, when that was adopted as the first ten amendments to the Constitution) remained constitutional today, unless intervening amendments provide otherwise; and what was *uncon*stitutional then is *un*constitutional now.

During the 1960s, in the courts and the law schools, this vision of the Constitution underwent a radical transformation. Two doctrinal developments were central to this transformation. The first was a repudiation of original meaning as the ultimate determiner of constitutional text. Opinions of the Supreme Court made it clear that what the text meant when adopted could simply be rejected in favor of a meaning that the Court found more desirable. This new approach is set forth most explicitly in the Court's case law dealing with the Eighth Amendment, the provision of the Bill of Rights prohibiting "cruel and unusual punishments." What sort of punishment is prohibited by the Eighth Amendment, the Court said, is not static, but changes from age to age, to comport with "the evolving standards of decency that mark the progress of a maturing society."

On the basis of this evolutionary approach, the Court came close, in the 1970s, to abolishing the death penalty—which was unquestionably constitutional in 1791, when the Eighth Amendment was adopted. Although the Court's Eighth Amendment jurisprudence purported to be simply applying a new "consensus" reflected in the laws and practices of the American people, that consensus tended to resemble whatever a majority of the Court thought to be a good idea. For example, in 2002 the Supreme Court held that the Eighth Amendment categorically forbade execution of the mentally retarded—even though twenty of the thirty-eight states that had the death penalty left it to the jury to decide the degree to which mental retardation diminished moral responsibility for the particular crime.

The second doctrinal development was a severing of constitutional guarantees from any substantial connection to the text of the Constitution. The Bill of Rights contained a discrete number of guaranteed liberties—freedom of speech, freedom of the press, freedom of religion, right to jury trial, and so on. Even if those guarantees were given an "evolutionary" interpretation, so that they now forbade more governmental action than they originally did, there was at least some textual limit upon the nature of the guarantees. No amount of mere "evolutionary interpretation" could convert the guarantee of freedom of speech into a guarantee of the right to abortion. Virtually complete liberation from the text of the Constitution was achieved by a distortion of the Due Process Clause. This provision of the Constitution states that no person "shall be deprived of life, liberty or property without due process of law." It is self-evidently a procedural, rather than a substantive, guarantee. Can one be deprived of life? Yes, but not without due process of law—which includes proper enactment of the law that was allegedly violated, and conviction beyond a reasonable doubt by a jury. And the same for liberty and property—one can be deprived of them, but not without due process.

Although there were traces of such an approach in some earlier opinions, in the 1960s the Supreme Court firmly entrenched within constitutional jurisprudence the doctrine of "substantive due process" (a contradiction in terms, of course, since substance is the opposite of process). This doctrine prescribes that *some* liberties are *so fundamental* that they simply cannot be taken away, no matter what procedure is followed. It is up to the Court, of course, to decide which particular liberties are entitled to this extraordinary protection. By a stroke of the pen, "substantive due process" gave the Supreme Court power to make all sorts of additions to the Bill of Rights, literally unencumbered by any textual limitation. A right to abortion, right to assisted suicide, right to a parental relationship with one's illegitimate child born to a married woman, right to visit one's grandchildren even if their parents don't approve—these and an inexhaustible number of other new rights could all be added to the guarantees of the Bill of Rights, if the Court was of a mind to do so.

The consequence of these twin jurisprudential developments— departure from the original meaning of the guarantees contained in the text of the Constitution, and departure from even the *text itself* insofar as the creation of new rights is concerned—has been the creation of a Constitution that is an instrument of change rather than of stability. It can be, and has been, the source of all sorts of new restrictions upon democratic government. Some of these consist of novel applications of guarantees specified in the Constitution (for example, interpreting the Eighth Amendment to prohibit certain criminal punishments that were formerly permissible, or interpreting the Due Process Clause to demand certain criminal-trial procedures that were formerly not used). Others consist of the announcement of newly guaranteed "liberties" not recognized in the text of the Constitution (for example, the right to abortion and the right to die). The attractive name given to this new Constitution, whose content changes from age to age, according to what the times demand—or what the Supreme Court thinks the times demand—is the "living Constitution." Its existence is so unquestioned, and so well known by now, even to the average man in the street, that I have had visiting schoolchildren recite to me— proud of what they had learned in school—"the Constitution is a living document."

You must understand that the power of the living Constitution as an instrument of change is much greater than that of any state legislature, or indeed even of the federal Congress. Whereas a state legislature's repeal of the state's law against assisted suicide would have effect only in that single state; and whereas the federal Congress probably would not have power to override state anti-suicide laws (and certainly would not have the inclination to do so); the Supreme Court, wielding the living Constitution, can make assisted suicide lawful in all fifty states, and with such finality that that disposition cannot be changed even by Congress itself. Small wonder that the courts have become the forum of first, rather than last, resort for organized interest groups seeking all sorts of legal change—from the repeal of laws banning assisted suicide, to the mandating of laws that permit grandparents to visit their grandchildren despite parental objection.

Once that has happened, however—once the courts are in the *forefront* of legal change, performing a function that used to be performed democratically, by the enactment of new rights-creating legislation—one must expect that, eventually, there will be demands for the courts, like the legislatures, to be accountable to the people. If the Constitution is not going to mean what its text said, but is rather to be a sort of empty bottle that each successive generation can fill with a different liquid, then by God it will be the People, and not some self-anointed judicial aristocracy, who will decide what that liquid will be. And within the federal system, the one way in which that accountability can be achieved is in the appointment process. The president will appoint, and the Senate will confirm, those judges who agree with the majority as to what the Constitution ought to mean. The qualities that used to be most important in judicial candidates—legal scholarship, judicial demeanor, capacity for impartial deliberation—all become of secondary importance. The primary inquiry is whether this candidate will "evolve" the Constitution in the direction that the constituents of the president (or the constituents of the particular senator) favor.

That is why one often hears it discussed in the United States whether a particular rumored candidate for a judgeship would be "moderate" or "extreme." What could these terms possibly mean as applied to a federal judge, who has no common-law powers but is *always* interpreting the text of a statute or of the Constitution? The interpretation of a text can be right or wrong, but how can it possibly be called "moderate" or "extreme"? The explanation, of course, is that the term refers to the nature of the new rights (or the elimination of old rights) that the candidate would find in *his* version of the evolving Constitution. If, by and large, those rights (and eliminations of rights) are "in the mainstream" of what the people would favor (or, more accurately, what the principal organs of elite opinion, such as *The New York Times*, would favor), he is a moderate; if not, he is "extreme."

There is of course a great irony in this new practice of selecting justices on the basis of what kind of Constitution *the People* desire. The whole purpose of the Bill of Rights is to protect individuals against the wishes of the people; and in enforcing the restrictions contained in those provisions, the courts act in a decidedly *anti-democratic* capacity. They tell the people that they cannot do what they would like to do. Thus, to turn the interpretation of the Constitution over to majority opinion is to place the Bill of Rights in the hand of precisely the entity it was meant to protect against.

YOU WILL HAVE misunderstood what I have said today if you interpret it as an unmitigated criticism of the politicization of the judicial appointment process. I assuredly do not like that politicization, but I think that it is the inevitable consequence of judicial overreaching—and that it is preferable to the alternative of rule by a judicial aristocracy. What we have been witnessing in the past few decades is simply application of the political check upon the courts that I described at the outset of this lecture. The courts have *invited* this application because their new construct of a living Constitution involves them regularly in the business, not of law but of politics—of deciding not what rights *have been* established in the Constitution, but what rights *ought to be* there.

What I urge, then, is the return of the courts to the traditional role that, until the last third of the twentieth century, made the application of outcome-based political accountability in the appointments process the rare exception rather than the rule. The abandonment, that is, of the notion of an "evolving" Constitution, and of the doctrine of "substantive due process." Unless that occurs, I fear that the independent and nonpolitical nature of the federal judiciary will be permanently impaired.

My remarks have some application to the judicial systems of other countries as well. Many foreign national and international judges have admired and indeed envied my court because of its enormous power to alter the course of American life by simply decreeing—with no text or prior American practice to support it—that abortion must be allowed, that uncoerced criminal confessions obtained without a prior *Miranda* warning cannot be introduced at trial, that the death penalty is in most instances impermissible. I suggest that before these foreign judges proceed from admiration to emulation, they should await the end of the play. It may turn out to be a tragedy rather than a romance. It is my firm belief that, in the long run, *no* court can expect to remain immune from severe political pressure—either in the appointment stage, or even more directly through various procedures for removal from office—if it assumes the role of *inventing* solutions for social problems instead of merely *applying* those solutions prescribed in democratically adopted statutory or constitutional text. A living Constitution designed by the Court will mean a court controlled by the people.

LEGISLATIVE HISTORY

According to Justice Elena Kagan, Justice Scalia's "most long-lasting legacy" will be in statutory interpretation, where his compelling arguments for textualism "changed the way all of us think and talk about the law."

Legislative history, as a legal dictionary defines the term, consists of the "background and events, including committee reports, hearings, and floor debates, leading up to enactment of a law." In a seemingly obscure but important part of his case for textualism, Scalia vigorously opposed using the legislative history of a statute to determine the meaning of the statute. In this September 1991 speech at Northwestern University law school, he explained why.

Although the Court never fully embraced Scalia's position against use of legislative history, its reliance on legislative history diminished dramatically during his tenure.

———

My view on legislative history is, quite simply, that it ought not to be used as an authoritative indication of the meaning of a statute. Ordinarily, this means that it should be consulted *not at all*. My friend and former colleague Judge Patricia Wald, in a piece published last year concerning the Supreme Court's use of legislative history in the 1988–89 term, concluded as follows: "The traditionalists still hold, but like the Maginot line, the strength of their dedication and the limits of their endurance is in some doubt." By "the traditionalists" Judge Wald means those who make extensive use (as she does) of legislative history. Pat really knows how to hurt a fellow. There is no truth to the suggestion that I am not in this, as in all else, a traditionalist. The school of analysis that regards the extensive use of legislative history as "traditional" is the school that believes American legal history began with the Warren Court.

As late as 1897, the Supreme Court says that there is "a general acquiescence in the doctrine that debates in Congress are not appropriate sources of information from which to discover the meaning of the language of a statute passed by that body." And as late as 1940, a treatise on statutory construction describes the landscape in this country as follows:

> Although there seems to be considerable conflict in the cases, the weight of authority apparently refuses to regard the opinions, the motives, and the reasons expressed by the individual members of the legislature, even in debate, as a proper source from which to ascertain the meaning of an enactment. . . . A number of cases, however, make a distinction between legislative debates and the reports of legislative committees, and it must be admitted that the latter undoubtedly do possess a more reliable or satisfactory source of assistance.

Extensive use of legislative history in this country dates from about the 1940s and was severely criticized by such respected justices as Frankfurter and Jackson as recently as the 1950s. Jackson, for example, wrote in one concurrence:

> I should concur in this result more readily if the Court could reach it by analysis of the statute instead of by psychoanalysis of Congress. When we decide from legislative history, including statements of witnesses at hearings, what Congress probably had in mind, we must put ourselves in the place of a majority of Congressmen and act according to the impression we think this history should have made on them. Never having been a Congressman, I am handicapped in that weird endeavor. That process seems to me not interpretation of a statute but creation of a statute.

Though it is not the traditional practice, there is no doubt that the extensive use of legislative history is the current one. Indeed, in the past few decades we have developed a legal culture in which lawyers routinely—and I do mean routinely—make no distinction between words in the text of a statute and words in its legislative history. I am frequently told, in briefs and in oral argument, that "Congress said thus and so"—when in fact what is being quoted is not the law promulgated by Congress, nor even any text endorsed by a single house of Congress, but rather the statement of a single committee of a single house, set forth in a committee report. I am sure you have heard the humorous quip that one should consult the text of the statute only when the legislative history is ambiguous. Well, that's no longer funny. Reality has overtaken parody. A few terms ago, I read a brief that *began* the legal argument with a discussion of legislative history and then continued (I swear I am quoting it *verbatim*): "Unfortunately, the legislative debates are not helpful. Thus, we turn to the other guidepost in this difficult area, statutory language."

I think that the use of legislative history is a great mistake, for reasons of principle and of practicality. As to principle: the premise upon which all use of legislative history is based is that the object of judicial construction is to ascertain the intent of the legislature. I do not agree with that, and I do not think our legal system agrees with it. Otherwise we would not have the rule (which even the most avid aficionados of legislative history acknowledge) that legislative history should not be consulted when the text of the statute is clear. But if intent of the legislature is the object of construction, why should that be? No matter how clear the text, a conclusive demonstration that the actual intention was otherwise ought to prevail—at least so long as no one has been *misled* by the text, which will not often be the case. We do not allow such a countertextual intent to prevail, I think, because we are, as the Constitution of Massachusetts describes it, a government of laws, not of men—which means government by legislated text, not by legislators' intentions. Though I am sure I have been guilty of it myself, I think it a mistake, in legal writing, to use the formulary phrase "the congressional intent" or "Congress did not intend." I agree with Justice Holmes's remark (quoted approvingly by Justice Frankfurter in his article on the construction of statutes):

> Only a day or two ago—when counsel talked of the intention of a legislature, I was indiscreet enough to say I don't care what their intention was. I only want to know what the words mean.

And I agree with Holmes's other remark, quoted approvingly by Justice Jackson: "We do not inquire what the legislature meant; we ask only what the statute means." In this, as in all else, I think Holmes, Frankfurter, Jackson, and I represent the traditional view.

Even assuming, however, that the object of statutory construction is to plumb the intent of Congress, the practical question arises whether the use of legislative history is, by and large, all in all, helpful or harmful to the determination of that intent. I have no doubt that it *sometimes* might be helpful. One can posit a lively floor debate, in both houses of Congress, on the precise question before the Court, in which many members of Congress participated, displaying the general understanding of the provision in question. Or one can posit a well-crafted committee report in each house, read by most of the members, that clearly addresses the point at issue and is the basis on which the members cast their votes. But the question of the utility of legislative history must be decided, it seems to me, not on the basis of whether it might, now and then, be helpful, but on the basis of whether—assuming one wishes to be governed by "legislative intent"—it is more likely, all in all, by and large, in the totality of cases, that legislative history will produce a genuine legislative intent or a phony one. I have no doubt it is the latter.

The first and most obvious reason this is true is that, with respect to 99.99 percent of the issues of construction reaching the courts, there *is* no legislative intent, so that any clues provided by the legislative history are bound to be false. Those issues almost invariably involve points of relative detail, compared with the major sweep of the statute in question. That a majority of both houses of Congress (never mind the president, if he signed rather than vetoed the bill) entertained *any* view with regard to such issues is utterly beyond belief. For a virtual certainty, the majority of members was blissfully unaware of the *existence* of the issue, much less had any preference as to how it should be resolved.

But assuming, contrary to all reality, that the search for "legislative intent" is a search for something that exists, is it likely to be found in the archives of legislative history? The answer is clearly no—and more obviously no as each year passes. In earlier days, when Congress had a much smaller staff and enacted much less legislation, it might have been reasonable to suppose that a significant number of senators or representatives were present for the floor debate, or read the committee reports, and actually voted on the basis of what they heard or read. Those days, if they ever existed, are long gone. The floor is rarely crowded for a debate, the members generally being occupied with committee business and reporting to the floor only when a quorum call is demanded or a vote is to be taken. And as for committee reports, it is not even certain that the members of the issuing *committees* have found time to read them.

Ironically, but quite understandably, the more courts have relied upon legislative history, the less worthy of reliance it has become. In earlier days, it was at least genuine and not contrived—a real part of the legislation's *history*, in the sense that it was part of the *development* of the bill, part of the attempt to inform and persuade those who voted. Nowadays, however, when it is universally known and expected that judges will resort to floor debates and (especially) committee reports as authoritative expressions of "legislative intent," affecting the courts rather than informing the Congress has become the primary purpose of the exercise. It is less that the courts refer to legislative history because it exists than that legislative history exists because the courts refer to it. Extraordinary in its candor, but quite characteristic in its substance, is an episode that I discussed in one of my recent opinions. A member of the House proposed a floor amendment to the committee's bill. The floor manager refused to accept it, on the ground that it was unnecessary, whereupon the member said he would not press the point, so long as they "made some legislative history" that would support the substance of the proposed amendment—which a colloquy between the member and the floor manager then proceeded to do. The Supreme Court's opinion (which I did not join) then used that colloquy to establish that a proposed amendment that was NOT adopted was part of the law. Given such a ready audience, it is no wonder that one of the routine tasks of the Washington lawyer-lobbyist is to draft language that sympathetic legislators can recite in a pre-written "floor debate"—or, even better, insert into a committee report.

Now there are several common responses to some of the points I have just made. One is "So what that most members of Congress do not themselves know what is in the committee report? Most of them do not know the details of the legislation itself, either—but that is valid nonetheless. In fact, they are probably more likely to read and understand the committee report than to read and understand the text." This is a cute response, but it ignores the central point that genuine knowledge is a precondition for the authoritativeness of a committee report, and not a precondition for the authoritativeness of a statute. The committee report has no claim to our attention except on the assumption that it was the *basis* for the House's vote, and thus represents the House's understanding, which we (presumably) are searching for. A statute, on the other hand, has a claim to our attention simply because Article I, section 7 of the Constitution provides that since it has been passed by the prescribed majority (*with* or *without adequate understanding*—indeed, even if they are all fall-down drunk) it is a law.

Another response challenges the last-stated proposition head-on: "Committee reports are *not* authoritative because the full House presumably knows and agrees with them, but rather because the full House *wants* them to be authoritative—that is, leaves to its committees the details of its legislation." It may or may not be true that the Houses entertain such a desire. But if it is true, it is unconstitutional. "All legislative powers herein granted," the Constitution says, "shall be vested in a Congress of the United States, which shall consist of a Senate and House of Representatives." The legislative power is the power to make laws, not the power to make legislators. It is nondelegable. Congress can no more authorize one committee to "fill in the details" of a particular law in a binding fashion than it can authorize a committee to enact minor laws. Whatever Congress has not *itself* prescribed is left to be resolved by the executive or (ultimately) the judicial branch. That is the very essence of the separation of powers. The only conceivable basis for considering committee reports authoritative, therefore, is that they are a genuine indication of the will of the entire House—which, as I have been at pains to explain, they assuredly are not.

Judge Wald and others have described my rejection of legislative history as a power grab for the executive branch, giving to executive agencies (under the *Chevron* doctrine) the power to resolve ambiguities that previously would have been resolved by congressional committees in their committee reports. That is certainly wrong as an attribution of motive, and I think it is wrong as a description of effect as well.

Some additional power will go to the executive, it is true. But by far the greater shift of power will go from defunct congressional committees to live ones. To begin with, it should not be thought that simply because courts are no longer bound by the details of committee reports the reports will be of no effect. To the contrary. In the overwhelming majority of cases, even though the courts do not read the committee reports into law, the agencies will read the committee reports into executive practice. Agencies do not normally antagonize their oversight committees except on important "fighting" issues—and important fighting issues are not normally left to be resolved in committee reports.

The principal change that will occur under a regime that rejects legislative history as binding upon the courts is that agencies will be enabled to accommodate (within the bounds of the statutory text) the desires of their *future* oversight committees (as well as their own evolving desires) instead of being ruled, in the most minute detail, by the dead hand of the committee that happened to be in office when the statute was passed. I am frankly surprised that scholars and judges who fancy themselves progressive argue for a system that converts textually flexible laws into straitjackets.

My position on legislative history has also been criticized on the grounds that it produces an increase in judicial activism and an abandonment of judicial restraint—results that Scalia, of all people, is not supposed to favor. Well, that depends upon what you mean by judicial activism and judicial restraint. By judicial activism I do not mean judges actively doing what they are *supposed* to be doing; and by judicial restraint I do not mean judicial indolence. What judges are *supposed* to do, to my way of thinking, is to make sense of the entire body of the law. To interpret all provisions, to the extent the language will bear it, so as to reconcile each section of a statute with the others, and yesterday's laws with today's. That harmonization is a traditional function of the courts, one that is obstructed rather than assisted by use of legislative history. A single remark in a committee report or floor statement can forever deprive the courts of the flexibility needed to do the job well. That is what I refer to in the subtitle of this talk, when I speak of *judicial abdication* to fictitious legislative intent. When there is ambiguity in the text of a law, it is our job to resolve it (within the permissible limits of the text) so as to create a reasonable, sensible whole, and we should not resign that responsibility to be governed instead by dispositions that Congress has not in fact adopted, and that there is not even any plausible reason to believe Congress had in mind.

It is the *use* of legislative history, rather than its abandonment, that produces judicial activism in the bad sense, concealing and facilitating decisions that are based upon the courts' policy preferences, rather than neutral principles of law. Since there are no rules for the use of legislative history, it can usually be either invoked or ignored with equal plausibility. If you don't like the committee report, well, don't use it; call the statute not ambiguous enough, the committee report too ambiguous, or the legislative history "as a whole" inconclusive. It is ordinarily very hard to demonstrate that this is false so convincingly as to produce embarrassment. To be sure, there are ambiguities involved, and hence opportunities for judicial willfulness, in other techniques of interpretation as well—the canons of construction, for example, are assuredly manipulable. But the ambiguity of legislative history is not *substituted* for those: it is *added* to them. We now have the canons of construction to play with *plus* legislative history to play with. What lusted-after result the one cannot be made to produce, the other surely can. Legislative history provides, moreover, a uniquely broad field of discretion. In any major piece of legislation, the legislative history is extensive, and there is something for everybody. As Judge Leventhal used to say, the trick is to look over the heads of the crowd and pick out your friends. The variety and specificity of result that legislative history can achieve is unparalleled. No canon of construction, for example, would permit a judge to conclude, as legislative history can, that a statute which contains no time limits on its face is meant to have a time limit of a year.

The changes in outcome that would be produced by repudiation of legislative history are fewer than you might think. Only one change will be unquestionable and dramatic: judges, lawyers, and clients will be saved an enormous amount of time and expense. When I was head of the Office of Legal Counsel in the Justice Department, I estimated that 60 percent of the time of the lawyers on my staff was expended finding, and poring over, the incunabula of legislative history. What a waste. We did not used to do it, and we should do it no more.

Natural Law

In honor of the eight-hundredth anniversary of the Dominican Order (formally, the Order of Preachers), Justice Scalia spoke on "Saint Thomas Aquinas and Law" at the Dominican House of Studies in Washington, D.C., on January 7, 2016. The celebration continued with Solemn Vespers in the beautiful chapel and a dinner in the refectory that featured an address by Justice Samuel Alito. My last memory of Justice Scalia that evening is seeing him on his knees in prayer in the chapel's choir stalls during Compline, the night prayer that brought a fitting end to the observance. That turned out to be the last time I would ever see him, as he died barely a month later. —EW

I am pleased to help you celebrate the eight-hundredth jubilee of the Order of Preachers. *Ad plures annos.** Since this is a celebration of the Dominicans, I thought it incumbent upon me not just to address my own perception of the role of the judge, but to reconcile that, if possible, with what your great predecessor and brother Thomas Aquinas had to say.

Aquinas is one of the beneficiaries of what I call the Shakespeare principle. When I was a sophomore at Xavier High School in Manhattan, I had as an English professor Father Tom Matthews—a crusty no-nonsense New England Jesuit (in those days Jesuits were allowed to be crusty and no-nonsense). In the same class with me was a student who was sophomoric even for a sophomore, and in a class on *Hamlet*, as I recall, he offered some silly criticism of the Bard's work. Father Matthews fixed him with a

---

* Loosely translated: May you have many more years.

withering stare and delivered a line that I have found most useful in later life, and in many contexts. "Mistah," he said in his Boston accent, "when you read Shakespeah, Shakespeah's not on trial; you ah."

And so it is with Aquinas. I was anxious, therefore, to see if the Angelic Doctor's view of the role of the judge comported with my own—or rather, if mine comported with his. My shtick, as you may know, is textualism. I believe that judges should adhere to the text of the law, and not amend or revise it to accord with what they think the law ought to be. Imagine my delight, then, when I find, in Aquinas's discussion of the question "Whether we should always judge according to the written law?" the following seemingly categorical conclusion:

> Hence it is necessary to judge according to the written law, else judgment would fall short either of the natural or of the positive right.

Bravo! I knew I have been right.

Now one of the things we textualists have learned, and have enjoined upon our followers, is that to understand a statutory text it is necessary to read *the whole thing*. So I read on in the *Summa*, and, alas, I found the following, in Aquinas's replies to earlier objections:

> Just as the written law does not give force to the natural right, so neither can it diminish or annul its force, because neither can man's will change nature. Hence if the written law contains anything contrary to the natural right, it is unjust and has no binding force. For positive right has no place except where "it matters not," according to the natural right, "whether a thing be done in one way or in another"; . . . Wherefore such documents are to be called, not laws, but rather corruptions of law . . . and consequently judgment should not be delivered according to them.

Horrors! A sentiment worthy of Chief Justice Earl Warren! And if that were not bad enough, in response to a second earlier objection Aquinas writes the following:

> Even as unjust laws by their very nature are, either always or for the most part, contrary to the natural right, so too laws that are rightly established, fail in some cases, when if they were observed they would be contrary to the natural right. Wherefore in such cases judgment should be delivered, not according to the letter of the law, but according to equity which the lawgiver has in view. Hence the jurist says: "By no reason of law, or favor of equity, is it allowable for us to interpret harshly, and render burdensome, those useful measures which have been enacted for the welfare of man." In such cases even the lawgiver himself would decide otherwise; and if he had foreseen the case, he might have provided for it by law.

Double horrors! Judging not by text but by equity. A sentiment worthy of Justice William Brennan.

I must say, telling the judge that he must judge according to the text, unless he thinks that contrary to natural law or to equity, reminds me of a doggerel song from my childhood: "Mother, may I go out to swim?" "Yes, my darling daughter. Hang your clothes on a hickory limb, but don't go near the water."

So, despite my adherence to the Shakespeare principle, and despite my veneration for Thomas Aquinas, I plan to contradict what Aquinas says about judging. Perhaps that is not too brash of me. He knows infinitely more about theology; but I have much more experience with judging. Aquinas was right the first time. It is necessary to judge according to the written law—period.

Let me address first Aquinas's proposition that in some cases "judgment should be delivered, not according to the letter of the law, but according to equity which the lawgiver has in view." That proposition is remarkably reminiscent of a famous case decided by the Supreme Court of the United States in 1892: *Church of the*

Holy Trinity v. United States. The Church of the Holy Trinity is the blackened old Gothic church on Wall Street. The church had hired one E. Walpole Warren, an English clergyman, to be its rector and pastor. Unfortunately, there was a federal statute that forbade the importation of any foreigners into the United States under contract to work here. The statute made exceptions for professional actors, artists, lecturers, singers, and domestic servants, but no exception for clergymen. The United States sued the church for the penalty provided by the act. The Supreme Court held that the act did not apply. "We cannot think," the Court said, "[that] Congress intended to denounce with penalties a transaction like that in the present case. It is a familiar rule that a thing may be within the letter of the statute and yet not within the statute because not within its spirit nor within the intention of its makers."

So the government lost that case, but ultimately came to love it. Whenever the Solicitor General's Office wanted us to ignore the text of the statute it would cite *Church of the Holy Trinity.* "It is a familiar rule that a thing may be within the letter of the statute and yet not within the statute because not within its spirit. . . ." I used to ask the assistant SG arguing the case, "Is this the *Holy Trinity* team today, or do you want us to follow the law?"

Well, I am happy to say that *Church of the Holy Trinity* has fallen into disrepute. It is not cited to us anymore. And with good reason. Changing the text because of "equity," or "the spirit of the law," or what must have been "the intention of its makers" is fundamentally contrary to the role of the judge—which is to apply the law, not to improve it. Who is it, I wonder, whom Aquinas envisioned as the judge applying equity and the spirit of the law, and intuiting the unexpressed intention of the lawgiver? I suppose an angel could do that pretty well—but not any of the human judges I am familiar with. Equity and spirit tend to be what the judge believes is a good idea; and the unexpressed intention of the lawgiver has an uncanny tendency to comport with the wishes of the judge.

The consequences of such judicial hegemony are often much more serious than the outcome of *Church of the Holy Trinity.* In 1928, in *Olmstead v. United States*, my court confronted for the first time the question whether wiretapping by the government violated the Fourth Amendment—which provides that "the people [shall] be secure in their persons, houses, papers, and effects against unreasonable searches and seizures." Easy case. A conversation is not a person, house, paper, or effect, and thus government eavesdropping—which can and should be made illegal by statute—is not covered by the Fourth Amendment. Thirty-nine years later, in the heyday of the Warren Court, *Olmstead* was overruled. "[T]he Fourth Amendment," we said sanctimoniously, "protects people—and not simply 'areas'—against unreasonable searches and seizures." *Katz v. United States* (1967). *Of course* it protects people—but it protects them, as the Fourth Amendment says, "in their persons, houses, papers, and effects."

One consequence of this judicial departure from text is this: a highly controversial issue nowadays is what telephone records the government is permitted to gather in order to protect against Islamic terrorists. What is a "reasonable" search, in that context as in all others, depends upon two things: the degree of intrusion and the degree of the danger it guards against. Is there anything more intrusive than the body search to which air travelers must submit in order to board a plane? But the search is a reasonable one, because without it the plane and its passengers might be destroyed. In the days when *Olmstead* and the real Fourth Amendment governed, the question of whether the terrorist threat was severe enough to justify telephonic snooping would be answered by Congress and the president. Today it will be answered by that institution of government least capable of providing the right answer. Congress and the president know the scope of the danger from Islamist terrorists; the Supreme Court of the United States does not. Yet it is that institution that will ultimately decide what telephonic searches the NSA can engage in.

I have to say one more word about Aquinas's statement that, when equity and the spirit of the law contradict its text, "even the lawgiver himself would decide otherwise; and if he had foreseen the case, he might have provided for it by law." Discerning what the lawgiver "might have done" or "would have done" is a tricky business—and was so even true in the days of Aquinas, when the law was written by King Roger or whoever at the time ruled the Kingdom of the Two Sicilies. But it is a hundred times more difficult to discern the lawgiver's unenacted intent today, when laws are written by assemblies of men and women who have differing views and often enact what is a compromise. What seems like an illogical omission may have been the quid pro quo for a congressional compromise, and it is certainly not the proper role of the judge to destroy that compromise. By far the best rule, expressed in one of the common law's ancient canons of interpretation, is *casus omissus pro omisso habendus est.*[*]

Let me say a few words now about Aquinas's other exception to the principle that the judge must judge according to the law. "[I]f," he says, "the written law contains anything contrary to the natural right, it is unjust and has no binding force. . . . Wherefore such documents are to be called, not laws, but rather corruptions of law . . . and consequently judgment should not be delivered according to them." Wow. Do you really want human judges setting aside positive law because they believe it contradicts natural law? Again, bear in mind that these judges are not angels—and are not even Thomas Aquinas. Do you not think that the five-justice majority that last term disregarded—"struck down"—numerous state laws providing that marriage was between a man and a woman, do you not think those judges believed that that is what natural law required? Do you really want judges—fallible judges—going about enforcing their vision of natural law, contrary to the dictates of democratically enacted positive law? Lord, no.

Now in my view natural law does make its demands upon judges—but not the demand that they render judgments that contradict positive law. Where positive law places a judge in the position of being the instrument of evil, the judge must recuse from the case or (if there are many such cases) resign from the bench. Thus, if I were a judge in Nazi Germany, charged with sending Jews and Poles to their death, I would be obliged to resign my of-

---

[*]   "A case omitted is to be held as intentionally omitted."

fice (and perhaps lead a revolution). That is, by the way, not the position that Catholic judges are in with respect to abortion. They in no way participate in the killing of the baby. They merely hold, in accordance with the Supreme Court's determination of what natural law requires, that the government cannot prevent that killing.

Natural law would require me to recuse—and probably to resign my office—if I believed (as a footnote in a papal encyclical suggested) that the death penalty is immoral. For I do participate in sending convicted murderers to their death. But I do not believe that the death penalty is immoral, because I do not believe (as the encyclical suggested) that the only valid purposes of punishment are disabling the criminal and deterring others—both of which can be achieved without the death penalty. One, and perhaps the most important, purpose of punishment is to set right the moral disorder that has been created by the crime. Call it retribution, if you will. Not only has the Church always approved the death penalty (St. Thomas More was accused of using it too liberally), but, to tell the truth, the whole story of the redemption makes no sense without the retributive imperative. Why did we have to be "redeemed"? Why couldn't the all-loving God simply have forgiven us? No, payment had to be made, and Jesus Christ had to redeem us.

So, with apologies to Aquinas, I follow the prescription of Justinian's Digest, *A verbis legis non est recedendum.* Do not depart from the words of the law. Will that produce a perfect world? Of course not. Some laws are stupid, and some are malevolent. But it will produce a better world than one in which judges run about enforcing their view of natural law and of equity. The rule of law will always be second best to the rule of love, but we have to leave the latter to the next world. One of my favorite quotations is from Grant Gilmore: "In Heaven there will be no law, and the lion will lie down with the lamb. . . . In Hell there will be nothing but law, and due process will be meticulously observed." Meantime, we live in an imperfect world that is best governed by the text of laws.

Foreign Law

In recent decades, the justices of the Supreme Court have been sharply divided over whether it is proper to look to contemporary foreign laws to determine the meaning of provisions of the Constitution. Justice Scalia was steadfast against the practice, for the reasons he spelled out in this 2006 speech at the American Enterprise Institute.

———

I will talk today about the use of foreign law in American judicial opinions. Since most of what I will have to say is unfavorable to the use of foreign law, I feel I should begin by pointing out that I am not a xenophobe. I do not mind foreign law. In fact, in my years as a law professor, I used to teach foreign law. One of my subjects was comparative law. I indeed believe that comparative law might well be made a mandatory subject in United States law schools. Just as you do not understand your own language until you have taken a foreign language (whether it be Latin, German, or any other one), you do not understand your own legal system until you see how the ordering of the same matters could be done in a different way. The only way to appreciate the distinctiveness of your system—what drives it—is to examine some other system.

Moreover, I do not take the position that foreign law is never, ever relevant to American judicial opinions. It sometimes is. One example is the interpretation of treaties. The object of a treaty is to bring nations into agreement on a particular course of action. If I am interpreting a treaty provision that has already been interpreted uniformly by several other signatories, I am inclined to follow that interpretation so long as it is within the realm of reasonableness. If other signatories have adopted an absolutely unreasonable interpretation, of course I would not follow it. But where it is within the bounds of the ambiguity contained in the text, I think it is a good practice to look to what other signatories to the treaty have said. Otherwise, you produce a treaty that is interpreted in different ways by different countries, which is certainly not the object of the exercise. I also think that foreign law is sometimes relevant to the meaning of an American statute. For example, if the statute is designed to implement a treaty provision, the interpretation of that treaty provision by foreign courts is relevant to what the treaty means, and hence relevant to what the statute means.

Sometimes, moreover, the issue that arises under a statute depends upon foreign law. We had a case a few terms ago that turned on whether, under a United States statute, a corporation organized in the British Virgin Islands was a "citizen or subject of a foreign state." I could not decide that question without consulting British law as to whether a corporation in the British Virgin Islands was a citizen or subject of Britain. Another example of the same phenomenon: the Foreign Sovereign Immunity Act permits suit against foreign sovereigns for property "taken in violation of international law." We had a case a few terms ago involving the seizure of some valuable paintings by the Nazis. Obviously, whether the person who was seeking to have the paintings restored was entitled to that relief depended upon whether or not she had owned the paintings. That question was a question of Austrian law, which we had to consult to decide the case.

Finally, I think foreign law can also be profitably discussed in the opinions of United States courts where it is consulted in response to the argument that if you interpret this statute this way, or if you interpret the Constitution this way, the skies will fall. You can look to foreign law and say, "Well, gee, they did this in Germany and the skies didn't fall." That is certainly a very valid use of foreign law.

But these are not the uses of foreign law that people are concerned about. They are concerned principally about the use of foreign law to determine the meaning of the United States Constitution. Even there, I have to tell you that I cannot say it is never relevant. Indeed, I probably consider it relevant more often than most of my colleagues on the Supreme Court. Of course, the foreign law I think is relevant is very old foreign law—very old English law, to be precise. Because what is meant by many terms of the federal Constitution—the writ of habeas corpus, due process of law, and cruel and unusual punishments, for example—depends upon what meaning they had for Englishmen in 1789 or 1791. So, I use foreign law all the time, but it is all very old English law.

What about *modern* foreign legal materials? Well, that is where I get off the boat. It is my view that foreign legal materials can never be relevant to an interpretation of the meaning of the United States Constitution. Sometimes the Supreme Court seems to have agreed with this view. For example, in a 1997 case called *Printz v. United States*, a case deciding whether the federal government could press state law officers into service to administer a federal statute—the statute provided that state sheriffs would have to do some paperwork for the implementation of the federal law—the Court rejected as irrelevant Justice Breyer's assertion that Switzerland, Germany, and the European Union all provide that the constituent states must themselves implement many of the laws enacted by the Central Federation. The Court's opinion (which I authored) rejected that citation of foreign law, saying the following: "We think such comparative analysis inappropriate to the task of interpreting a constitution, though it was of course quite relevant to the task of writing one."

In many other cases, however, opinions for the Court have used foreign law for the purpose of interpreting the Constitution. The first such case I am familiar with was a 1958 decision involving the Eighth Amendment, the Cruel and Unusual Punishments Clause. In *Trop v. Dulles*, the Court held that the Eighth Amendment forbids the penalty of forfeiture of citizenship because, inter alia, "The civilized nations of the world are in virtual unanimity that statelessness is not to be imposed as punishment for crime."

Reliance upon foreign law has been made with increasing frequency in Eighth Amendment cases. In *Coker v. Georgia*, a 1977 case, the Court noted that "out of 60 major nations in the world surveyed in 1965, only 3 retained the death penalty for rape where death did not ensue." In *Enmund v. Florida*, a 1982 case, the Court noted that the doctrine of felony murder (murder that occurs in the course of a felony is made a capital crime under the laws of many states) "has been abolished in England and India, severely restricted in Canada and a number of other Commonwealth countries, and is unknown in continental Europe." In a 1988 case, *Thompson v. Oklahoma*, the Court noted that "other nations that share the Anglo-American heritage" and "the leading members of the Western Europe community" opposed the death penalty for a person less than sixteen years old at the time of the offense. (I must interject that almost all those countries also opposed the death penalty when a person was more than sixteen years old at the time of the offense—but never mind.) In *Atkins v. Virginia*, decided in 2002, the Court thought it relevant that, "within the world community, the imposition of the death penalty for crimes committed by mentally retarded offenders is overwhelmingly disapproved." That was deemed relevant to the Court's interpretation of our Eighth Amendment.

Recently the Court has expanded the use of foreign law beyond the area of the Eighth Amendment. For example, in *Lawrence v. Texas*, decided in 2003, the Court relied upon action of the British Parliament and a decision of the European Court of Human Rights in declaring that laws punishing homosexual conduct were unconstitutional under the American Constitution. Individual justices have urged the relevance of foreign law in other cases as well.

I expect, or rather I fear, that the Court's use of foreign law in the interpretation of the Constitution will continue at an accelerating pace. That is so for three reasons. First, because the "living Constitution" paradigm for the task of constitutional interpretation prevails on the Court and indeed in the legal community generally. Under this view, it is the task of the Court to make sure that the current Constitution comports with, as we have put the point in the Eighth Amendment context, "the evolving standards of decency that mark the progress of a maturing society." Thus, a constitutional right to abortion, which assuredly did not exist during the first few centuries of our country's, and of the predecessor colonies', existence, does exist today. Likewise, a constitutional right to homosexual conduct.

Of course I disagree with this "living Constitution" approach, but my purpose here is not to debate originalism. Rather, my point is that once you assume the power to revise what the Constitution requires in order to keep it up to date, then the criticism voiced by my opinion for the Court in *Printz*—that comparative analysis is inappropriate to the task of interpreting a Constitution, though it was quite relevant to the task of writing one—no longer has any bite. You *are* engaged in the process of writing a new Constitution and there is no reason not to consult foreign materials in doing it.

I suppose it could be argued that one can be a living constitutionalist who wants to create only a new *American* Constitution— the sort of living constitutionalist who does not care what foreign countries think, but only wants to update the American Constitution according to the likes of Americans. Well, the existence of such chauvinistic living constitutionalists is certainly a theoretical possibility, but I have never met one. The American people can make their will well enough known by creating new rights legislatively through the federal and state legislatures or, in the last analysis, by amending the Constitution in the democratic method that the Constitution contains. One who believes that it falls to the courts to update the list of rights guaranteed by the Constitution is in my experience invariably one who believes in a Platonic right and wrong in these matters, which wise judges are able to discern when the people at large cannot.

In fact, it has occurred to me that this notion of an overarching moral law, binding upon all the nations of the world and discerned by the world's judges, has replaced the common law. Those of you who are lawyers remember that in the bad old days, that is to say before *Erie Railroad v. Tompkins* in 1938, courts believed (or at least behaved as though they believed) that there was a True Common Law up there in the stratosphere. The state courts of California said it meant one thing, the state courts of New York said it meant something else, and the federal courts something different still. But two of them (or perhaps all three) had simply got it wrong— and it was the task of judges in other jurisdictions to figure out The Truth. In those days, a common-law decision in one state would often cite as authority common-law decisions of other states, because all judges were engaged in the same enterprise of figuring out the content of what Justice Holmes called the "brooding omnipresence in the sky" that was the common law. As I say, we have abandoned that notion and have replaced it with the reality that the supreme court of each jurisdiction creates its own common law according to what it considers best. But belief in a universal common law has been replaced, I think, by belief in a universal Law of Human Rights. Human rights, after all, implicate *moral* issues, as to which there *must* be right and wrong answers: whether there is a natural right to abortion, a natural right to homosexual conduct, a natural right to suicide, and so forth.

Well, I in fact believe that there are right and wrong answers to these questions. But it surpasses my understanding why judges believe that they are authorized, or are suited by their legal training, to provide answers to those questions that supersede the answers arrived at by the democratic societies over which they preside. But that is where we are. A worldwide brotherhood of the judiciary believes that it is our function to determine the true content of human rights. And the wisdom that judges in one country bring to this enterprise is quite relevant to the decisions of their brother and sister judges in other countries. That is why I think if you are a living constitutionalist, you are almost certainly an international living constitutionalist.

The second reason foreign law is likely to be used increasingly in our "living Constitution" decisions is George Leigh Mallory's reason: because it's there. Let's face it. It's pretty hard to put together a respectable number of pages setting forth, as a legal opinion is supposed to do, analytical reasons for newly imposed constitutional constraints upon the people that do not at all rest on the text of the Constitution or centuries of practice under that text. How can one logically explain why some long-accepted government limitations on sexual freedom (such as laws against bigamy or adultery or incest) are perfectly constitutional while other long-accepted limitations on sexual freedom (such as laws making homosexual relations a crime) are not? Decisions on such matters, whether taken democratically by society or undemocratically by courts, have nothing to do with logic, but rest upon one's moral sentiments, one's view of natural law, one's philosophy, or one's religion. So, without something concrete to rely on, judicial opinions will be driven to such philosophic or poetic musings as appeared in one of our recent decisions: "At the heart of liberty is the right to define one's own concept of existence, of meaning, of the universe, and of the mystery of human life." Surely, this is not a happy state of affairs for a law court. Published decisions will seem much more like real judicial opinions if they can cite some legal authority to support the philosophic, moral, or religious conclusions that they pronounce. Foreign authority can serve that purpose. You can set forth the name of the case, followed by numbers and letters, just as in a real opinion—33 Uganda Law Reports 295 (2002). It looks very legal.

The third reason foreign law will be increasingly used is an intensely pragmatic one: adding foreign law to the box of available legal tools is enormously attractive to judges because it vastly increases the scope of their discretion. In that regard, it is much like legislative history, which ordinarily contains something for everybody and can be used or not used, used in one part or in another, deemed controlling or pronounced inconclusive, depending upon the result the court wishes to reach. Consider *Lawrence*, where the Court cited European law to strike down sodomy laws. But of course Europe is not representative of the whole world. Zero out of fifty countries in Europe prohibit sodomy. (Not necessarily, by the way, because of the democratic preferences of those fifty countries, but because of the uniformity imposed by the European Court of Human Rights.) But 33 out of 51 countries in Africa prohibit it; 8 out of 43 countries in the Americas; 27 out of 47 Asian Pacific countries, and 11 out of 14 countries in the Middle East.

Thus, the rest of the world aside from Europe is about evenly split on the issue.

The Court's reliance on foreign sources has been selective not only with regard to which foreign law is consulted, but also with regard to whether foreign law is consulted at all. For example, although the United States was in the minority in allowing states to prohibit sodomy, it was not in the minority in allowing states to restrict abortion. According to the United Nations, the United States is now one of only 53 countries classified as allowing abortion on demand, versus 139 countries allowing it only under particular circumstances or not at all. Among those countries the UN classified in 2001 as not allowing abortion on demand were the United Kingdom, Finland, Iceland, India, Ireland, Japan, Luxembourg, Mexico, New Zealand, Portugal, Spain, Switzerland, and virtually all of South America. But the Court has generally ignored foreign law in its abortion cases. *Casey* does not mention it at all. *Roe* discusses only modern British law, which in any event is more restrictive than what *Roe* held. I will become a believer in the ingenuousness, though never in the propriety, of the Court's newfound respect for the wisdom of foreign minds when it applies that wisdom in the abortion cases.

Let me make clear that, although I believe the use of foreign law in our constitutional decisions is the wave of the future, I do not think it is a good idea. The men who founded our republic did not aspire to emulating Europeans, much less the rest of the world. I wrote an opinion for the Court a few terms back overruling an earlier case that had held that the Confrontation Clause is satisfied so long as the unconfronted testimony has "particularized guarantees of trustworthiness." The opinion pointed out that the Confrontation Clause was designed precisely to prevent a procedure considered trustworthy by continental European nations and others that followed the civil law tradition. "Examinations of witnesses upon interrogatories," wrote John Adams, "are only by the civil law. Interrogatories are unknown at common law and Englishmen and common lawyers have an aversion to them, if not an abhorrence of them." As recently as 1993, France was still defending its use of ex parte testimony before the European Court of Human Rights, arguing that a defendant's accusers in a drug trafficking case had a "legitimate interest in remaining anonymous" and that the defendant's rights were adequately protected so long as "the judge held hearings which enabled him to satisfy himself" that the witnesses stood by their statements. Should we have loosened up our Confrontation Clause in light of foreign opinion on this subject?

France permits suits against the executive branch only in an executive branch court called the Conseil d'Etat, whose members are appointed and promoted by the executive and who regularly alternate between performing executive functions and adjudicating the lawfulness of other people's performance of executive functions. Other European countries have somewhat similar systems, though the extent of their participation in executive functions may be more limited. This is a practice that Tocqueville contrasted unfavorably with our own as long ago as 1835. Should we change our mind?

In number 46 of the *Federalist Papers*, James Madison speaks contemptuously of the governments of Europe, which are "afraid to trust the people with arms." Should we revise the Second Amendment because of what these other countries think?

In November of 2002, the Council of Europe approved what was called "An Additional Protocol to the Convention on Cybercrime," which makes it illegal to distribute anything online which "advocates, promotes or incites hatred or discrimination." A spokesman for the United States Department of Justice said, quite correctly, that this country could not be a party to such a treaty because of the First Amendment. If all of Europe thinks that such a provision does not unduly limit speech, should we reconsider? And I could go on.

If there was any thought absolutely foreign to the founders of our country, surely it was the notion that we Americans should be governed the way Europeans are governed. Nothing has changed. I dare say that few of us here would want our life, liberty, or property subject to the disposition of French or Italian criminal justice.

Not because those systems are unjust, but because we think ours is better. What reason is there to believe that dispositions of a foreign country are so obviously suitable to the morals and manners of our people that they can be judicially imposed through constitutional adjudication? And is it really an appropriate function of judges (that is to say, lawyers) to decide which are and which aren't? I think not.

JUDGES AS MULLAHS

In Justice Scalia's view, Supreme Court justices have no authority to impose their "abstract moralizing" about what is best for American society, nor do they have any special competence in the matter. Over the last decade of his life, Justice Scalia presented his objections on multiple occasions and under various titles—for example, "Mullahs of the West: Judges as Moral Arbiters"—throughout the world, from Europe to South America to Australia to the United States.

———

In the first half of the last century, American political theory was obsessed with the expert. The key to effective government, it was thought, was to take the direction of government agencies out of the hands of politicians, and to place it within the control of men experienced and knowledgeable within the various fields of government regulation.

Accordingly, despite the fact that the United States Constitution calls for all executive power to reside in a nationally elected president, Congress created a series of agencies insulated from presidential control, in that their managers were not subject to presidential direction and could not be removed from office by the president except for malfeasance. Typically, these so-called "independent regulatory agencies" were headed by a board of five or more members, no more than a bare majority of whom could be from the same political party, appointed for staggered terms of years exceeding the president's four-year term. In this way, it was thought, politics could be taken out of the job of managing the economy; it would be done by experts. Thus there was created what came to be known as the "headless fourth branch" of American government—a series of alphabet agencies such as the ICC (Interstate Commerce Commission), the FTC (Federal Trade Commission), the SEC (Securities and Exchange Commission), the FCC (Federal Communications Commission), and the CAB (Civil Aeronautics Board).

It is fair to say that the project was a grand failure—for two basic reasons. First, and most important, it was discovered (and this should have been no surprise) that many of the most important issues to be decided by government agencies—even agencies dealing with seemingly technical fields such as telecommunications and transportation—have no right or wrong answers that experts can discover. They involve social preferences that, in a democracy, can only be expressed through the political process. How many television stations should the FCC permit a single company to own? It depends upon how much you care about quality of programming (by and large, bigger operations can deliver more expensive programs) compared with how much you fear big-company domination of television, including its news and public-affairs programming. There is no right answer to the question, only a policy preference.

How much should the ICC permit railroads to charge for the hauling of municipal waste? If they are allowed to charge their cost (including a reasonable profit), it will be very expensive to dispose of waste in this fashion. But perhaps we want to subsidize the burying of municipal waste in landfills, so that cities will not pollute the environment by incineration. We can apply that subsidy by requiring railroads to charge below their cost for carrying municipal waste, the deficit to be made up for by permitting overcompensatory rates for other cargos—which amounts to a tax imposed on the consumers of those other cargos. So, how much you permit railroads to charge depends upon (1) how much you care about the environment, and (2) how much you are willing to subsidize cities. There is no right answer to the question, only a policy preference.

And the second reason the project of the so-called independent agency was a failure is that it is quite utterly impossible to take politics out of policy decisions. (That is not just a reality; it is, for those of us who believe in democracy, a blessed reality.) The reduction in the elected president's control over the independent regulatory agencies was simply replaced by augmentation of the elected Congress's control. Agency heads were no longer removable by the elected president, but they were also no longer protected by his political power; he had no interest in protecting them since their acts were not his acts, their failures not his failures. Thus, the independent regulatory agencies became all the more subservient to the policy direction of the committees of Congress responsible for their budgets and for their oversight.

By the end of the twentieth century, independent regulatory agencies were no longer fashionable. Indeed, two of the oldest of them, the Interstate Commerce Commission and the Civil Aeronautics Board, were abolished. But in the United States, and indeed throughout the world, belief in the expert has been replaced by belief in the judge-moralist. Whereas *technical* questions, we have come to learn, do not have any single right answer, surely *moral* questions do. Whether a woman has a natural right to an abortion. Whether society has the right to take a man's life for his crimes. Whether it is unfair (and hence, in the terminology of the American Constitution, a denial of equal protection) to permit marriage between people of opposite sexes, but not between people of the same sex. Whether a human being has an unalienable right to take his own life, and to have the assistance of others in doing so. These, and many similar questions, involve basic morality, basic human rights—and *surely* there is a right and wrong answer to them.

Well, I believe firmly that indeed there is. That is to say, I believe in natural law. The problem is that my view of what natural law prescribes is quite different from others' views—and none of us has any means of demonstrating, with anything approaching scientific certainty, the correctness of his position. Thus, as a matter of democratic theory, there is no more reason to take *these* issues away from the people than there is to take away issues of economic policy—because there is no moral expert to answer them. This is not to say that the people's conclusion can always override my own conscience on these questions of right and wrong. In Nazi Germany, for example, even if it had been democratically determined that Jews and Poles had no right to live, I would be obliged to protect and defend them, in defiance of the law if necessary. But we are not talking about individual responsibility; we are talking about who, in a democratic society, should have the power to determine the *government*'s view of what the natural law is. That seems to me obvious. Given that there is a natural law, the question becomes: What do the American people, or the Dutch people, or the Italian people, believe the natural law to be? Does it permit abortion or forbid abortion? And in an open democratic society the people can debate these issues, each side trying to persuade the other to its way of thinking. And the people (unlike the courts) can even *compromise* on these issues—for example, by leaving the issue of abortion to be dealt with in divergent fashion by the sub-units of a federal state, or by prohibiting only abortion performed in a particularly brutal fashion, or by permitting abortion in case of rape or incest.

But in these early years of the twenty-first century, that is not the way we proceed. We have become addicted to abstract moralizing. That is relatively harmless when it appears in the operating documents of such international organizations as the United Nations—which can implement the moralization or not implement it, as political convenience dictates. Stop, or do not stop, for example, what our Congress has termed the genocide occurring in the Sudan; nothing forces the UN's hand. But abstract moralizing is a dangerous practice when it is reflected in the operating documents of a nation-state (or a federation of nation-states), which require the moralizing *to be judicially enforced*. There is nothing inherently wrong, for example, with Article 8 of the Council of Europe's Convention for the Protection of Human Rights and Fundamental Freedoms, which provides, in part, that "[e]veryone has the right to respect for his private . . . life." Who could possibly disagree with such an inspiring sentiment? Any more than one could disagree with the inspiring sentiment of Article V of the

1789 French Declaration of the Rights of Man and of the Citizen, that "[t]he law ought to prohibit only actions hurtful to society." But whereas the latter was left to languish as an inspiring sentiment, with no attempt to have judges enforce it against the French Parliament, the former—the "right to respect for . . . private . . . life"—has been made enforceable against the democratic governments of Europe by judgment of the European Court of Human Rights. What does "respect for private life" consist of? Who knows, other than the European Court of Human Rights?

Nine years ago, that provision was held to invalidate a provision of the United Kingdom's law against gross indecency that said that the law's permission of private homosexual conduct did not apply "when more than two persons take part or are present." The Court of Human Rights held that the gross indecency law could not, by reason of the required "respect for *private* life," be applied against a five-man homosexual orgy, which the participants considered so little confidential that they videotaped it. (The court did not specify how many people had to be participating in the sexual conduct before it would cease to qualify as part of each one's "private life." Presumably it is some number between five and the number required to fill the Colosseum. Unless, of course, all sexual activity not intentionally displayed to nonparticipants is part of one's "private life," in which case even Yankee Stadium is a permissible venue for the living out of one's private life.)

In the course of its opinion, not only did the seven-judge chamber of the Court of Human Rights definitively resolve for the people of Europe the scope of legally protected privacy. It also ruled definitively upon what is "necessary in a democratic society . . . for the protection of health or morals." For Article 8 of the Convention makes that an explicit exception to the right of privacy. I take no position, of course, on whether the prohibition of sex orgies is necessary for the protection of morals. I do assert, however, that in a democratic society the binding answer to that value-laden question should not be provided by seven unelected judges.

The European Court of Human Rights does not, of course, stand alone in making value-laden judgments for the society. My court does it all the time. *Roe v. Wade* is perhaps the prime example, requiring abortion on demand throughout the United States. But there are many more examples. Six terms ago, we held laws against private consensual sodomy, laws that had existed in perfect conformity with the Constitution for over two hundred years, to be impermissible, citing, inter alia, the Court of Human Rights's *Dudgeon* case to prove the meaning of the Due Process Clause of the American Constitution. We have held it impermissible to let juries decide (as they have done in the past) that a murderer should be condemned to death despite his mental retardation, or despite the fact that he was under eighteen years of age when he killed. We have held it impermissible for a state to maintain a military college for men only, despite the fact that West Point, the Citadel, and the Virginia Military Institute had for more than a century not been thought to be in violation of the Constitution's requirement of equal protection of the laws. We have rejected, for the time being, a constitutional right to assisted suicide, but have reserved the right to revisit that issue. And I could go on.

Why have judges not *always* been such pioneering policymakers? The answer is that until relatively recently the meaning of laws, including fundamental laws or constitutions, was thought to be *static*. What vague provisions such as a right to "respect for . . . private life," or a right to "equal protection" meant at the time of the Constitution's enactment could readily be determined (in most controversial areas) from the accepted and unchallenged practices that existed at that time. And what the Constitution permitted at the time of its enactment it permitted forever; only the people could bring about change, by amending the Constitution. Thus, in 1920, when there had come to be general agreement that women ought to have the vote, the United States Supreme Court did not declare that the Equal Protection Clause of the Constitution had "acquired" a meaning that it never bore before; rather, the people adopted the Nineteenth Amendment, requiring every state to accord women the franchise.

Under a regime of static law, it was not difficult to decide whether, under the American Constitution, there was a right to abortion, or to homosexual conduct, or to assisted suicide. When the Constitution was adopted, all those acts were criminal throughout the United States, and remained so for several centuries; there was no credible argument that the Constitution made those laws invalid. Of course society remained free to decriminalize those acts, as some states have; but under a static Constitution *judges* could not do so.

A change occurred in the last half of the twentieth century, and I am sorry to say that my court was responsible for it. It was my court that invented the notion of a "living Constitution." Beginning with the Cruel and Unusual Punishments Clause of our Eighth Amendment, we developed the doctrine that the meaning of the Constitution could change over time, to comport with "the evolving standards of decency that mark the progress of a maturing society." And it is we, of course, the justices of the Supreme Court, who will determine when there has been evolution, and when the evolution amounts to progress. On the basis of this theory, all sorts of entirely novel constitutional requirements were imposed, from the obligation to give a prior hearing before terminating welfare payments to the obligation to have law libraries in prisons.

For a time, the American Supreme Court was the envy of the judicial world. *Ah*, judges thought, *if only we all could have such power to do good!* And then, with the creation of constitutional courts in Europe, and ultimately creation of the European Court of Human Rights, the Power to Do Good came into every judge's hands—or at least the hands of every judge empowered to override legislative acts. The Court of Human Rights was quick to adopt the proposition that the Convention was (as the Court put it in 1978) a "living instrument which . . . must be interpreted in the light of present-day conditions." And thus the world, or at least the West, has arrived at its current state of judicial hegemony.

Let me make it clear that the problem I am addressing is not the social evil of the judicial dispositions I have described. I accept for the sake of argument, for example, that sexual orgies eliminate social tensions and ought to be encouraged. Rather, I am questioning the propriety—indeed, the sanity—of having a value-laden decision such as this made for the entire society (and in the case of Europe for a number of different societies) by unelected judges. There are no scientifically demonstrable "right" answers to such questions, as opposed to answers that the particular society favors. And even if there were scientifically "right" answers, there would be no reason to believe that law-trained professionals can discern them more readily than, say, medical doctors or engineers or ethicists or even the fabled Joe Six-Pack. Surely it is obvious that nothing I learned in my law courses at Harvard Law School, none of the experience I acquired practicing law, qualifies me to decide whether there ought to be (and hence is) a fundamental right to abortion or to assisted suicide.

Judges' lack of special qualification to deal with such questions is disguised by the fact that they provide their answers in classic legal-opinion form, with boring recitations of the facts, the procedural history of the case, the relevant provisions of law, the arguments of the parties, and finally, the court's analysis, which takes pains to demonstrate the consistency of today's result with earlier decisions of the court. The problem is that those earlier decisions, like the present one, fail to address the real issues, which are of a nature too fundamental to be logically resolved by a law court. Thus, the Court of Human Rights' opinion in the *Dudgeon* case, which held that the prohibition of homosexual sodomy violated Article 8, found that the prohibition was not necessary for the protection of morals while yet purporting not to "mak[e] any value-judgment as to the morality of homosexual relations between adult males." Surely the morality of the practice was central to the question whether proscription of it is necessary for the protection of morals. I suggest that the court disclaimed any determination of the morality of homosexual conduct, not because it was irrelevant to the case, but because it is blindingly clear that judges have no greater capacity than the rest of us to determine what is moral. The same phenomenon of disclaiming resolution of the central issue in the case appeared in *Roe v. Wade*, where my court said that, in order to decide whether a state must allow termination of a fetus's life at the wish of the mother, it was unnecessary to decide when human life begins. Of course that question is central to intelligent discussion of the issue—but judges obviously know no more about it than the rest of us.

WHICH BRINGS ME back to the comparison I suggested at the outset of these remarks. Just as scientific "experts" were unqualified to give the people's answer to the many policy judgments that inhere in any economic regulation, so also judges are unqualified to give the people's answer to the moral questions that inhere in any a priori assessment of human rights. And just as it proved impossible to take politics out of economic regulation, it will prove impossible to take politics out of the year-by-year refashioning of society's official views on human rights.

In the United States, the mechanism for the infusion of politics has been the appointment and confirmation process. Federal judges in general, and Supreme Court justices in particular, are nominated by the president and confirmed by the Senate. Every Republican presidential candidate since Richard Nixon has complained about an activist Supreme Court and has promised to appoint justices who believe in "judicial restraint." And every Democratic presidential candidate since Michael Dukakis has promised to appoint justices who will uphold *Roe v. Wade*, which is synonymous with judicial activism. Each year the conflict over judicial appointments has grown more intense. Recently, it has expanded to the court of appeals level, Democrats in the Senate refusing to permit a vote on court of appeals nominees whom they expect to disagree with *Roe v. Wade*. Because of this political controversy, a number of seats on our courts of appeals remain unfilled.

The lesson is, that in a truly democratic society—or at least the one in America—one way or another the people *will* have their say on significant issues of social policy. If judges are routinely providing the society's definitive answers to moral questions on which there is ample room for debate—rather than merely determining the meaning, when enacted, of democratically adopted texts—then judges *will* be made politically accountable. The people, through their representatives the president and the Senate, will no longer select candidates for the bench according to the traditional criteria—legal ability, integrity, judicial temperament, etc. Those qualities are all well and good, but they are no longer the most important thing we should be looking for. We should be looking for people who agree *with us* as to what the annually revised Constitution ought to say. And you have seen this revision of criteria come to pass, now that the people—after about fifty years of the living Constitution—have figured out the name of the game. I was confirmed to the Supreme Court twenty-three years ago by a vote of 98–0; today, an originalist like me cannot even get sixty votes to sit on a court of appeals.

What has occurred is betrayed even by the terminology with which the confirmation debates are conducted. The Senate is looking for "moderate" judges—"mainstream" judges. What in the world is a moderate interpretation of a constitutional text? Halfway between what it says and what we would like it to say? It makes no sense to speak of a "moderate" lawyer. But it makes a lot of sense to speak of a moderate policymaker—a moderate draftsman of an ever-evolving new Constitution. The "moderate" judge is one who will interpret the Constitution to mean what most people would like it to mean; and the "extremist" judge is one who will invent a new Constitution that most people would not approve. Once one adopts this criterion, of course, the Constitution ceases to perform its principal function: to *prevent* the majority from doing some things it *wants* to do.

I would predict the same politicization of the European judicial process, but I frankly do not know what mechanism would make that possible. One of the checks upon judicial power that the Framers inserted into the American Constitution was precisely the appointment of judges in a highly visible and highly political fashion—so that judicial appointments can be an important issue in a presidential election. I am not aware that effective political checks exist with respect to European constitutional courts, the Court of Justice, or the Court of Human Rights. Moreover, unlike in America, political hostility toward your courts cannot be personalized. Your courts have many members, and in numbers there is anonymity. Adding to the inability to assess blame is the fact that your judges ordinarily sit in panels rather than en banc—so that any single judge can be criticized for only a portion of the judgments. And the opinions for the court are not signed by a particular judge, but are anonymous. For all these reasons, you will not see in Europe placards that are the equivalent of IMPEACH EARL WARREN or IMPEACH HARRY BLACKMUN—or political mailings similar to the *in terrorem* letter a fundraiser for the Democratic Party recently sent to my house (I presume in error), reading, on the front of the envelope, "Imagine *Chief Justice* Scalia."

I am not happy about the intrusion of politics into the judicial appointment process in my country. But frankly, I prefer it to the alternative, which is government by judicial aristocracy. I shall observe with interest the development of this issue in Europe.

DISSENTS

Justice Scalia was famous for his brilliant and forceful dissents. In this 1994 speech to the Supreme Court Historical Society, he discussed the history of Supreme Court dissents and celebrated the practice.

———

I have chosen to speak this afternoon about the dissenting opinion. It is not a subject I aspire to become an expert in—but it is one, I think, of some interest and importance.

First of all, some definitions of terms: In speaking of dissenting opinions, I mean to address opinions that disagree with the Court's *reasoning*. Some such opinions, when they happen to reach the same disposition as the majority (that is, affirmance or reversal of the judgment below), are technically concurrences rather than dissents. To my mind, there is little difference between the two, insofar as the desirability of a separate opinion is concerned. Legal opinions are important, after all, for the *reasons* they give, not the *results* they announce; results can be announced in judgment orders without opinion. An opinion that gets the *reasons* wrong gets *everything* wrong that it is the function of an opinion to produce. There is a couplet spoken by Thomas à Becket in T. S. Eliot's *Murder in the Cathedral*, in which the saint, tempted by the devil to stay in Canterbury and resist Henry IV in order to achieve the fame and glory of martyrdom, rebuffs him with the words: "The last temptation is the greatest treason: to do the right deed for the wrong reason." Of course the same principle applies to judicial opinions as to eternal salvation: to get the reasons wrong is to get it all wrong, and that is worth a dissent, even if the dissent is called a concurrence.

But though I include in my topic concurrences, I include only *genuine* concurrences, by which I mean separate writings that disagree with the grounds upon which the court has rested its decision, or that disagree with the court's omission of a ground which the concurring judge considers central. I do not refer to, and I do not approve of, separate concurrences that are written only to say the same thing better than the court has done, or, worse still, to display the intensity of the concurring judge's feeling on the issue before the court. I regard such separate opinions as an abuse, and their existence as one of the arguments against allowing any separate opinions at all.

As you know, dissents and concurrences are commonplace in the practice of the United States Supreme Court. That has not always been so. During the first decade of the Court's existence, there was not a single dissent—for the simple reason that, in significant cases at least, there was no opinion of the Court from which to dissent. Whenever more than a mere memorandum judgment was called for, we followed the custom of the King's Bench and the other common-law courts: each justice filed his own separate opinion. Not all have cheered the abandonment of that system. In one of his concurrences, Justice Felix Frankfurter regretted that "[t]he volume of the Court's business has long since made impossible the early healthy practice whereby the Justices gave expression to individual opinions." The reason for departure from the practice, however, was really not the press of business, but the forceful personality of Chief Justice John Marshall, who established the system we currently use, whereunder one of the justices announces an opinion "for the Court." Dissents from that court opinion were very rare at first—only a single one-sentence concurrence during the first four years of Marshall's chief justiceship, and very few during his entire tenure.

The new system instituted under Marshall made Thomas Jefferson furious. Since 1811 the appointees named to the Court by

Jefferson and by his successor and political ally Madison, had constituted a majority on the Court. Yet the Court continued to come out with unanimous, pro-federal opinions written by Marshall, as though nothing had changed and the Federalists were still in control. In an 1820 letter, Jefferson complained about opinions "huddled up in conclave, perhaps by a majority of one, delivered as if unanimous, and with the silent acquiescence of lazy or timid associates, by a crafty chief judge, who sophisticates the law to his mind, by the turn of his own reasoning." In 1822, he finally wrote directly to Justice William Johnson, whom he had appointed to the Court in 1804, urging Johnson to return to the English practice of seriatim opinions:

> The Judges holding their offices for life are under two responsibilities only. 1. Impeachment. 2. Individual reputation. But this practice [of unanimous opinions] compleatly withdraws them from both. For nobody knows what opinion any individual member gave in any case, nor even that he who delivers the opinion, concurred in it himself. Be the opinion therefore ever so impeachable, having been done in the dark it can be proved on no one. As to the 2d guarantee, personal reputation, it is shielded compleatly. The practice is certainly convenient for the lazy, the modest and the incompetent. It saves them the trouble of developing their opinion methodically and even of making up an opinion at all. That of seriatim argument shews whether every judge has taken the trouble of understanding the case, of investigating it minutely, and of forming an opinion for himself, instead of pinning it on another's sleeve.

Justice Johnson's response suggested that Jefferson may not have been too far off the mark. While some have attributed the unified Marshall Court to Marshall's great political skills, Johnson was more inclined to credit it to the lack of juridical skills on the part of Marshall's colleagues. "Cushing," he wrote to Jefferson, "was incompetent, Chase could not be got to think or write—

Paterson was a slow man and willingly declined the Trouble, and the other two [Marshall and Washington] are commonly estimated as one judge."

In any event, since Marshall's time, separate opinions have become steadily more frequent: One scholar has calculated that up until 1928, dissents and concurrences combined were filed in only about 15 percent of all Supreme Court cases. Between 1930 and 1957, dissents alone were filed in about 42 percent of all Supreme Court cases. Last term, a dissent or separate concurrence was filed in 71 percent of all cases.

In assessing the advantages and disadvantages of separate opinions, one must consider their effects both within and without the court. Let me discuss the latter first: The foremost and undeniable external consequence of a separate dissenting or concurring opinion is to destroy the appearance of unity and solidarity. From the beginning to the present, many great American judges have considered that to be a virtually dispositive argument against separate opinions. So high a value did Chief Justice Marshall place upon a united front that according to his colleague, Justice William Johnson, he not only went along with opinions that were contrary to his own view, but even announced some. Only toward the end of his career—when his effort to suppress separate opinions had plainly failed—did he indulge himself in dissents: a total of only nine dissents in thirty-four years. In more recent times, no less a judicial personage than Judge Learned Hand warned that a dissent "cancels the impact of monolithic solidarity upon which the authority of a bench of judges so largely depends."

I do not think I agree with that. It seems to me that in a democratic society the authority of a bench of judges, like the authority of a legislature, or the authority of an executive officer, depends quite simply upon a grant of power from the people. And if the terms of the grant are that the majority vote shall prevail, then *that* is all the authority that is required—for a court no less than for a legislature or for a multi-member executive. Now it may well be that the people will be more inclined to accept without complaint a unanimous opinion of a court, just as they will be more inclined to accept willingly a painful course decided upon unanimously by their legislature. But to say that the *authority* of a court *depends* upon such unanimity in my view overstates the point. In fact, the argument can be made that artificial unanimity—the suppression of dissents—deprives genuine unanimity of the great force it can have when that force is most needed. United States Supreme Court lore contains the story of Chief Justice Warren's heroic and ultimately successful efforts to obtain a unanimous Court for the epochal decision in *Brown v. Board of Education*, which prohibited racial segregation in all public education. I certainly agree that that unanimity was important to achieving greater public acceptance. But would it have had that effect if *all* the decisions of the Supreme Court, even those decided by 5–4 vote, were announced as unanimous? Surely not.

Perhaps things are different when a newly established court is just starting out. Or perhaps they were different, even for a well-established court, in simpler, less sophisticated, less bureaucratic times. But I have no doubt that for the United States Supreme Court, at its current stage of development and in the current age, announced dissents augment rather than diminish its prestige. Almost half a century ago—when the number of staff personnel in the executive and legislative branches was even a good deal less than it is today—Justice Brandeis made his oft-quoted observation that the reason the justices of the Supreme Court enjoyed such a high level of popular respect was that, as he put it, "[we] are almost the only people in Washington who do [our] own work." Dissents make that clear. Unlike a unanimous institutional opinion, a signed majority opinion, opposed by one or more signed dissents, makes it clear that these decisions are the product of independent and thoughtful minds, who try to persuade one another but do not simply "go along" for some supposed "good of the institution."

I think dissents augment rather than diminish the prestige of the Court for yet another reason. When history demonstrates that one of the Court's decisions has been a truly horrendous mistake, it is comforting—and conducive of respect for the Court—to look back and realize that at least some of the justices saw the danger clearly, and gave voice, often eloquent voice, to their concern. I think, for example, of the prophetic dissent of Justice Harlan (the earlier Justice Harlan) in *Plessy v. Ferguson*, the case essentially overruled by *Brown v. Board of Education* a half century later, which held that, despite the provision of the Constitution requiring equal protection of the laws, the State of Louisiana could require railroads to carry white people and black people in separate cars. Harlan wrote:

> In respect of civil rights common to all citizens, the Constitution of the United States does not, I think, permit any public authority to know the race of those entitled to be protected in the enjoyment of such rights. . . .
>
> [I]n view of the Constitution, in the eye of the law, there is in this country no superior, dominant, ruling class of citizens. There is no caste here. Our Constitution is color-blind. In respect of civil rights, all citizens are equal before the law. The humblest is the peer of the most powerful. The law regards man as man. . . .
>
> The destinies of the two races in this country are indissolubly linked together, and the interests of both require that the common government of all shall not permit the seed of race hate to be planted under the sanction of law.

Or Justice Jackson's dissent in *Korematsu v. United States*, the 1944 case in which the Court upheld a military order providing for the internment of Japanese Americans on the West Coast. He wrote:

> A military order, however unconstitutional, is not apt to last longer than the military emergency. . . . But once a judicial opinion . . . rationalizes the Constitution to show that the Constitution sanctions such an order, the Court for all time has validated the principle of racial discrimination in criminal procedure and of transplanting American citizens. The principle then lies about like a loaded weapon, ready for the hand

of any authority that can bring forward a plausible claim of an urgent need. . . . All who observe the work of the courts are familiar with what Judge Cardozo described as "the tendency of a principle to expand itself to the limit of its logic." A military commander may overstep the bounds of constitutionality, and it is an incident. But if we review and approve, that passing incident becomes the doctrine of the Constitution. There it has a generative power of its own, and all that it creates will be in its own image.

A second external consequence of a concurring or dissenting opinion is that it can help to change the law. That effect is most common in the decisions of intermediate appellate tribunals. When a judge of one of our circuit courts of appeals dissents from an opinion of his colleagues, he warns the courts of appeals of the other twelve circuits (who are not bound by the precedential effect of that opinion) that they should not too readily adopt the same legal rule. And if they do not, of course—if they are persuaded by the view set forth in his dissent, pressed upon them by counsel in some later case—a conflict in the circuits will develop, ultimately requiring the attention of my court. At the court of appeals level, a dissent is also a warning flag to the Supreme Court: the losing party who seeks review can point to the dissent as evidence that the legal issue is a difficult one worthy of our attention.

At the Supreme Court level, on the other hand, a dissent rarely helps change the law. Even the most successful of our dissenters—Oliver Wendell Holmes, who acquired the sobriquet "The Great Dissenter"—saw somewhat less than 10 percent of his dissenting views ultimately vindicated by later overrulings. Most dissenters are much less successful than that. It sometimes happens that a separate concurring opinion has the effect of shaping the future law, not because it announces a different rule from that of the Court's opinion, but simply because it expresses that rule much more felicitously. What immediately comes to mind is Justice Harlan's separate concurrence in *Katz v. United States*, which held that our constitutional protection against "unreasonable searches and seizures" forbade the police from eavesdropping upon a telephone conversation conducted from a public phone booth. Harlan joined the opinion of the Court, but he also wrote separately to say:

> My understanding of the rule that has emerged from prior decisions is that there is a twofold requirement [for the provision against unreasonable searches and seizures to apply], first that a person have exhibited an actual (subjective) expectation of privacy and, second, that the expectation be one that society is prepared to recognize as "reasonable."

That formulation, rather than the opinion of the Court in *Katz*, is repeatedly cited in later cases, and has become the classic (if somewhat circular) statement of Fourth Amendment protection.

The dissent most likely to be rewarded with later vindication is, of course, a dissent that is joined by three other justices, so that the decision is merely a 5–4 holding. That sort of a dissent, at least in constitutional cases (in which, under the practice of our court, the doctrine of *stare decisis*[*] is less rigorously observed), emboldens counsel in later cases to try again, and to urge an overruling— which sometimes, although rarely, occurs. And that observation leads me to the last external effect of a dissenting opinion, which is to inform the public in general, and the bar in particular, about the state of the Court's collective mind.

Let me give a concrete example: Two terms ago the Court held, in a case called *Lee v. Weisman*, that the Establishment Clause of our Bill of Rights, which prohibits an "establishment of religion," forbids public officials from making a nondenominational invocation part of the ceremonies at a public high school graduation. Had the judgment been rendered by an institutional opinion for the Court, that rule of law would have the appearance of being as clear, as unquestionable, and as stable as the rule that denominational prayers cannot be made a mandatory part of the school day. In fact, however, the opinion was 5–4. It is clear to all that the de-

---

[*]   Adherence to precedent.

cision was at the very margin of Establishment Clause prohibition, that it would not be extended much further and may even someday be overruled.

Or to take another example, one that involves the provision of our Bill of Rights that forbids laws which prohibit the free exercise of religion. Four terms ago, in a case called *Employment Division v. Smith*, the Court held that this did not form the basis for a private exemption from generally applicable laws governing conduct—so that a person could not claim a right to use a proscribed psychotropic drug (peyote) in religious ceremonies. There again, the decision on the point was 5–4, making clear to one and all (and to future litigants, in particular) that this is a highly controverted and thus perhaps changeable portion of our jurisprudence.

I have tried to be impartial in the examples I have chosen: I wrote the dissent in the first case, and the opinion for the Court in the second. In the one as in the other I think it was desirable, and not destructive, that the fragility of the Court's holding was apparent. This is not to suggest, by the way, that every 5–4 decision of our court is a sitting duck for future overruling. In cases involving statutory law, rather than the Constitution, we will almost certainly not revisit the point, no matter how closely it was decided. But even there, disclosure of the closeness of the vote provides useful information to the legal community, suggesting that the logic of the legal principle at issue has been stretched close to its utmost limit and will not readily be extended further. Assume, for example, a statute prescribing a supplementary penalty of five years for the second conviction of a crime of violence. If the Court has held, by only a 5–4 vote, that a robbery committed by brandishing (though not discharging) a firearm is a "crime of violence" within the meaning of the statute, it is not likely to hold that kidnapping by trick followed by false imprisonment qualifies. And it is useful for prosecutors and lower-court judges to have that information.

It would be wrong to exaggerate this point. Dissenting or concurring opinions can sometimes obfuscate instead of clarify. Justice Jackson put it well in one of his essays:

There has been much undiscriminating eulogy of dissenting opinions. It is said they clarify the issues. Often they do the exact opposite. The technique of the dissenter often is to exaggerate the holding of the Court beyond the meaning of the majority and then to blast away at the excess. So the poor lawyer with a similar case does not know whether the majority opinion meant what it seemed to say or what the minority said it meant.

But it is always within the power of the justice writing the Court's opinion to disavow the exaggerations and distortions of the dissent, and to make clear the precise scope of the holding. Which is one reason why it is my practice, when writing for the Court, always to respond to the dissent, rather than adopting the magisterial approach of grandly ignoring it.

Of course the likelihoods and unlikelihoods, the fragilities and rock-solid certainties, signaled by unanimous or closely divided opinions have a relatively short shelf life. They become stale, so to speak, as the justices who rendered the opinion in question are, one by one, replaced. And that raises what seems to be one of the undesirable external effects of a system of separate opinions. It produces, or at least facilitates, a sort of vote-counting approach to significant rules of law. Whenever one of the five justices in a 5–4 constitutional decision has been replaced, there is a chance, astute counsel must think, of getting that decision overruled. And worse still, when the decision in question is a highly controversial constitutional decision, that thought occurs not merely to astute counsel but to the president who appoints the new justice, to the senators who confirm him, and to the lobbying groups that have the power to influence both. If the decision in question is controversial enough—*Roe v. Wade* is the prime modern example—the appointment of the new justice becomes something of a plebiscite upon the meaning of the Constitution in general and of the Bill of Rights in particular, in effect giving the majority the power to prescribe the meaning of an instrument designed to restrain the majority. That could not happen, or at least it could not happen as readily, if the individual positions of all the justices were not known.

I confess not to be quite as aghast at this consequence of separate opinions as I expect most of my listeners are. It seems to me a tolerable, and indeed perhaps a necessary, check upon the power of the Court in a system in which the adoption of a constitutional amendment to reverse a Court decision is well nigh impossible. In the United States system, constitutional amendments must be proposed by a two-thirds vote of both Houses of Congress, or by a national convention called for by two-thirds of the states, and then must be approved by three-fourths of the states by either the state legislature or a special convention. In such a system, the ability of the people to achieve correction of what they deem to be erroneous constitutional decisions through the appointment process seems to me not inappropriate. I think that corrective has been overused in recent years—but I would attribute that to a popular legal culture which encourages the people to believe that the Constitution means whatever it *ought* to mean.

Avoiding the grave temptation to pursue that controversial topic, let me turn to the last, but by no means the least, of the "external" consequences of our system of separate opinions. By enabling, indeed compelling, the justices of our court, through their personally signed majority, dissenting and concurring opinions, to set forth clear and consistent positions on both sides of the major legal issues of the day, it has kept the Court in the forefront of the intellectual development of the law. In our system, it is not left to the academicians to stimulate and conduct discussion concerning validity of the Court's latest ruling. The Court itself is not just the central organ of legal *judgment*; it is center stage for significant legal *debate*. In our law schools, it is not necessary to assign students the writings of prominent academics in order that they may recognize and reflect upon the principal controversies of legal method or of constitutional law. Those controversies appear in the opposing opinions of the Supreme Court itself and can be studied from that text; for example, whether the Constitution guarantees a generalized "right of privacy," or whether it protects unenumerated rights through the Due Process Clause, questions you will have heard put to the latest appointee to our court in her confirmation hearings—as they have been put in all confirmation hearings, at least since *Roe v. Wade*. The affirmative side of those questions appears in a number of court opinions, including *Griswold v. Connecticut*, a 1965 case establishing a federal constitutional right to contraception. To hear the case for the negative side, you might read the relevant portion of the book that Judge (and ex–Yale professor) Robert Bork published several years ago. But you need not. You will find that negative side put quite concisely and quite elegantly in *Griswold* itself, in the dissenting opinions of Justice Black and Justice Stewart.

Our dissents convey knowledge, not only about what legal issues are current, but also about what legal controversies are timeless. Judicial activism, for example—which in our federal system means giving an overly expansive meaning to the text of the Constitution— is criticized first from the Left and later from the Right, as the practitioners of that philosophy have moved in the opposite direction. In 1905, when the Court held unconstitutional a New York law limiting bakery workers to a ten-hour day (on the theory that it deprived them of "liberty of contract" without the "due process of law" that the Fourteenth Amendment requires), Justice Holmes protested that "[t]he Fourteenth Amendment does not enact Mr. Herbert Spencer's Social Statics." And in another dissent he wrote:

> I have not yet adequately expressed the more than anxiety that I feel at the ever increasing scope given to the Fourteenth Amendment in cutting down what I believe to be the constitutional rights of the States. As the decisions now stand, I see hardly any limit but the sky to the invalidating of those rights if they happen to strike a majority of this Court as for any reason undesirable. I cannot believe that the Amendment was intended to give us *carte blanche* to embody our economic or moral beliefs in its prohibitions.

More than half a century after Holmes began his protests, listen to the second Justice Harlan making the same objection, but now complaining about the Court's imposition of a *liberal* moral belief, in a case that used the Fourteenth Amendment to invalidate a state poll tax:

Property and poll-tax qualifications, very simply, are not in accord with current egalitarian notions of how a modern democracy should be organized. It is, of course, entirely fitting that legislatures should modify the law to reflect such changes in popular attitudes. However, it is all wrong, in my view, for the Court to adopt the political doctrines popularly accepted at a particular moment of our history and to declare all others to be irrational and invidious, barring them from the range of choice by reasonably minded people acting through the political process.

Justice Black wrote, in the same case:

The Court's justification for consulting its own notions, rather than following the original meaning of the Constitution, . . . apparently is based on the belief of the majority of the Court that for this Court to be bound by the original meaning of the Constitution is an intolerable and debilitating evil; that our Constitution should not be "shackled to the political theory of a particular era," and that, to save the country from the original Constitution, the Court must have constant power to renew it and keep it abreast of this Court's more enlightened theories of what is best for our society.

It seems to me that this is an attack not only on the great value of our Constitution itself, but also on the concept of a written constitution which is to survive through the years as originally written.

In sum, the system of separate opinions has made the Supreme Court the central forum of current legal debate and has transformed its reports from a mere record of reasoned judgments into something of a History of American Legal Philosophy with Commentary. I have no doubt that this has contributed enormously to the prominence of the Court and of the *United States Reports.*

Let me turn now to what I have called the "internal" consequences of separate opinions—their effect within the Court itself. Let me assure you at the outset that they do not, or at least need not, produce animosity and bitterness among the members of the Court. Dissenting will have that effect, I suppose, if it is an almost unheard-of occurrence, subjecting the writer of the Court's opinion to what may be viewed as a rare indignity. I am indebted to an article by the former Judge Stanley Fuld of the New York Court of Appeals for preservation of the following item from *The New York Times* of March 27, 1957:

> The Italian Constitutional High Court . . . accepted today the resignation of its president, Senator Enrico de Nicola.
>
> The reasons for Judge de Nicola's resignation were not given, [but] . . . it is understood . . . that . . . he was . . . irritated by the fact that some of the fourteen judges who sit with him on the High Court had dissented from some of his decisions.

Needless to say, none of the justices of my court would take such umbrage at a dissent. In part that is because we come, as I have described, from a tradition in which each judge used to write his own opinion. But mostly it is because dissents are simply the normal course of things. Indeed, if a justice's opinions were never dissented from, he would begin to suspect that his colleagues considered him insipid, or simply not worthy of contradiction. I doubt whether any two justices have dissented from each other's opinions any more regularly, or any more sharply, than did my former colleague Justice William Brennan and I. I always considered him, however, one of my best friends on the Court, and I think that feeling was reciprocated.

The most important internal effect of a system permitting dissents and concurrences is to improve the majority opinion. It does that in a number of ways. To begin with, the mere *prospect* of a separate writing renders the writer of the majority opinion more receptive to reasonable suggestions on major points. I do not mean to minimize the extent to which, even in the absence of a system of dissenting opinions, the colleagues of the judge who drafts the opinion can suggest and obtain desirable changes; that happens in our court as well, not only when the opinion is unanimous, but even among the five (or six or seven or eight) justices who form the majority in a split decision. However, human nature being what it is, nothing causes the writer to be as solicitous of objections on major points as the knowledge that, if he does not accommodate them, he will not have a unanimous court, and will have to confront a separate concurrence.

The second way in which separate opinions improve the majority opinion is this: though the fact never comes to public light, the first draft of a dissent often causes the majority to refine its opinion, eliminating the more vulnerable assertions and narrowing the announced legal rule. When I have been assigned the opinion for the Court in a divided case, nothing gives me as much assurance that I have written it well as the fact that I am able to respond satisfactorily (in my judgment) to all the onslaughts of the dissent or separate concurrence. The dissent or concurrence puts my opinion to the test, providing a direct confrontation of the best arguments on both sides of the controverted points. It is a sure cure for laziness, compelling me to make the most of my case. Ironic as it may seem, I think a higher percentage of the worst opinions of my court—not in result but in reasoning—are unanimous ones.

And finally, the last way in which a separate opinion can improve the majority opinion is by *becoming* the majority opinion. Not often, but much more than rarely, an effective dissent or concurrence, once it is circulated, changes the outcome of the case, winning over one or more of the justices who formed the original majority. Objections to the proposed majority opinion made at oral conference, or even in an exchange of written memoranda, will never be as fully developed, as thoroughly researched, and as forcefully presented as they are in a full-dress dissenting or concurring opinion prepared for publication.

I am so persuaded of this value of the separate opinion that I wish it were the practice of my court, though it is not, for the justices to refrain from the joining the circulated majority opinion until the dissent appears.

Besides improving the Court's opinions, I think a system of separate writing improves the Court's judges. It forces them to think systematically and consistently about the law, because in every case their legal views are not submerged within an artificially unanimous opinion but are plainly disclosed to the world. Even if they do not personally write the majority or the dissent, their name will be subscribed to the one view or the other. They cannot, without risk of public embarrassment, meander back and forth—today providing the fifth vote for a disposition that rests upon one theory of law, and tomorrow providing the fifth vote for a disposition that presumes the opposite.

Finally, and to me most important of all, a system of separate opinions renders the profession of a judge—and I think even the profession of a lawyer—more enjoyable. One of the more cantankerous of our justices, Justice William O. Douglas, once wrote that "the right to dissent is the only thing that makes life tolerable for a judge of an appellate court." I am not sure I agree with that, but I surely agree that it makes the practice of one's profession as a judge more satisfying. To be able to write an opinion solely for oneself, without the need to accommodate, to any degree whatever, the more-or-less-differing views of one's colleagues; to address precisely the points of law that one considers important *and no others*; to express precisely the degree of quibble, or foreboding, or disbelief, or indignation that one believes the majority's disposition should engender—that is indeed an unparalleled pleasure.

And it blesses him who receives, I think, as well as him who gives—that is, those who read separate opinions as well as those who write them. Legal scholars often bemoan the fact that ours is the one profession in which one does not necessarily study the best of what has been produced, but often the worst. If one is a student of Italian literature, he will read Dante. If a student of physics, Newton. If biology, Darwin. And so forth. But if his field of study is law, he will—at least in a common-law system such as ours—be condemned to reading, as often as not, the likes of Lord Tindal or Justice Duvall, not because they write well or think well (they do not), but because what they say is authoritative; it is the law. Dissents and separate concurrences provide a small parole from this awful sentence. Unlike majority opinions, they need not be read after the date of their issuance. They will not be cited, and will not be remembered, unless some quality of thought or of expression commends them to later generations. That is often the case, however, since dissents can have a character and flair ordinarily denied to majority opinions—for reasons well put by Justice Cardozo:

> Comparatively speaking at least, the dissenter is irresponsible. The spokesman of the court is cautious, timid, fearful of the vivid word, the heightened phrase. He dreams of [the consequences] of careless *dicta*. . . . The result is to cramp and paralyze. Not so, however, the dissenter. . . . For the moment, he is the gladiator making a last stand against the lions. The poor man must be forgiven a freedom of expression, tinged at rare moments with a touch of bitterness, which magnanimity as well as caution would reject for one triumphant.

How much poorer the patrimony of American law would be without those dissents and concurrences that have been thus preserved.

I quoted earlier from the eloquent dissents of the first Justice Harlan in *Plessy v. Ferguson*, and of Justice Jackson in *Korematsu*. There are many others, which have become part of our legal literature and our legal culture. For example, the marvelous dissent of Justice Holmes in *Northern Securities Co. v. United States*, the antitrust case challenging the merger of two of the nation's greatest railroads, the Great Northern and the Northern Pacific. It was a merger that Teddy Roosevelt, the great trustbuster, vigorously opposed and appointed Holmes to the Court with the expectation that *Holmes* would oppose (and never forgave him, by the way, for *not* opposing). Holmes wrote:

> Great cases, like hard cases, make bad law. For great cases are called great not by reason of their real importance in shaping the law of the future, but because of some accident of immediate overwhelming interest which appeals to the feelings and distorts the judgment. These immediate interests exercise a kind of hydraulic pressure which makes what previously was clear seem doubtful, and before which even well settled principles of law will bend.

Or the many memorable dissents of Holmes regarding freedom of speech, including such passages as:

> Persecution for the expression of opinions seems to me perfectly logical. If you have no doubt of your premises or your power, and want a certain result with all your heart, you naturally express your wishes in law and sweep away all opposition. . . . But when men have realized that time has upset many fighting faiths, they may come to believe . . . that the ultimate good desired is better reached by free trade in ideas—that the best test of truth is the power of the thought to get itself accepted in the competition of the market. . . . That at any rate is the theory of our Constitution. It is an experiment, as all life is an experiment. Every year, if not every day, we have to wager our salvation upon some prophecy based upon imperfect knowledge.

Or Justice Jackson's classic defense of freedom of speech:

> [F]reedom to differ is not limited to things that do not matter much. That would be a mere shadow of freedom. The test of its substance is the right to differ as to things that touch the

heart of the existing order. If there is any fixed star in our constitutional constellation, it is that no official, high or petty, can prescribe what shall be orthodox in politics, nationalism, religion, or other matters of opinion or force citizens to confess by word or act their faith therein.

Or, come to think of it, Justice Jackson's pithy remarks on a number of subjects. On judicial activism:

This Court is forever adding new stories to the temples of constitutional law, and the temples have a way of collapsing when one story too many is added. So it was with liberty of contract, which was discredited by being overdone.

On judicial humility:

[R]eversal by a higher court is not proof that justice is thereby better done. There is no doubt that if there were a super-Supreme Court, a substantial proportion of our reversals of state courts would also be reversed. We are not final because we are infallible, but we are infallible only because we are final.

Or (and with this I shall conclude) Justice Jackson on changing one's mind. This was written in a concurrence explaining why Jackson joined an opinion that reached precisely the opposite result of an opinion that Jackson himself had rendered ten years earlier, when he was attorney general. It includes the following:

Precedent . . . is not lacking for ways by which a judge may recede from a prior opinion that has proven untenable and perhaps misled others. . . . Baron Bramwell extricated himself from a somewhat similar embarrassment by saying, "The matter does not appear to me now as it appears to have appeared to me then." And Mr. Justice Story, accounting for his contradiction of his own former opinion, quite properly put the matter: "My own error, however, can furnish no ground for its being adopted by this Court. . . ." Perhaps Dr. Johnson really went to the heart of the matter when he explained a blunder in his dictionary—"Ignorance, sir, ignorance." But an escape less self-depreciating was taken by Lord Westbury, who, it is said, rebuffed a barrister's reliance upon an earlier opinion of his Lordship: "I can only say that I am amazed that a man of my intelligence should have been guilty of giving such an opinion." If there are other ways of gracefully and good-naturedly surrendering former views to a better considered position, I invoke them all.

Legal Canards

Concerned that legal practice in New York City was not compatible with family life, Antonin Scalia moved to Cleveland, Ohio, in 1961 to begin his legal career with the law firm of Jones, Day, Cockley & Reavis. He spent six years there before he decided to teach law. In October 1989, Scalia returned to Cleveland to present the Sumner Canary Lecture at Case Western Reserve law school. His lecture exposes and analyzes several clichés of legal writing.

———

Every judge, and indeed perhaps every lawyer, acquires over the years an intense dislike for certain oft-repeated statements that he is condemned to read, again and again, in the reported cases. It gets to be a kind of Chinese water torture: one's intelligence strapped down helplessly by the bonds of *stare decisis* that require these cases to be read, and trickled upon, time after time, by certain ritual errors, vapidities, and non sequiturs. It is usually impossible to cry out, even in a dissent, for these statements typically have little actual impact upon the decision of the case. They are part of its atmospherics, or of its overarching philosophy; it is fruitless to complain about the weather, and unlawyerlike to discuss philosophy rather than the holdings of the cases.

I thought I would indulge myself this evening, therefore, by lashing out against these instruments of torture. Here follow, in no particular order of aversion, my most hated legal canards.[*]

---

[*]   Omitting discussion of first canard, "Remedial statutes are to be liberally construed."

"A FOOLISH CONSISTENCY IS THE HOBGOBLIN OF LITTLE MINDS."

You are all familiar with this aphorism of Ralph Waldo Emerson. I am enormously happy to say that as far as I can discern it is not yet so deeply imbedded in the legal culture that it has appeared in a Supreme Court opinion. But it has been used by federal district courts and courts of appeals—and is surely among the ten most favorite *bons mots* of law professors. My main point is that it is, in the legal culture, an unacceptable proposition. But before proceeding to that, I cannot avoid the more general observation that it is a pretty silly proposition in any context. Perhaps no more is needed to demonstrate that than quotation of the entire paragraph in Emerson's essay "Self-Reliance" from which the phrase has been taken.

> A foolish consistency is the hobgoblin of little minds, adored by little statesmen and philosophers and divines. With consistency a great soul has simply nothing to do. He may as well concern himself with his shadow on the wall. Out upon your guarded lips! Sew them up with packthread, do. Else, if you would be a man, speak what you think today in words as hard as cannon balls, and tomorrow speak what tomorrow thinks in hard words again, though it contradict every thing you said to-day. Ah, then, exclaim the aged ladies, you shall be sure to be misunderstood. Misunderstood! It is a right fool's word. Is it so bad then to be misunderstood? Pythagoras was misunderstood, and Socrates, and Jesus, and Luther, and Copernicus, and Galileo, and Newton, and every pure and wise spirit that ever took flesh. To be great is to be misunderstood.

I am sure Emerson's reputation will long outlive mine, but I must believe (though I am not an Emerson scholar) that it rests upon both style and substance better than this. As for style: One can forgive the mistaken imagery of sewing up guarded lips rather than unsealing them, and perhaps even the imagery of "words as hard as cannon balls," which resembles a Monty Python cartoon; but it is quite impossible to forgive the line "To be great is to be misunderstood," which has been cribbed from the same book of banalities as "Love means never having to say you're sorry."

As for substance: It should be noted that Emerson is condemning not just that portion of consistency he considers "foolish." His point is that *all* desire for consistency is foolish. "With consistency a great soul has nothing to do." At the risk of being considered a little statesman, a philosopher, a divine, or even an aged lady (at least many of the last category, by the way, seem quite wise to me), this strikes me as unmitigated nonsense. One should assuredly not shrink from changing his views when persuaded that they are wrong. But the person who finds himself repeatedly in that situation, who quite readily speaks today what he thinks today, and tomorrow what he thinks tomorrow, with no concern for— with "simply nothing to do" with—the inconsistency between the two, is rightly regarded, it seems to me, not as a "great soul" but as one who habitually speaks without reflection, that is to say, a right fool. It is an even bet, by the way, whether Emerson would agree with this. Since he undoubtedly considered himself a great soul rather than a little statesman, etc., there is no reason to believe that what he thought yesterday has anything to do with what he might think today.

Now all of this would not have been worth commenting upon if Emerson had not been inflicted upon the law. I think it a generally sound policy to leave poets alone if they leave you alone. But the fact is that Emerson's aphorism—which, as I have observed, is even inaccurate in its more general application—has been regularly and repeatedly applied to the law, where it would be destructive beyond measure. Consistency is the very foundation of the rule of law. If you go through our Bill of Rights, I daresay it does not contain a single provision that various cultures, in various ages, have not in principle rejected: freedom of speech, freedom of press, freedom of religion, even the prohibition of cruel and unusual punishment. But you will search long and hard to find anyone, in any age, who would reject the fundamental principle underlying the equal protection clause: that persons similarly situated should be similarly treated—that is to say, the principle that the law must be consistent. Some societies, of course—even our own, alas, before the Civil War—have not been willing to regard all human beings as "persons," or to consider them all "similarly situated" insofar as their inherent human dignity is concerned, and it was the elimination of those blind and erroneous classifications (rather than expression of the universally accepted principle of consistency) that was the purpose of the Equal Protection Clause. But even where those blind and erroneous classifications existed, no one would have argued, for example, that two freedmen, or two Brahmans, or two serfs, or two noblemen should be treated differently. Indeed, it is the very primeval passion for consistency in the law that prompts the construction of such classifications, for without them the underlying inconsistency in the treatment of human beings becomes unacceptably obvious.

Besides its centrality to the rule of law in general, consistency has a special role to play in judge-made law—both judge-pronounced common law, and judge-pronounced determinations of the application of statutory and constitutional provisions. Legislatures are subject to democratic checks upon their lawmaking. Judges less so, and federal judges not at all. What checks their arbitrariness is only the insistence upon consistency, and application of the teachings of the mother of consistency, logic. Courts in a precedent-based system such as ours do not resolve each case in isolation from the cases that went before, deciding what seems "fair" or in accord with statutory or constitutional text on the basis of stated reasons that are plausible but quite incompatible with equally plausible reasons set forth in an earlier case. Rather, courts apply to each case a system of abstract and entirely fictional categories developed in earlier cases, which are designed, if logically applied, to produce "fair" or textually faithful results. Without such a system of binding abstractions, it would be extraordinarily difficult for even a single judicial lawgiver to be confident of consistency in his many ad hoc judgments; and it would be utterly impossible to operate a hierarchical judicial system, in which many individual judges are supposed to produce "equal" protection of the laws. (That is why, by the way, I never thought Oliver Wendell Holmes and the legal realists did us a favor by pointing out that all these legal fictions were fictions: those judges wise enough to be trusted with the secret already knew it.)

Sometimes, of course, the highest court in the judicial system may come to the conclusion that the result inescapably produced by the binding abstractions is simply wrong—which means a return to the drawing board, and the construction of a superseding scheme that leads to the right result. Such overrulings, I must acknowledge, involve a sacrifice of consistency. Yet even while abandoning consistency in the particular case, the court will affirm its enduring value for the system as a whole. For even as the old rationale is abandoned, a new one is announced, which forms the basis for a new scheme that is to be consistently followed.

In short, if Emerson is right, he must include in his rogues' gallery of those who value consistency not only little statesmen and philosophers and divines, but also good judges.

"THE FAMILIAR PARADE OF HORRIBLES"

This canard tends to be popular with the same people who like the previous one—for quite logical reasons that I shall in due course discuss. The phrase is often used, as you know, to denigrate the majority's or the dissent's contention that the principle embraced by the other side will produce certain specified undesirable consequences. Those consequences are dismissed, with a wave of the hand, as "the familiar parade of horribles."

I do not know for certain when the phrase was introduced into legal writing, but it appears in Supreme Court opinions at least half a century ago, in a 1948 Felix Frankfurter dissent. Frankfurter, I should note, did not use it as the projectile for a cheap shot at the majority, but rather was defending his own opinion against the anticipated argument that it contained a "parade of horribles."

The reason I say that the "parade of horribles" put-down

appeals to the Emersonian school of jurisprudence is this: just as one cannot conceive of a parade unless one believes in organization, so also one cannot take seriously a jurisprudential parade of horribles unless one believes in the demands of logic and consistency as the determinants of future judicial decisions. The judge without that belief—the judge who lacks the underlying assumption that he must not only decide who wins the case before him, but must decide on the basis of a general principle that he is willing to apply consistently in future cases—that judge can simply dismiss the predictions of future mischief by quoting Holmes's reply to Chief Justice Marshall's venerable dictum that the power to tax is the power to destroy. "The power to tax is not the power to destroy," Holmes said, "while this Court sits."

The notion that predicted evils cannot occur "while this Court sits" is comforting, of course, but hardly a response to how they can be avoided without repudiating the legal principle adopted in the case at hand. I would have thought it a better response to Marshall's dictum that the power to tax the activities of the federal government cannot constitute the power to destroy the federal government so long as the tax is generally applicable and nondiscriminatory—because it is implausible that the state would destroy its own citizens as well. Instead, however, Holmes simply said "Not while this Court sits,"—and excused Marshall's ignorance with the observation that "[i]n those days it was not recognized as it is today that most of the distinctions of the law are distinctions of degree." (Here Holmes flatters himself and his legal realist disciples. Perhaps it was not as *generally* recognized, but I am sure Marshall was quite aware of it.) "The question of interference with Government," Holmes concluded, "is one of reasonableness and degree and it seems to me that the interference in this case is too remote."

Of course if one is to adopt as the controlling legal principle "reasonableness and degree," one need fear no parade of horribles. As soon as the result seems "unreasonable," or goes "too far," the remaining marchers will be sent home. But what guidance does such a principle provide for the lower courts, and what check is it against the personal preferences of future judges? "Be reasonable and do not go too far" is hardly more informative than "Do justice," or "Do good and avoid evil." Once one departs from such platitudes and insists upon an analytical principle that is not value-laden—then, and only then, does the parade of horribles become a meaningful threat.

It is not my wish to banish the phrase "parade of horribles" from legal discourse—as it is, I must confess, to banish the Emersonian hobgoblin. Some arguments deserve to be dismissed as a "parade of horribles," but the careful legal writer will proceed to explain why—why all of the untoward results asserted to follow from the principle the Court is adopting indeed do not follow, why the logical principle governing the Court's decision does not have those consequences, or can be limited by another logical principle to avoid them. That was the approach adopted, for example, by Justice Brennan's dissent in *Goldman v. Weinberger* (1986), the case that upheld an Air Force regulation prohibiting the wearing of yarmulkes in uniform. Justice Brennan wrote:

> The Government dangles before the Court a classic parade of horribles, the specter of a brightly-colored, "rag-tag band of soldiers." Although turbans, saffron robes, and dreadlocks are not before us in this case, and must each be evaluated against the reasons a service branch offers for prohibiting personnel from wearing them while in uniform, a reviewing court could legitimately give deference to dress and grooming rules that have a *reasoned* basis in, for example, functional utility, health and safety considerations, and the goal of a polished, professional appearance. It is the lack of any reasoned basis for prohibiting yarmulkes that is so striking here.

That is the "parade of horribles" argument employed *comme il faut*—with an explanation of why the parade will not occur. But do not scoff at the "parade of horribles" in principle, as though the marchers in fact never materialize. To disabuse yourself of that notion, it is enough to read Justice Harlan's dissent in *Plessy v. Ferguson* (1896), the case that upheld a Louisiana law requiring rail carriers to provide separate coaches for blacks and whites. "The judgment this day rendered," he said, "will, in time, prove to be quite as pernicious as the decision made by this tribunal in the *Dred Scott* case":

> If a State can prescribe, as a rule of civil conduct, that whites and blacks shall not travel as passengers in the same railroad coach, why may it not so regulate the use of the streets of its cities and towns as to compel white citizens to keep on one side of a street and black citizens to keep on the other? Why may it not, upon like grounds, punish whites and blacks who ride together in streetcars or in open vehicles on a public road or street? Why may it not require sheriffs to assign whites to one side of a courtroom and blacks to the other? And why may it not also prohibit the commingling of the two races in the galleries of legislative halls or in public assemblages convened for the consideration of the political questions of the day?

Those horribles, or horribles very much like them, did indeed ensue from the decision in *Plessy v. Ferguson*. So use the phrase "parade of horribles," if you wish, to identify predictions that you can demonstrate are ill founded, because the legal rule asserted to produce them *has* a limiting principle that will prevent their occurrence. But do not dismiss the parade of horribles as an inherently unacceptable method of argumentation. The marchers are necessarily phantoms only if consistency is a hobgoblin.

"IT IS THE ESSENCE OF THE JUDICIAL FUNCTION TO DRAW LINES."

I will say only a few words about this one, because it belongs to the same family of ducks as the last. Like "the familiar parade of horribles," it can be true enough properly applied but is usually employed for the unworthy purpose of evading analysis. It is, moreover, generally aimed at the same target as that earlier canard (a marvelous mixed metaphor), namely, the argument that it is impossible to distinguish situation X, covered by the majority's or the dissent's proposed disposition, from situation Y, which quite obviously should *not* be subjected to that disposition. It simply does not suffice to refute such an argument to say that "it is the essence of the judicial function to draw lines."

Of course it is the essence of the judicial function to draw lines—because it is the essence of the judicial function to be governed by lines, the lines of the logical and analytical categories I discussed earlier. The dispute is not over whether lines should be drawn, but whether they should be drawn now or later. The right answer is ordinarily now, for two reasons. First, because the correctness of today's decision as the application of a neutral legal principle cannot be assessed unless that principle also appears to produce acceptable results in other contexts. If it does not, and if there is no rational exception that shows how it can be limited, then it is an erroneous principle—not only for the future, but also for the case before the court today.

The second reason line-drawing must be done in advance, at least in appellate opinions, is that most lawyers and their clients do not have the luxury of waiting for it to be done at a later date. Perhaps in the infancy of the common law it would have sufficed to say, in response to the alleged future mischief that a decision might detail: "We will cross that bridge when we come to it. We will draw the necessary line when the occasion arises." But when one is operating, as we are today, in a judicial system in which the Supreme Court of any jurisdiction reviews a minuscule proportion of the decided cases, the function of a good decision is to make the distinctions—or at least the obviously necessary distinctions—clear from the outset, so that hundreds of cases will not be decided incorrectly before the Supreme Court has the opportunity to revisit the field.

In short, the riposte that should usually be made to the argument that "it is the essence of the judicial function to draw lines" is: "Quite so; and you have not done it."

"WE MUST NEVER FORGET THAT IT IS *A CONSTITUTION* WE ARE EXPOUNDING."

There are, alas, so many canards in the law that once one gets rolling discussing them it is hard to know where to stop. I will conclude, however, with the misuse of this famous statement of Chief Justice Marshall, written in *McCulloch v. Maryland* (1819). It is often trotted out, nowadays, to make the point that the Constitution does not have a fixed meaning—that it must be given different content, from generation to generation, retaining the "flexibility" needed to keep up with the times. There are many instances of this use. I will give you as an example of one that is perhaps not the best, but that does conform to the principle *de vivis nil nisi bonum*:* Justice Fortas's dissent in *Fortson v. Morris* (1966). That case involved an Equal Protection Clause challenge to the provision of the Georgia constitution which provided that, if no candidate for governor should receive a majority of the votes cast, the General Assembly would choose between the two candidates having the most votes. The Court upheld the provision, in an opinion by Justice Black that ended:

> Article V of Georgia's Constitution provides a method for selecting the Governor which is old as the Nation itself. Georgia does not violate the Equal Protection Clause by following this article as it was written.

Fortas's dissent summons up Marshall's dictum in support of the proposition that "[m]uch water has gone under the bridge since the late 1700's and the early 1800's," making it appropriate

---

* Of the living, say nothing but good.

for "[n]otions of what constitutes equal treatment for purposes of the Equal Protection Clause [to] change."

Now it is not my object here to discuss the substantive accuracy of such reasoning. It does seem to me that a constitution whose meaning changes as our notions of what it *ought* to mean change is not worth a whole lot. To keep government up-to-date with modern notions of what good government ought to be, we do not need a constitution but only a ballot box and a legislature. But never mind that dispute. What I am addressing here is not whether the "evolutionary" theory of the Constitution is correct, but whether it is shown by the above quote to be endorsed by as orthodox an authority as John Marshall himself. The answer is not only *pas du tout* but *au contraire*.

Marshall's words, you will recall, were written in the course of considering whether Congress had the constitutional power to incorporate a Bank of the United States. Establishing a bank or creating a corporation were not among the powers *expressly* conferred; but Marshall's point, in the passage at issue here, was that it is the nature of a constitution not to set forth everything in express and minute detail. The nature of the document at issue, he said, "requires, that only its great outlines should be marked, its important objects designated, and the minor ingredients which compose those objects be deduced from the nature of the objects themselves." A constitution that went beyond that, "to contain an accurate detail of all the subdivisions of which its great powers will admit, and of all the means by which they may be carried into execution, would partake of the prolixity of a legal code, and could scarcely be embraced by the human mind." In assessing the significance of the fact that the power to incorporate a bank is not specifically mentioned, then, "we must never forget that it is *a constitution* we are expounding."

None of this, of course, has anything to do with whether the meaning of a constitution changes from age to age. That Marshall did not believe the latter is conclusively shown when he turns to his next argument, the provision of the Constitution that gives

Congress power "[t]o make all Laws which shall be necessary and proper for carrying into Execution" the specifically conferred legislative powers. He acknowledges that the word *necessary* can be used to mean "essential" or "indispensable." In this context, however, he says that it must reasonably be given another of its common meanings: "convenient," "appropriate," or "useful." He explains why:

> This provision is made in a constitution intended to endure for ages to come, and consequently to be adapted to the various crises of human affairs. To have prescribed the means by which Government should, in all future time, execute its powers ... would have been an unwise attempt to provide by immutable rules for exigencies which, if foreseen at all, must have been seen dimly, and which can be best provided for as they occur.

This argument rests entirely upon the premise that the interpretation given today must be adhered to. Otherwise, there would be no need to bear in mind the "exigencies of the future"—which could be met by saying, as Justice Fortas said, well, our notions of what the Constitution permits have changed.

More faithful to John Marshall's philosophy, it seems to me, is Justice Black's use of his words, dissenting in *Bell v. Maryland* (1964):

> We are admonished that in deciding this case we should remember that "it is a constitution we are expounding." We conclude as we do because we remember that it is a Constitution and that it is our duty "to bow with respectful submission to its provisions." [Quoting Marshall in *Cohens v. Virginia* (1821).] And in recalling that it is a Constitution "intended to endure for ages to come," we also remember that the Founders wisely provided the means for that endurance: changes in the Constitution, when thought necessary, are to be proposed by Congress or conventions and ratified by the States. The Founders gave no such amending power to this Court. Our duty is

simply to interpret the Constitution, and in doing so the test of constitutionality is not whether a law is offensive to our conscience or to the "good old common law," but whether it is offensive to the Constitution.

Or as Felix Frankfurter put it more concisely: "Precisely because 'it is *a constitution* we are expounding,' we ought not to take liberties with it."

I have come to the end of my remarks—not, I am sorry to say, because I am out of canards but because I am out of time. The catharsis has done me good, and I return, reinvigorated, to reading opinions and biting my tongue. Much of what I have said has been in a humorous vein, but I hope I have not entirely obscured the serious purpose behind it. The fallacy that passes for truth by the mere frequency of its repetition is a particular peril for lawyers working in the common-law system. Like all men and women, we are comfortable with familiar formulations, and in addition are trained to follow what has been said before. It is sometimes worth pausing to consider whether it has been said aright.

On Virtue and
the Public Good

---

*"Because human institutions succeed or fail in large
part because of the good traditions or the
bad traditions that animate them—and because
good traditions, once lost, are difficult
if not impossible to re-establish—we must guard and
nourish all of our valuable traditions."*

COURAGE

In May 2011, Justice Scalia returned to his alma mater, Xavier High School in New York City, to pay homage to the school's tradition of military training.

Scalia graduated from Xavier in 1953. During his senior year, a profile of him in the school paper praised his "exceptional accomplishment in the field of studies," his "skill in the science of debating and the art of dramatics" (including the lead role in Macbeth*), his talents with the French horn and the rifle, and his "full Catholic life."*

————

Men of Xavier: Many thanks for your warm and generous welcome. It is my great pleasure to be with you this evening to celebrate the Regiment and to recognize the achievements of those being honored with awards. The Regiment, as I remember it, is a place where awards are earned; so I have no doubt you and your families are deservedly proud of what you have accomplished. Congratulations.

Whatever Regimental glory I won when I graduated in 1953 is unrecorded. The one distinctively military item I recall is that I rose to the rank of lieutenant colonel, commanding officer of the Marching Band. I count that an honor because traditionally the post had been held by a major. Xavier's official history—published in 1997 on the occasion of the school's 150th birthday—notes only one achievement of mine: while an underclassman, I represented Xavier on a panel of students from schools throughout the city on a Sunday-morning television show called *Mind Your Manners*. It was reported afterward that my "keen sensible answers, well seasoned with a bit of humor, stole the show." I think that may have been the peak of my favorable press coverage.

My talk this evening is about the legacy to which you and I are heirs. Xavier High School was the most formative institution in my life; and as I look back on those times, fifty-eight years later, it is the Regiment I remember most. Then as now, military training was the distinctive tradition that set Xavier apart (and Xavier men apart) from the other Jesuit schools in the city—a link to the broader tradition of American military academies. And situated in New York, in the heart of American Catholicism, the Regiment has also been a visible sign of the patriotism of the Catholic citizens of this country.

Xavier's contribution to the armed forces began even before it became a military school. At the outset of the Civil War, about half the population of the city was made up of Catholics; and in those days, to put it mildly, Catholics were not universally beloved, or even trusted, by their Protestant brethren. Military service on behalf of the Union did much to dispel that mistrust. In 1861, eight regiments of predominantly Catholic New Yorkers volunteered to fight for the Union. Many of them were Irish—no surprise there, since the Irish National Anthem begins "Soldiers are we."

Although Xavier was small and young then, she sent a number of her sons to the Union Army, including James Rowan O'Beirne, who won the Medal of Honor for holding a line under withering enemy fire, and later, as provost marshal of Washington, led the manhunt for Lincoln's assassins.

Xavier also sent three of her priests to serve as chaplains. One of them, Father Michael Nash, had been a prefect at Xavier, and evidently a strict one. Father Nash was assigned to minister to a famously rough company of volunteers called the Wilson Zouaves. When they first met Father Nash, the Wilson Zouaves had less interest in confession than they did in drinking and brawling. But Father Nash stuck it out, and by the time the whole company had sailed to Florida where they were to serve, they carried him ashore on their shoulders. According to an 1897 history of Xavier, thanks to Father Nash the Zouaves "proved to be true patriots, obedient and brave, a bulwark of the country, the terror of the enemy." If that seems to you a bit much to attribute to a chaplain, you should know the aforementioned history was written by the Alumni Association. But whatever its motivations, the account properly recognizes that the military service of Xavier's priests was in the best tradition of the Church and the Society of Jesus. It says:

> Called from the professor's chair to bear all the hardships of military life, they showed again and again that they sons of the knightly Loyola have inherited the undaunted soul of their founder. . . . By their faithful work as Christian priests they infused into their men greater and nobler and purer patriotism. On the field of battle, scorning fear and danger, they sought the wounded and dying amidst flying bullets, and were good Samaritans alike to Catholic and non-Catholic, to friend and foe.

A few decades later, Xavier's military tradition began in earnest. By the 1890s, Xavier would become "the Catholic military school." Military training became compulsory for all students; and the Regiment became the public image of the school in New York. Captain John Drum, an Army officer who would later give his life on San Juan Hill, organized students into separate companies and taught them military drill. A fife-and-bugle corps was established, and Xavier's cadets began to assume a place of honor in New York City parades on public holidays like St. Patrick's Day, Decoration Day (what we now call Memorial Day), and Columbus Day. Those honors culminated in 1897, Xavier's golden-jubilee year, when the corps of cadets was invited to participate in the dedication of Grant's Tomb. An account written that year records that "[t]he department of Military Science has become more and more a part of the life of the College."

I have no doubt those first Xavier cadets played a small but important role in reinforcing public perceptions of Catholic loyalty and civic virtue. The need for such reinforcement should not be underestimated. In the late nineteenth century, religious hostilities were real and deep. In 1884, Republican presidential candidate James G. Blaine came to New York to attend a morning meeting. Blaine looked good to win the election, which was just days away. But on that fated morning, a Presbyterian minister named Samuel Burchard rose to give a speech supporting Blaine. Burchard assailed the Democrats as "the party whose antecedents have been rum, Romanism, and rebellion." Blaine failed to rebuke Burchard, and Irish Catholics in this city, as you may imagine, did not care for that a'tall a'tall. They turned out in droves and defeated Blaine in New York by just over one thousand votes— costing him the election.

That was the era when Xavier's students began to put on the cadet's uniform, and I think it improved the public's perception of Catholics. For once, *The New York Times* agrees that I am right— even if you have to go back to May 31, 1894, to read about it. The *Times* published a rebuke of an anti-Catholic organization called the American Protective Association and its leader, the Reverend Madison C. Peters. The APA and Peters accused Catholics of "Romanizing the army and navy" and proposed to prevent them from holding public office or command positions in the armed forces, on the grounds (I suppose) that if given a battalion to command, a Catholic colonel might turn the unit over to the Pope. To its credit the *Times* published a piece entitled "Object Lesson for Bigots: Catholic and Protestant in the Memorial Parade." The article reminded the reader that the previous day New York had hosted a parade for the Grand Army of the republic—a procession of veterans of the Civil War. The procession comprised "men of all creeds and nationalities who had followed the Stars and Stripes together in many a hard fight regardless whether the men in front of them or behind them were Roman Catholics or Protestants, Jews or Gentiles." The article described a memorial service that had been held that day in the Church of St. Francis Xavier, at which "the students of [the college], to the number of 300," who have been "under the instruction and drill of Capt. Drum of the United States Army," "appeared in full military costume in honor of the occasion." The *Times* continued:

It is instructive to turn from these terrible and distorted pictures of the Roman Catholics and their Church, as Mr. Peters draws them, to the reality as witnessed yesterday at St. Francis Xavier's. . . . The great edifice was crowded to the doors with devout worshippers, who were privileged to listen to a sermon that was as full of glowing, broad-minded patriotism as are the sermons of Mr. Peters full of prejudice and bigotry.

That sermon was delivered right here, in this church. It reminded those present that obedience to lawful authority is the religious duty of every Catholic, and that Catholics had proved their loyalty on the battlefield.

It is easy for us, more than a century later, to take for granted that no serious person seriously doubts the patriotism of his Catholic neighbors—though the ugly old slanders do occasionally rear their heads. But we should not forget the small debt we owe to the members of this Regiment who were willing to become conspicuous examples of Catholics living their faith by serving their country. Probably the most striking symbol of that union between faith and service was the military Mass. One historian reports that by the end of the nineteenth century (and partly as a protest against the Reverend Peters and his APA) Xavier began holding special military Masses to open the month of May and its special devotions to Mary. At that Mass, "the cadets processed into church and the officers sat in the front pews with their swords unsheathed— imitating the crusading knights of the past—during the reading of the Gospel and the profession of the Creed. A trumpet sounded during the Consecration of the bread and wine." It was ceremonial flair with a purpose. The tradition was still alive during my days here. On First Fridays the regiment would attend morning Mass in dress blues (dress blues were the uniform of the day on Fridays). Just before the consecration, the regimental officers would march down the center aisle in a column of twos, swords drawn and resting on their right shoulders; the front of the column would divide left and right at the altar rail, producing a single line across the transepts and forming, with the officers remaining in the main aisle, a cross of regimental blue. The elevation of the Host would be announced by a bugle's flourishes instead of a bell, and the officers, from front to rear, would present swords.

By the 1930s, the Regiment had become a part of the pageantry of the city. In 1932, New York held the biggest parade since World War I to celebrate the bicentennial of George Washington's birthday. Xavier was the only high school unit to participate—a great honor. The entire Regiment assembled for the parade, stretched out for three or four blocks east of Fifth Avenue. They did draw dreary duty, however: they marched last, so they were stuck where they stood from morning until late afternoon. The whole regiment continued to march in major New York parades during my days here—and its place in the pageant had improved considerably. We used to march right behind the first military unit in the parade, the Fighting 69th, New York City's regiment. I will never forget participating in what I have been told was the last real ticker-tape parade, before the ticker-tape machine became technologically obsolete: the parade celebrating General Douglas MacArthur's return from Japan.

Over the years, it became commonplace to see Xavier cadets in their ROTC uniforms, or in dress blues on Fridays, on the subways from four boroughs (Staten Islanders took the ferry), on the trains from New Jersey, and even from as far up the Hudson as Verplanck, New York (one of my classmates was from there). I was a member of the JV rifle team, so I occasionally had to bring my .22 carbine on the subway from Queens to school, or to the gunsmith in Brooklyn. (Imagine that today.) Periodically, on the occasion of major liturgical celebrations, the police would stop traffic on 16th Street while the whole Regiment marched, to the music of the band and the drum-and-bugle corps, down the impressive front steps of the school, column left along 16th Street, and column left again into the Church of St. Francis Xavier for Mass; and afterward we would parade back—all in dress blues.

But the Regiment's most important legacy, of course, was not pageantry; it was discipline, and duty, and sacrifice. Nearly a thousand of Xavier's sons served in the First World War—including

Captain Drum's son, Hugh, a Xavier man who eventually rose to the rank of lieutenant general. World War II saw nearly fifteen hundred Xavier men fight for their country, fifty-four of whom gave their lives. Like Father Nash in the Civil War, ten Jesuit teachers and nine lay faculty left the school to serve. Historian Helen McNulty writes that Xavier was "one of the few high schools in the country which had thoroughly prepared students to participate in modern military warfare. . . . It is believed that no high school in the United States made a greater contribution in manpower and effort during WWII than Xavier High School." I believe it. And at a military Mass in 1947, with the war over, Cardinal Spellman— who was archbishop of both New York and the United States military—read aloud Pope Pius XII's handwritten letter to Xavier's president, Father Tynan, offering the Holy Father's "prayerful remembrance . . . of those whose courage and self-sacrifices made the proud present possible."

But as you know, the tradition of Xavier as a thoroughly military academy did not survive the anti-military sentiment of the Vietnam War. I lamented when the school announced that the Regiment would no longer be compulsory, and I continue to think that was a mistake. This country has a rich tradition of military schools. It was born partly of necessity—since with independence from Britain came the need to have an army and to run it competently—but it was also born partly of democratic theory. Congress first authorized the creation of the United States Military Academy at West Point in 1802. But that academy, of course, could not educate the whole country in military matters—and in those days, the whole country might well be called upon to serve as militia. Following the War of 1812, the Committee on Militia of the House of Representatives reported to Congress its belief that:

> The safety of a republic depends as much upon the equality in the use of arms amongst its citizens, as upon the equality of rights; nothing can be more dangerous in such a government than to have a knowledge of the military art confined to a part of the people—for sooner or later that part will govern.

Military schools followed different paths in the North and South. In the South, it became common for states to establish and fund public military academies. Two of them—the Virginia Military Institute and South Carolina's Citadel—were resurrected after the Civil War and continue an illustrious tradition. But in the North, states took a more laissez-faire approach. Private military schools sprang up, including many run by religious denominations. Xavier was one of a number of Catholic military secondary schools established in the nineteenth century—including LaSalle Military Academy on Long Island, and Canisius College (Jesuit, of course) in Buffalo. All Hallows College in Utah was a military school, and Catholic universities, such as Notre Dame and St. Louis University (Jesuit), had compulsory military training. It was, as I have said, part of the long connection between Catholics and the armed forces. West Point has had a disproportionate share of Roman Catholics, enough to justify a separate chapel since 1899.

Xavier has been a prominent part of that Catholic tradition. Catholicism, of course, has never had that contempt for the soldier that came to the fore in Vietnam-era America. The Roman centurion at the Crucifixion who said "Truly this was the son of God" was not one of the bad guys. Nor the centurion who asked Jesus to heal his servant without the necessity of going there (the famous line, echoed at Mass, "Lord, I am not worthy that you should enter under my roof, but only say the word and my servant will be healed"). Of him, Jesus said he had not seen such faith in Israel. And while Jesus said that he who lives by the sword will die by the sword, He did not regard soldiers as men who lived by the sword. His advice to them was not "Throw down your arms," but be content with your wages. (The real villains in the Gospels, I am sorry to say, were the lawyers—though to be fair they were lawyers in a theocratic state, so that their closest modern equivalent is probably, imagine that!, theologians.) Two of the earliest and most venerated of Christian martyrs, St. Sebastian and St. George, were soldiers of Diocletian. And come to think of it, Ignatius Loyola—"the knightly Loyola," as the Alumni Association puff piece I quoted earlier described him—was a soldier. And his successors are still called generals.

The defining virtue of a soldier is courage. What chastity is to a nun, or humility to a friar, courage is to a soldier. In *The Screwtape Letters*, C. S. Lewis imagines a senior demon, Screwtape, sending advice to his nephew Wormwood on how to ensnare the soul of an Englishman living on the brink of World War II. Screwtape tells Wormwood that the demons have managed to fool mankind into believing that many virtues are vices—that modesty is prudishness, for example. But that has not worked for the virtue of courage.

> We have made men proud of most vices, but not of cowardice. Whenever we have almost succeeded in doing so, the Enemy [that is, God] permits a war or an earthquake or some other calamity, and at once courage becomes so obviously lovely and important even in human eyes that all our work is undone, and there is still at least one vice of which they feel genuine shame.

I believe that military service is not only appropriate for Christians, it is conducive to Christian virtue. I know of no other profession where one *commits* to laying down his life for his friends. I have nine children, whom I have sent to many different colleges, including two Jesuit colleges. I can say in all honesty that the school which took most seriously, which made a large part of each day's *instruction*, the task of *moral formation*—of developing character, and instilling fidelity to duty, honor, country—was West Point. And training oneself to be a soldier, preparing oneself to make that sacrifice if needed, is not just one more interchangeable way for a Christian to develop good character. Let no one demean it. It is good training indeed.

Let me leave you with this illustration: There was a Xavier man in the class above me named Donald Cook. On New Year's Eve, 1964, Marine Captain Donald Cook was taken prisoner by the Viet Cong—and remained their prisoner until his death. For his conduct as a prisoner of war, Cook was posthumously promoted to colonel and awarded the Medal of Honor. His citation for conspicuous gallantry reads in part:

> Despite the fact that by doing so he would bring about harsher treatment for himself, [Cook] established himself as the senior prisoner, even though in actuality he was not. Repeatedly assuming more than his share of [responsibility for] their health, Colonel Cook willingly and unselfishly put the interests of his comrades before that of his own well-being and, eventually, his life. Giving more needy men his medicine and drug allowance while constantly nursing them, he risked infection from contagious diseases while in a rapidly deteriorating state of health. This unselfish and exemplary conduct, coupled with his refusal to stray even the slightest from the Code of Conduct, earned him the deepest respect from not only his fellow prisoners, but his captors as well. Rather than negotiate for his own release or better treatment, he steadfastly frustrated attempts by the Viet Cong to break his indomitable spirit and passed this same resolve on to the men with whose well-being he so closely associated himself. Knowing his refusals would prevent his release prior to the end of the war, and also knowing his chances for prolonged survival would be small in the event of continued refusal, he chose nevertheless to adhere to a Code of Conduct far above that which could be expected. His personal valor and exceptional spirit of loyalty in the face of almost certain death reflected the highest credit upon Colonel Cook, the Marine Corps, and the United States Naval Service.

It also reflected great credit on the Regiment. To return to C. S. Lewis (I can't resist): Screwtape warns Wormwood that a war can be dangerous for their satanic cause, because it awakens men from their moral stupor. He says:

> This, indeed, is probably one of the Enemy's motives for creating a dangerous world—a world in which moral issues really

come to the point. He sees as well as you do that courage is not simply *one* of the virtues, but the form of every virtue at the testing point, which means, at the point of highest reality. A chastity or honesty, or mercy, which yields to danger will be chaste or honest or merciful only on conditions. Pilate was merciful till it became risky.

The indispensability of courage is easier for the soldier to appreciate, whose very life may depend upon the courage of his comrades. Its value is harder to appreciate in the layman's endless days of peace, where the type of courage that is called for is rarely the physical courage to risk one's life. But for most of us, that is the long fight we are in for—courageously setting things right in the world God has created, starting with ourselves. The habit of courage is not acquired by study; it is forged by practice. And there is no better practice than the Regiment. By demanding obedience to duty, manly honor and discipline, frank and forthright acknowledgment of error, respect for ranks above and solicitude for ranks below, assumption of responsibility including the responsibility of command, willingness to sacrifice for the good of the corps—by demanding all those difficult things the Regiment develops *moral courage*, which, in the Last Accounting we must give, is the kind that matters. That is why military training is not, and never will be, just one more interchangeable way for young Christians to develop good character or learn to serve others. It is one of the noblest ways, and never let anyone tell you otherwise.

Thank you for inviting me to be with you this evening. I am tremendously proud to be a part of the tradition of this Regiment. What I have seen at this awards ceremony—and what I have learned: that four of your officers have been admitted to West Point, and two awarded ROTC scholarships—fills me with confidence that the tradition continues, and will endure.

TRADITION

The Marine Corps Air Station in remote Cherry Point, North Carolina, might not seem an obvious locale for a Supreme Court justice to give a speech. But that didn't stop longtime Navy chaplain Captain Thomas Dansak from inviting Justice Scalia to be the guest speaker at the Air Station's annual prayer breakfast in 1998. Figuring that he had nothing to lose, Father Dansak contacted Scalia out of the blue—and "his favorable response surprised me!" The event, Father Dansak reports, drew a full house and was a great highlight of his thirty years of service in the Navy.

———

M en and women of the United States Marine Corps assigned to the Second Marine Aircraft Wing:

I want to speak to you this morning about tradition. The Marine Corps understands the value of that elusive, intangible quality. It is there in your motto: Always Faithful. Not just faithful today; not just faithful from now on; but faithful always, from 1775 to the present, and for as long as the republic will call upon you. It is there in the Marine's Hymn, which recalls expeditions against enemies of the republic so long gone and so long forgotten that few Americans, alas, even know what the Halls of Montezuma were. And it is there, of course, in your battle pendants, giving witness to a long road of fidelity and honor from Tripoli to Iwo Jima to Iraq.

It is a strange thing, tradition. It can be squandered, but not bought. It can be lost, but not given to someone else. In the field of human activity in which I toil—the law—the newly emerged democracies of Eastern Europe are trying to establish independent judiciaries, and we are trying to help them. But to tell you the truth, we cannot help them very much. We can tell them of our two-century-long tradition of proud judicial independence, and urge them to emulate it. But we cannot *give* them a tradition of independence to replace their own lengthy traditions of judicial subservience to political authority. When we think "judge," we think of an impartial arbiter between the power of the state and the rights of the citizen; when they think "judge," they think of one of the faithful instruments of state power.

Because human institutions succeed or fail in large part because of the good traditions or the bad traditions that animate them—and because good traditions, once lost, are difficult if not impossible to re-establish—we must guard and nourish all of our valuable traditions with the same care and devotion that the Corps devotes to *Semper Fidelis*. I want to speak this morning about one of our oldest and I think most important national traditions that has for some years been in grave and imminent peril: the traditional belief, expressed unashamedly in our national pronouncements and reflected faithfully in our public policies, that we are a nation under God. That tradition appears, of course, in the first document to issue from us as a nation. The Declaration of Independence, which appeals to the "Laws of Nature, and of Nature's God," affirms that "all men . . . are endowed by their Creator with certain unalienable Rights," and asserts in its concluding sentence "a firm reliance on the protection of divine Providence." The First Congress to be elected under the new Constitution adopted a joint resolution requesting the president to "recommend to the people of the United States a day of public thanksgiving and prayer." President Washington responded to that request by issuing the first Thanksgiving Day proclamation, and of course we have had Thanksgiving Day proclamations ever since. We have also had, from the very beginning, publicly supported army and navy chaplains, House and Senate chaplains who open each day's sessions with a prayer, exemptions from state property taxes for houses of worship, "In God We Trust" on the coinage (since the Civil War), and yes, even opening of the sessions of the Supreme Court with the invocation "God save the United States and this Honorable Court."

This religious tradition of ours has consistently affirmed a national belief in God—but not a national belief in a particular religion. That has been the key distinction: between official encouragement of religion, which was always practiced, and official favoritism of particular religious sects, which was prohibited. The best exemplar of this distinctively American approach toward church and state was the greatest American of them all, the indispensable man, your first commander in chief, George Washington. When he presided over the 1787 Convention in Philadelphia that drafted the Constitution, Washington wrote home to his wife, Martha, that "this morning, I attended the Popish mass." Imagine this aristocratic Virginian attending a Roman Catholic church service. He attended, of course, in his capacity as the virtual personification of the new nation that was in the process of forming; everyone knew he would be elected president, if the Constitution-drafting project were ever a success. And he attended to demonstrate that this new nation would not favor one sect over another. This was the same extraordinary man who, in the first year of his presidency, would write a letter addressed "To the Hebrew Congregation in Newport, Rhode Island," thanking them for their letter to him and saying among other things the following:

> It is now no more that toleration is spoken of, as if it was by the indulgence of one class of people, that another enjoyed the exercise of their inherent natural rights. For happily the Government of the United States, which gives to bigotry no sanction, to persecution no assistance requires only that they who live under its protection should demean themselves as good citizens, in giving it on all occasions their effectual support.

He concludes the letter:

> May the children of the Stock of Abraham, who dwell in this land, continue to merit and enjoy the good will of the other inhabitants, while everyone shall sit in safety under his own vine and fig tree, and there shall be none to make him afraid.

May the Father of all mercies scatter light and not darkness in our paths, and make us all in our several vocations useful here, and in his own due time and way everlastingly happy.

This long American tradition of official encouragement of religion, but strict neutrality among religious sects, was acknowledged by my court as recently as 1952. In a case upholding New York City's so-called "released time" program, whereby public-school children whose parents so requested were released from school early one day each week so that they might attend religious instruction programs at their churches or synagogues, the Supreme Court said the following:

> We are a religious people whose institutions presuppose a Supreme Being. . . . When the state encourages religious instruction or cooperates with religious authorities by adjusting the schedule of public events to sectarian needs, it follows the best of our traditions. For it then respects the religious nature of our people and accommodates the public service to their spiritual needs. . . . The government must be neutral when it comes to competition between sects. . . . It may not coerce anyone to attend church, to observe a religious holiday, or to take religious instruction. But it can close its doors or suspend its operations as to those who want to repair to their religious sanctuary for worship or instruction.

That opinion for the Court was written, by the way, by William O. Douglas, hardly one of the more conservative justices.

Why, then, do I say that our national tradition of public religiousness is imperiled? Because many people, particularly opinion leaders, no longer believe what Justice Douglas wrote, but rather espouse the view that the government must be scrupulously impartial, not merely as between various religious sects and denominations, but even as between religion in general and atheism. The Constitution, these people believe, forbids government from bestowing any special favor upon religion, even if it is done in a nonsectarian fashion. How serious the situation is may become apparent when I tell you that these people include (insofar as one can tell from the cases) a majority of the justices of the Supreme Court. For the Court has explicitly abandoned Justice Douglas's approach and has demanded a scrupulously secular state. In a 1968 opinion, for example, the Court said the following:

> Government in our democracy, state and national, must be neutral in matters of religious theory, doctrine, and practice. . . . The First Amendment mandates governmental neutrality between religion and religion, and between religion and nonreligion.

That position—mandated neutrality between religion and nonreligion—is where the Court's jurisprudence in theory remains today. It was the basis, for example, for the Court's striking down in 1989 a Texas statute (which had counterparts in the laws of many other states) that exempted from state sales tax the sales of doctrinal religious publications—Bibles, Korans, and Talmuds. It was unconstitutional, the Court held, thus to favor religious belief.

I dissented from that opinion, because I do not believe in the principle of neutrality between religion and nonreligion on which it is based. Indeed, it seems to me that the First Amendment itself is a repudiation of that principle, since the Free Exercise Clause gives special favor to the free exercise of religion. The neutrality principle is also contradicted by the many national practices, dating back to the earliest times, which I have described earlier.

The Court has changed its position on this matter once—and hopefully will change it back once again. Indeed, to put it that way makes the Court's current jurisprudence sound much more logical than it in fact is—since the Court has continued to approve practices that are flatly inconsistent with the new principle of "neutrality between religion and nonreligion." It has approved, for example, the longstanding practice of legislative chaplains who open sessions of both state and federal legislatures with nondenominational prayers. And it has approved property-tax exemptions for church property. If you can figure out how these holdings are consistent with the principle that religion in general cannot be favored, you are sharper than I am.

If I were you, I would not look to Supreme Court opinions to figure out our national tradition on matters of this sort. A good person to look to, in this as in many other matters, is your first commander in chief. I will conclude with a few of his more prominent pronouncements, and you can judge for yourself whether he thought we somehow had to suppress the notion that we were a nation under God.

On November 2, 1783, at Rock Hill, near Princeton, New Jersey, Washington issued his Farewell Orders to the bulk of the armies of the United States, which the Continental Congress had released from federal service. In the concluding paragraph of those orders he offered to the departing troops "his recommendations to their grateful country, and his prayers to the God of Armies. May ample justice be done them here, and may the choicest of heaven's favours, both here and hereafter, attend those who, under divine auspices, have secured innumerable blessings for others." About a month and a half later, on December 23, Washington addressed the Continental Congress at Annapolis on resigning his commission. The next-to-last sentence of his brief address was this: "I consider it an indispensable duty to close this last solemn act of my Official life, by commending the Interests of our dearest Country to the protection of Almighty God, and those who have the superintendence of them, to his holy keeping." One of the congressmen present reported that as he spoke the words "our dearest Country to the protection of Almighty God" his voice "faltered and sank and the whole house felt his agitations." He rode on horseback that day for Mount Vernon; he came up the driveway lined by trees that he had planted, Martha standing in the doorway, on Christmas Eve.

Washington left us another famous Farewell Address, the one he gave to all the citizens of the republic on September 19, 1796, when he advised them of his resolution not to stand for a third term as president. That lengthy address had something quite specific to say about his view of the relationship between religion and politics:

> Of all the dispositions and habits which lead to political prosperity, Religion and morality are indispensable supports. In vain would that man claim the tribute of Patriotism, who should labour to subvert these great Pillars of human happiness, these firmest props of the duties of Men and citizens. The mere Politician, equally with the pious man ought to respect and to cherish them. A volume could not trace all their connections with private and public felicity. Let it simply be asked where is the security for property, for reputation, for life, if the sense of religious obligation *desert* the oaths, which are the instruments of investigation in Courts of Justice? And let us with caution indulge the supposition, that morality can be maintained without religion. Whatever may be conceded to the influence of refined education on minds of peculiar structure, reason and experience both forbid us to expect that National morality can prevail in exclusion of religious principle.

Finally, as a stellar example of what I mean by the religious faith central to our American political tradition, and also as the most appropriate conclusion imaginable to this prayer breakfast, let me read President Washington's and the nation's first Thanksgiving proclamation, issued in the Capitol of New York on October 3, 1789:

> Whereas it is the duty of all Nations to acknowledge the providence of Almighty God, to obey his will, to be grateful for his benefits, and humbly to implore his protection and favor—and whereas both Houses of Congress have by their joint Committee requested me "to recommend to the People of the United States a day of public thanksgiving and prayer to be observed by acknowledging with grateful hearts the many signal favors of Almighty God especially by affording them an opportunity

peaceably to establish a form of government for their safety and happiness."

Now therefore I do recommend and assign Thursday the 26th day of November next to be devoted by the People of these States to the service of that great and glorious Being, who is the beneficent Author of all the good that was, that is, or that will be—That we may then all unite in rendering unto him our sincere and humble thanks—for his kind care and protection of the People of this Country previous to their becoming a Nation—for the signal and manifold mercies, and the favorable interpositions of his Providence which we experienced in the course and conclusion of the late war—for the great degree of tranquillity, union, and plenty which we have since enjoyed—for the peaceable and rational manner, in which we have been enabled to establish constitutions of government for our safety and happiness, and particularly the national One now lately instituted—for the civil and religious liberty with which we are blessed; and the means we have of acquiring and diffusing useful knowledge; and in general for all the great and various favors which he hath been pleased to confer upon us.

And also that we may then unite in most humbly offering our prayers and supplications to the great Lord and Ruler of Nations and beseech Him to pardon our national and other transgressions—to enable us all, whether in public or private stations, to perform our several and relative duties properly and punctually—to render our national government a blessing to all the people, by constantly being a Government of wise, just, and constitutional laws, discreetly and faithfully executed and obeyed—to protect and guide all Sovereigns and Nations (especially such as have shewn kindness unto us) and to bless them with good government, peace, and concord—to promote the knowledge and practice of true religion and virtue, and the encrease of science among them and us—and generally to grant unto all Mankind such a degree of temporal prosperity as he alone knows to be best.

CHARACTER

Justice Scalia delivered this speech to Langley High School's class of 1994, which included his son Christopher. He delivered versions of this speech elsewhere, most recently at his granddaughter's high school graduation in 2015.

———

One of the professional conveniences of being a justice of the Supreme Court is having the assistance of four talented law clerks; and one of the professional luxuries is being located right next door to the Library of Congress. When I was invited to give this address, I made use of both these advantages to get some research done on the subject of commencement speeches. The results, I am sorry to say, are disappointing. I have learned that since the first formal institution of learning, the University of Bologna, was founded some nine hundred years ago, there have been exactly six million commencement addresses. Of those six million, approximately five and a half million have been too long, four million have been too pompous, and two million have been wrong. But those statistics are not as bad as they seem, because—and for this I have the precise figure—of the 6 million, exactly 5,999,999 have been forgotten.

The one that has not been forgotten, of course, is the one I gave at the Langley High School graduation six years ago, when my son Paul was in the graduating class. And that has made it necessary for me to write another. It's some trouble to write a graduation address, particularly this time of year when the Court is trying to finish the last cases on its docket to adjourn by July. But as my wife reminded me when I was muttering about having to prepare this talk the other night, there are two enormous advantages that make it all worthwhile. The first, of course, is that if you are the graduation speaker you do not have to listen to somebody else. And the second is that you make sure the speech will be brief. This latter advantage is one that I can share with all of you—and I intend to do so.

There is one genre of graduation address that talks about some matter of national or international importance: the need to use the environment responsibly, the war in Bosnia, the need for a strong national defense, etc. I have some subjects like that up my sleeve—for example, the need for a democratic society not to expect the Constitution to make all its important decisions. But on this occasion, which can be regarded, I suppose, as the last lecture you will ever attend at Langley High School, I thought I would talk (briefly) about something more important: yourselves. For devotion to these grand global causes—war and peace, the environment, world hunger, feminism, even patriotism—becomes for many of us an exciting escape from the routine and difficult duties and responsibilities of our own private lives. Like the lady in Dickens (I don't recall her name now, but I'm sure one of your teachers does) who is so wrapped up in running the activities of the Child Welfare League that her own children are a bunch of little monsters, ill behaved, ill kempt, ill fed, and ill cared for. We have all known—or if you teenagers have not, you soon will—the person whose eyes are ablaze with energy and zeal to save the nation or the world, and whose private life is a shambles of opportunities neglected and responsibilities disregarded.

So first things first. I will speak to you—briefly—this afternoon not about the world but about yourselves. About what Langley has provided to make each of you a better, more perfect, and hence more happy individual and about what you can hope to acquire in the future that will continue that process. The first thing that comes to mind which Langley has given you is, of course, knowledge. Certainly you've spent the last four years cramming your heads full of that—or, for those of you who regard it as a more passive exercise, your teachers have spent the last four years trying to cram your heads full of that. Knowledge is good. Unless I am mistaken, almost all the Langley graduates before me have not yet gotten their fill of that commodity, and intend to go on to college for more of it—if not immediately, then at least eventually. Since I tend to be a rather contrary character, however, I do not intend to praise knowledge and learning. I don't intend to run them down, either, but I do want to get you to put them in proper perspective.

Let us consider the subject of knowledge and learning in the context of the Founders of our country. Those men included, as you may recall, some extraordinarily brilliant intellects, who had received college degrees in an era when few persons, even among the rich, did so. James Madison and William Patterson had BAs from Princeton (and Patterson an MA); John Jay had a degree from King's College (now Columbia), and Alexander Hamilton was attending that college when the war interrupted. Jefferson, of course, had his BA from William and Mary, and James Wilson his BA from St. Andrew's University in Scotland. But who was the unquestioned leader of that brilliant circle of men—the one whom all consulted, whose advice all heeded, whose mere presence seemingly overawed them all? It was, of course, George Washington, who was no dummy, but who had little formal education. Around him, I have no doubt, the likes of Jefferson and Hamilton could do intellectual cartwheels. Yet somehow, for whatever reason, this was a man who commanded their respect as no other did.

So there are some qualities, whatever they are, that must be added to knowledge and learning insofar as leadership abilities are concerned. That is not to say that knowledge and learning are unimportant; but they are not alone enough. But of course you should all have figured that out already. Surely you all know—not in this class, I am sure, but in some other classes at Langley—the disembodied "brain." The student who knows absolutely everything in the books, but you wouldn't trust him to take the dog for a walk without getting lost.

One of those qualities that must be added to knowledge and learning to make a truly outstanding human being is called judgment. Judgment is the difference between a wise person, and the person who, as the saying goes, knows the price of everything and the value of nothing. It is possible to be enormously erudite, and to have no judgment at all—and, contrariwise, it is possible to have enormously good judgment and be poorly educated. If it comes to a choice between the two, go for judgment. That is why we do not require a college degree, or even a high school degree, for voting. And it is why one smart-aleck political commentator once remarked that he would sooner be governed by the first fifty names in the Boston telephone book than by the faculty of Harvard.

No one has described the importance of judgment more powerfully—and more accurately—than William Penn. Remember William Penn? We all of us know him as a great American figure, but have never read anything he said. Well, this is the only one of his sayings you will ever have to know—and the only part of this graduation address you will ever have to remember. Penn wrote, in a book of philosophy and proverbs called *Some Fruits of Solitude*:

> Knowledge is the Treasure, but Judgment the Treasurer of a Wise Man. He that has more Knowledge than Judgment, is made for another Man's use more than his own.

And don't we all know people like that, who are smart but (in the vernacular) simple tools. Made for someone else's use. These people lack judgment.

So, we have identified one quality that must be added to knowledge to make a great human being: judgment. Is there anything else? There must be. Just as knowledge does not make us wise, so also knowledge does not make us virtuous. It always surprises me that so many people, in this century of all others, should think otherwise—should believe that education will, alone and automatically, produce goodness and virtue. The greatest possible disproof of that thesis is the horror of Nazism, which possessed not the dullest nation in the world but the brightest. You have missed the greatest lesson of the twentieth century if you have not appreciated that Germany was, at the time Adolf Hitler took it over, the envy and the model of the world in all matters of mind and culture. It was the leader in the physical sciences, in medicine, in music, in archaeology, in philosophy, in art, in education. What the Third Reich teaches is that knowledge is not virtue.

There are probably many different names for this quality that enables a smart person to be a good person—and an educated nation to be a good nation (for never forget that the whole is the sum of its parts). Let us call this quality character. My father, who was a college professor and therefore had the utmost respect for the value of knowledge and learning, used to impress upon me the importance of character this way. (And this, by the way, is the second and last thing in this talk that I insist you remember: just William Penn and my dad.) Brains, he said, can be hired by the hour, just like muscles. Only character is not for sale at any price.

If I may advert to the Founding Fathers again: one of the reasons that generation of Americans was so great, one of the reasons they got our republic off to such a fine start, is that they were constantly emphasizing the importance of character and of virtue— not only for the individual, but for the society at large. In George Washington's Farewell Address, you may recall, he called religion and morality two "great pillars of human happiness," which were indispensable to "private and public felicity." Pretty preachy stuff. Can you imagine a modern American president, when leaving office, speaking of such moral matters?

Or consider Washington's first Thanksgiving Proclamation, in October of 1789. I have always been impressed with the last line, because it shows character. Nowadays, we would hope or (if religious) pray for prosperity. Washington's last prayer in his proclamation was that God "grant unto all mankind"—not prosperity—but "such a degree of temporal prosperity as he alone knows to be best." In other words, too much prosperity might not be a good thing, and if not we should not have it. What a virtuous thought.

So there are, then, these three qualities. I would call them the triad of human perfection. Knowledge, and Judgment, and

Character. I have spoken to you about them because I want to warn you that up until now you have been receiving the second two imperceptibly and automatically—and that process is about to come to an end. You have learned judgment and character at home, whether you realize it or not: by example and by correction. And you have learned them at school, because even if the days of the McGuffey Reader are gone, many of your studies, from lower school up until now—from the story of the three little pigs to your American history course—have been selected for what they taught you about judgment and character. And your teachers have taken the formation of judgment and character to be part of their task.

There was a time when that process continued even in college—when institutions of higher learning undertook some responsibility for forming the judgment and the character of their students. In our colonial days, to revert to that theme: when Thomas Jefferson founded the University of Virginia he provided (though he was hardly a religious man) for ministers to be part of the faculty. As recently as my own college days—which, it may be difficult for you young people to appreciate, were much more than midway between Thomas Jefferson and now—we had required curriculums that were meant to convey much more than knowledge, and disciplinary sanctions for infractions of what the colleges thought to be sound morality, rather than political correctness.

At most institutions, all that is gone. You may perhaps applaud the change—in fact I have no doubt you will applaud it—and it is not my purpose to criticize it. But my purpose is to tell you this: You will automatically be provided with a lot more knowledge in your coming college years, but you will be pretty much on your own to get judgment and character. You will have to develop those qualities for yourselves—by what subjects you choose to study; what reading you choose to do outside of class; what extracurricular activities you choose to engage in; what adult advisers or counselors you seek out or permit to seek you out; and, of course, what friends you choose to make. I hope you will bear in mind the need to take control of that part of your lives yourselves. Your parents will no longer be there to see to it; your teachers will no longer consider it part of their responsibility. But don't neglect it your-selves. Unless you increase, in equal measure with your knowl-edge, your judgment and character, you will fail in the only thing that is really important, and from which all else follows. You will not be making yourself the best person you can be.

Right and Left

Speaking at the Pontifical Gregorian University in Rome in May 1996, Justice Scalia posed and addressed the question, "Is the political philosophy of the left or of the right more compatible with the public good?"

————

If there was ever a topic that cried out for a definition of terms, it is this one. "Right" and "left," "right wing" and "left wing" are terms that have virtually no fixed meaning in American political discourse, except that they all connote (as they do not in European political discourse) a degree of extremism. In America, both categories of term are pejorative. Thus, we have in American political commentary that familiar villain, the "right-wing extremist"; and, more recently, that ominous political force, the "Christian right." The terms "left-wing extremist" and "Christian left" would have similar overtones of foreboding if they were ever used by the American media—but they are not, which is an interesting phenomenon.

Once one gets beyond their pejorative content, it is hard to pin down the meaning of "right" and "left" in American political usage. Sometimes they are used to denote, respectively, statists and libertarians—those who favor strong and authoritarian government versus those who favor a high degree of individual freedom. In this sense, Richard Nixon would be a man of the Right and Eugene McCarthy a man of the Left. But if that were the only meaning of the terms, both Augusto Pinochet and Fidel Castro would have to be referred to as right-wingers. A second, quite different, connotation of the terms uses them to distinguish between laissez-faire capitalists and socialists. This is not only different from, it is sometimes the opposite of, the first connotation—since those who favor a high degree of individual freedom in other matters often favor a high degree of individual freedom in economic matters as well. Thus, the American Libertarian Party is a party of the Left under the first connotation, and a party of the Right under the second.

Yet a third meaning of "right" and "left" is much more relativistic: it draws a distinction between those who favor the *status quo* and those who favor change—between conservatives and progressives. Since over most of the past century change has been moving from a *status quo* of capitalism toward socialism, this third connotation tends to produce the same results as the second—Castro can be called a man of the Left in both these senses. But if and when the tide of history moves in reverse, the equivalence between the two connotations disappears. The old-line Communists in Russia, who resist the change toward democracy and capitalism, are referred to in the American press (believe it or not) as the "Right." And finally, "right" and "left" may connote a distinction between nationalism and one-worldism. This may be merely one aspect of the first connotation I mentioned: those who favor a strong, authoritarian government are ordinarily nationalists. But it really must be an entirely separate connotation, since I can think of no other basis for calling Nazis a party of the Right and Communists a party of the Left. They are both authoritarian, they are both socialist, and they are both untraditional; but the Communists are internationalists.

For purposes of my remarks today, I am assuming the second meaning of "right" and "left," the meaning that refers to the difference between capitalism and socialism. I take that approach in part because that probably comes closest to the meaning of the terms in European political discourse, and thus is more likely to be what the conveners of this conference had in mind; and in part because that is the only one of the dichotomies I have mentioned that is the subject of widespread current debate. In the waning years of the twentieth century, few have been urging a return to authoritarianism, vigorous nationalism, or traditionalism, whereas capitalism has made something of a comeback.

I must make a second clarification about the subject of my remarks. I have chosen to interpret "the common good" to mean "the Christian common good." Thus, I take that system to be conducive to the common good which is conducive to virtue (as Christianity understands virtue) and sanctification. I assume that this is the meaning of the common good that the organizers of the conference had in mind—the Gregorianum being, as I understand it, a school of theology and not of government or economics.

Having fully defined my topic, the first thing I wish to say about it is that I do not believe in it. That is to say, I do not believe that a Christian ought to choose his form of government on the basis of which will be most conducive to his faith, any more than he ought to choose a toothpaste on that basis. To be sure, there are certain prohibitions. A Christian should not support a government that suppresses the faith, or one that sanctions the taking of innocent human life—just as a Christian should not wear immodest clothes. But the test of good government, like the test of good tailoring, is assuredly *not* whether it helps you save your soul. Government is not meant for saving souls, but for protecting life and property and assuring the conditions for physical prosperity. Its responsibility is the here, not the hereafter—and the needs of the two sometimes diverge. It may well be, for example, that a governmental system which keeps its citizens in relative poverty will produce more saints. (The rich, as Christ said, have a harder time getting to heaven.) But that would be a bad government, nonetheless. This recognition of the separate spheres of church and state is not just the teaching of the First Amendment to the United States Constitution. It is also, I think, the teaching of Jesus Christ—who spoke of rendering to Caesar the things that are Caesar's and is not recorded as having indicated any preference about government, except one: He did not want the people to make *Him* king.

If I were to engage in the search for the form of government most conducive to Christianity, however, I would certainly not settle upon the candidate that seems to have such a great attraction for modern Catholic thinkers: socialism. It is hard to understand that attraction. Surely it does not rest upon the teachings of experience. I know of no country in which the churches have grown fuller as the governments have moved leftward. The churches of Europe are empty. The most religious country in the West by all standards—belief in God, church membership, church attendance—is that bastion of capitalism least diluted by socialism, the United States.

When I say least diluted by socialism, you must understand that I say it in a modern context, in which we are all socialists. In the United States, that battle was fought and decided with the New Deal. No one, even in the most conservative quarters of American society, now denies that there should be a so-called "safety net" provided by the government for our citizens. The only real argument is over how many services that safety net should provide, and how poor one must be in order to qualify. Few of us even understand, anymore, what a truly non-socialist mentality was like. I happened to encounter it, by accident, when I was a young law professor, doing research for an article on sovereign immunity— the legal doctrine that says that a state cannot be sued without its consent. I came across a debate in the Massachusetts legislature, during the eighteenth century, concerning a proposed bill that would provide compensation to a woman who had been seriously injured through the negligence of one of the agents of the state—a policeman, or a fireman, or whatever. Those members of the Massachusetts legislature opposing the legislation argued that they *had no right*—that it was *morally wrong*—to use public funds for private benefit, for a purpose that did not benefit the public at large. Because of the doctrine of sovereign immunity, they argued, the Commonwealth of Massachusetts owed this woman nothing in law, and to agree to pay her, out of public funds, money that was not legally owed was in effect to use public funds for a private gift, which (they said) was wrong. And this, I point out, was a woman *who had been injured* by the commonwealth; you can imagine what their attitude would have been toward dispensing public funds to the poor!

In the United States, a remnant of that non-socialist attitude lasted into the present century. Our federal Constitution, you may recall, gives Congress, not a general power to expend funds, but only the power to expend funds "for the general welfare." Until the triumph of the New Deal, there were many who thought that prohibited the expenditure of funds for any private assistance. Neither to the rich, nor to the poor. But that fight, as I have said, is over. We now believe that any expenditure for any citizen is an expenditure for the general welfare—whether to the poor, such as food-stamp recipients; or to the middle class or even fairly well-to-do, such as the victims of a tornado in Florida; or even to the downright rich, such as shareholders of Chrysler Corporation. All of these are now regarded as entirely proper objects of the state's beneficence.

The allure of socialism for the Christian, I think, is that it means well; it is, or appears to be, altruistic. It promises assistance from the state for the poor, and public provision of all the necessities of life, from maternity care to geriatric care, and from kindergarten through university. Capitalism, on the other hand, promises nothing from the state except the opportunity to succeed or fail. Adam Smith points unabashedly to the fact that the baker does not provide bread out of the goodness of his heart, but for profit. How uninspiring. Yet if you reflect upon it, you will see that the socialistic message is not necessarily Christian, and the capitalist message not necessarily non-Christian. The issue is not whether there should be provision for the poor, but rather the degree to which that provision should be made through the coercive power of the state. Christ said, after all, that you should give *your* goods to the poor, not that you should force someone else to give *his*.

Bear in mind that in this discussion I am not arguing about whether socialism is good or bad *as a system of government*. If private charity does not suffice to meet the needs of the poor, or if we do not want the poor to have to regard themselves as the objects of charity, or if we even wish to go beyond merely assisting the poor and want to redistribute the wealth of the rich to the middle class, socialism may be a better way to meet worldly needs. But that can be decided on the economic and secular merits of the matter. The question I am asking is whether Christian faith must incline us toward that system, and the answer, I think, is no. Christ did not preach "a chicken in every pot," or "the elimination of poverty in our lifetime"; those are worldly, governmental goals. If they were His objectives, He certainly devoted little of His time and talent to achieving them—feeding the hungry multitudes only a couple of times, as I recall, and running away from the crowds who wanted to put Him on the throne, where He would have had an opportunity to engage in some real redistribution of wealth. His message was not the need to eliminate hunger, or misery, or misfortune, but rather the need for each individual to love and help the hungry, the miserable, and the unfortunate. To the extent the state takes upon itself one of the corporal works of mercy that could and would have been undertaken privately, it deprives individuals of an opportunity for sanctification and deprives the body of Christ of an occasion for the interchange of love among its members.

I wonder to what extent the decimation of women's religious orders throughout the West is attributable to the governmentalization of charity. Consider how many orphanages, hospitals, schools, and homes for the elderly were provided by orders of nuns. They are almost all gone; the state provides or pays for these services. Even purely individual charity must surely have been affected. What need for me to give a beggar a handout? Do I not pay taxes for government food stamps and municipally run shelters and soup kitchens? The man asking me for a dollar probably wants it for liquor. There is, of course, neither any love nor any merit in the taxes I pay for those services; I pay them under compulsion.

The governmentalization of charity affects not just the donor but also the recipient. What was once asked as a favor is now demanded as an entitlement. When I was young, there used to be an expression applied to a lazy person: "He thinks the world owes him a living." But the teaching of welfare socialism is that the world does owe everyone a living. This belief must affect the character of welfare recipients—and not, I suggest, for the better. Or at least not for the better in the distinctively Christian view of things. Christ's special love for the poor was attributable to one quality that they possessed in abundance: meekness and humility. It is humbling to be an object of charity—which is why mendicant nuns and friars used to beg. The transformation of charity into legal entitlement has produced both donors without love and recipients without gratitude.

It has also produced a change in the product that is distributed. Most particularly, and most relevantly for purposes of the present discussion, social services distributed by the state in my country, for example, cannot be intermingled with Christian teaching, or even (increasingly) with Christian morality. They do not say the Angelus in public orphanages; there are no crucifixes on the walls of public hospitals; and the Ten Commandments are not posted in public schools. The religiously driven and religiously funded social welfare movements of the nineteenth century sought to achieve not merely the alleviation of poverty and hardship, but also what was called moral uplift. Of course that is no part of the function of state-administered social welfare today. The state-paid social worker, whose job is to see to the distribution of welfare funds to those who are legally entitled to them, is not—cannot legally be—concerned with improving not only the diet but also the virtue of her "clients" (which is the coldly commercial terminology that welfare bureaucracies use). It is quite simply none of her business.

Perhaps the clearest effects of the expansion of the state accompanied by the contraction of the church are to be found in the field of primary and secondary education. A relatively small proportion of Americans are nowadays educated in religious schools; Catholic schools are much less numerous than they were in mid-century. As the costs of primary and secondary education have risen, it has become very difficult for churches to run a system competitive with the tax-funded public schools. Simultaneously, litigation has caused the public schools to eliminate all religiously doctrinal materials from their curriculum. That is good and proper under our American system, which forbids the official establishment of any sect. But the nonsectarian state's increasing monopoly over primary and secondary education can hardly be considered beneficial to Christianity. Whereas such overtly religious texts as *The Pilgrim's Progress* were once the staple of the American schoolchild's education, religious instruction, if received at all, is obtained one evening a week in confraternity classes, or on Sunday. In more recent years, as society has become more and more diverse in its views on morality, the state's control of education deprives children not only of Catholic doctrine, but even of essentially Catholic moral formation. Schools distribute condoms, provide advice on birth control and abortion, and teach that homosexuality must not be regarded as shameful or abnormal. Again, it is not my place or my purpose to criticize these developments, only to observe that they do not suggest that expanding the role of government is good for Christianity.

Finally, I may mention that even the seeming Christian virtue of socialism—that it *means* well and seeks to help the poor—may be greatly exaggerated. It is true in the United States, and I believe it is true in all of the Western democracies, that the vast bulk of social spending does not go to the poor, but rather to the middle class (which also happens to be the class most numerous at the polls). The most expensive entitlement programs, Social Security and Medicare, for example, overwhelmingly benefit those who are not in dire financial straits. So one may plausibly argue that welfare-state democracy does not really have even the Christian virtue of altruism. The majority does not say to the rich, "Give your money to the poor," but rather, "Give your money to us."

Just as I believe the Left is not necessarily endowed with Christian virtue, so also I believe the Right is not necessarily bereft of it. Laissez-faire capitalism, like socialism, speaks to the degree of involvement of the state in the economic life of the society. Like socialism also, it does not speak to the nature of the human soul. There have been greedy and avaricious capitalists, but there have also been generous and considerate ones; just as there have been altruistic and self-deprecating socialists, but have also been brutal and despotic ones. The cardinal sin of capitalism is greed; but the cardinal sin of socialism is power. I am not sure there is a clear choice between those evils.

While I would not argue that capitalism as an economic system is inherently more Christian than socialism (so long as we are talking about a form of socialism that permits the acquisition and ownership of property), it does seem to me that capitalism is more *dependent* upon Christianity than socialism is. For in order for capitalism to work—in order for it to produce a good and a stable society—the Christian virtues are essential. Since in the capitalist system each individual has more freedom of action, each individual also has more opportunity to do evil. Without widespread practice of such Christian virtues as honesty, self-denial, and charity toward others, a capitalist system will be intolerable.

Let me conclude as I began, with a disclaimer: the burden of my remarks is not that a government of the Right is more Christlike, only that there is no reason to believe that a government of the Left is. To tell you the truth, I do not think Christ cares very much what sort of economic or political system we live under. He certainly displayed little interest in that subject during His time among us—as did His apostles. Accordingly, we should select our economic and political systems on the basis of what seems to produce the greatest material good for the greatest number, and leave theology out of it. The minimum wage, for example—which is a current political issue in Washington—is a good or a bad idea depending upon whether it produces good or bad economic consequences. It has nothing to do with the Kingdom of God.

THE HOLOCAUST

On May 8, 1997, the annual Days of Remembrance commemoration for victims of the Holocaust was held in the Rotunda of the U.S. Capitol. Justice Scalia gave the principal address at the ceremony.

———

Distinguished members of the United States Senate and House of Representatives; members of the Diplomatic Corps; survivors of the Holocaust; ladies and gentlemen:

I was profoundly honored to have been invited to speak at this annual ceremony in remembrance of those consumed in the Holocaust. But it is not, I must tell you, an easy assignment for a non-Jew to undertake. I am an outsider speaking to an ancient people about a tragedy of unimaginable proportions that is intensely personal to them. I have no memories of parents or children, uncles or cousins caught up in and destroyed by the horror. I have not even that distinctive appreciation of evil that must come from knowing that six million people were killed for no other reason than that they had blood like mine running in their veins.

More difficult still, I am not only not a Jew, but I am a Christian, and I know that the anti-Semitism of many of my uncomprehending co-religionists, over many centuries, helped set the stage for the mad tragedy that the National Socialists produced. I say uncomprehending co-religionists, not only because my religion teaches that it is wrong to hate anyone, but because it is particularly absurd for a Christian to hate the people of Israel. That is to hate one's spiritual parents, and to sever one's roots.

When I was a young man in college, spending my junior year

abroad, I saw Dachau. Later, in the year after I graduated from law school, I saw Auschwitz. I will of course never forget the impression they made upon me. If some playwright or novelist had invented such a tale of insanity and diabolical cruelty, it would not be believed. But it did happen. The one message I want to convey today is that you will have missed the most frightening aspect of it all, if you do not appreciate that it happened in one of the most educated, most progressive, most cultured countries in the world.

The Germany of the late 1920s and early 1930s was a world leader in most fields of art, science, and intellect. Berlin was a center of theater; with the assistance of the famous producer Max Reinhardt, playwrights and composers of the caliber of Bertolt Brecht and Kurt Weill flourished. Berlin had three opera houses, and Germany as a whole no less than eighty. Every middle-sized city had its own orchestra. German poets and writers included Hermann Hesse, Stefan George, Leonhard Frank, Franz Kafka, and Thomas Mann, who won the Nobel Prize for Literature in 1929. In architecture, Germany was the cutting edge, with Gropius and the Bauhaus school. It boasted painters like Paul Klee and Oskar Schlemmer. Musical composers like Anton Webern, Alban Berg, Arnold Schoenberg, and Paul Hindemith. Conductors like Otto Klemperer, Bruno Walter, Erich Kleiber, and Wilhelm Furtwängler. And in science, of course, the Germans were preeminent. To quote a recent article in the *Journal of the American Medical Association*:

> In 1933, when the National Socialist Party came to power in Germany, the biomedical enterprise in that country was among the most sophisticated in the world. German contributions to biochemistry, physiology, medicine, surgery, and public health, as well as to clinical training, had shaped to an important degree the academic and practice patterns of the time, and clinical training and research experience in the great German clinics and laboratories had been widely sought for decades by physicians and basic scientists from around the world.

To fully grasp the horror of the Holocaust, you must imagine (for it probably happened) that the commandant of Auschwitz or Dachau, when he had finished his day's work, retired to his apartment to eat a meal that was in the finest good taste, and then to listen, perhaps, to some tender and poignant lieder of Franz Schubert.

This aspect of the matter is perhaps so prominent in my mind because I am undergoing, currently, the task of selecting a college for the youngest of my children—or perhaps more accurately, trying to help her select it. How much stock we place in education, intellect, cultural refinement! And how much of our substance we are prepared to expend to give our children the very best opportunity to acquire education, intellect, cultural refinement! Yet those qualities are of only secondary importance—to our children, and to the society that their generation will create. I am reminded of words written by John Henry Newman long before the Holocaust could even be imagined.

> Knowledge is one thing, virtue is another; good sense is not conscience, refinement is not humility. . . . Liberal Education makes . . . the gentleman. It is well to be a gentleman, it is well to have a cultivated intellect, a delicate taste, a candid, equitable, dispassionate mind, a noble and courteous bearing in the conduct of life;—These are the connatural qualities of a large knowledge; they are the objects of a university. . . . [B]ut . . . they are no guarantee for sanctity or even for conscientiousness; they may attach to the man of the world, to the profligate, to the heartless.

Yes, to the heartless.

It is the purpose of these annual Holocaust remembrances—as it is the purpose of the nearby Holocaust museum—not only to honor the memory of the six million Jews and three or four million other poor souls caught up in this twentieth-century terror, but also, by keeping the memory of their tragedy painfully alive, to prevent its happening again. The latter can be achieved only by acknowledging, and passing on to our children, the existence of absolute, uncompromisable standards of human conduct. Mankind has traditionally derived such standards from religion; and the West has derived them from and through the Jews. Those absolute and uncompromisable standards of human conduct will not endure without an effort to make them endure, and it is to that enterprise that we rededicate ourselves today. They are in the Decalogue, and they are in the question put and answered by Micah: "What doth the Lord require of thee, but to do justly, to love mercy, and to walk humbly with thy God."

For those six million Jews to whom it was not done justly, who were shown no mercy, and for whom God and his laws were abandoned: may we remember their sufferings, and may they rest in peace.

ON HEROES
AND FRIENDS

"It is the greatest curse of advancing years that our world contracts, as friends who cannot be replaced, with insights into life that are not elsewhere available to us, leave us behind."

GEORGE WASHINGTON

In June 2004, the custodians of George Washington's Mount Vernon estate broke ground on a new museum and presidential library. Helping to mark the occasion, Justice Scalia praised his favorite Founding Father. Scalia drew from various biographies in presenting his account of Washington the Virginian.

———

We have gathered here tonight at Mount Vernon to celebrate the lord of the manor, George Washington. A man who has been called the Father of his Country. A man who served as our first president and against whom all other presidents are measured. He bore us through the violent birth of our nation and presided over the creation of the Constitution, a document that my court still interprets on occasion.

But I am not here to talk to you about those aspects of Washington that won him fame at the national level. I will not be talking about General Washington, for example. For if I were to do that, I would quickly take up all my allotted time. I think we all agree that he is properly numbered among the greatest generals in American history, not only for the types of daring tactics that brought victory in New Jersey and Yorktown, but also for his iron will that held together an army whose status waffled between desperate and dire. A general who, unlike so many that came before, *voluntarily* relinquished the power with which his people entrusted him. His other qualities testify to his great leadership, but it is that last fact, perhaps more than any other, that shows his love of the republic.

Nor am I going to discuss Washington the president. By the end of his two terms, the United States was at last a nation. And, it bears mention, he *voluntarily* declined to seek a third term, preferring instead to return here to the comforting shadow of his vine and fig tree.[*]

What I am going to talk about is George Washington as a Virginian. It seems appropriate, standing here at his home in the commonwealth, to discuss the life George Washington led on this local stage.

George Washington was, of course, the first Virginian to become president. His commonwealth coattails were quite long, for his fellow Virginians Thomas Jefferson, James Madison, and James Monroe followed in his footsteps shortly thereafter. (I do not, of course, forget the intervening four years of John Adams's presidency. The length of *his* commonwealth coattails will be measured this November.) In fact, Virginia has produced more presidents than any other state—eight native-born Virginians have served as president, out of a total of forty-three. My own native New Jersey has produced only one president, Grover Cleveland, although, thanks to Benjamin Harrison's intervening presidency, I may double-count him since he served as both the twenty-second and twenty-fourth president. It is thus to Washington that Virginia owes, at least in part, one of its nicknames—"mother of presidents." One of its other nicknames—the "birthplace of a nation"—is also directly attributable to him.

Washington was born on Pope's Creek plantation in Westmoreland County on February 22, 1732, to Augustine Washington and his second wife, Mary Ball Washington. (Washington was actually born on February 11, but in 1751 Great Britain changed from the Julian to the Gregorian calendar, and Parliament added eleven days to make the adjustment complete.) Westmoreland County lies in the Tidewater Region of Virginia, between the Potomac and Rappahannock Rivers on a peninsula known as the Northern

---

[*] A reference to Washington's Letter to the Hebrew Congregation at Newport, quoted in full in "Only in America."

Neck. Westmoreland County was a good neighborhood; Stratford Hall, the home of the remarkable Lee family, is also located there.

When George was three, his parents moved from Westmoreland County farther up the Potomac to the plantation at Little Hunting Creek. The plantation would later be renamed Mount Vernon by George's older half-brother, Lawrence, likely in honor of Admiral Edward Vernon, with whom Lawrence had served. A few years later, the family moved again, this time to a plantation, later called the Ferry Farm, in present Stafford County, on the left bank of the Rappahannock across from Fredericksburg. When his father died in 1743, George went to live with Lawrence at Mount Vernon, where he studied arithmetic, geography, astronomy, composition, the "rules of civility," and surveying. He did not attend college.

At age seventeen, George entered the workforce and the public service. Lawrence had married into the powerful Fairfax family, and his connections with Lord Fairfax helped secure George his first job as a county surveyor. On July 20, 1749, Washington presented to the justices of the newly formed county of Culpeper a commission that appointed him county surveyor, and he took the oaths of public office for the first time in his life. Surveying required Washington to traverse some of the roughest parts of the frontier. He slept on a straw mat (which once caught fire), and, when he was lucky, he slept in a tent (which on occasion blew away in the wind).

While surveying proved a useful and lucrative occupation, it was in defense of Virginia that Washington first honed the military skills that would later win him lasting fame. George Washington's early military career was marked by equal parts valor and ambition. On December 13, 1752, George, who was not yet twenty-one, was given the rank of major by Governor Dinwiddie and appointed adjutant of the Southern District of Virginia. In 1753, hostilities between the English settlers and the French, with their Indian allies, were on the rise. Learning of French advances in the upper Ohio Valley, King George II approved construction of a series of forts and ordered Governor Dinwiddie, if either Indians or Europeans should presume to hinder building these forts, to require them "peaceably to depart" and, if they paid no heed to his message, to "drive them off by force of arms." Of course, someone had to be chosen to convey this message to the French, and, as has always been the case, there was significant peril in being the bearer of bad tidings, not only because the recipient was likely to be hostile, but also because the delivery would take the bearer to distant Lake Erie. For this difficult task, the Virginia Council turned to George Washington, who immediately accepted. Washington performed superbly, making the arduous journey with celerity, gathering information on the disposition of French forces from friendly Indians and French deserters, noting in his diary the terrain through which he passed, and delivering the message to the captain of the French fort, Fort Le Boeuf. (The French declined to withdraw.)

Washington was rewarded for his excellent performance soon thereafter when Governor Dinwiddie commissioned him a captain of the Virginia militia. Then, when the time came to raise a force to defend Virginia's borders, Washington was named second in command, and made a lieutenant colonel. Washington saw his first battle at the age of twenty-two, when he led his troops in a surprise attack against French forces near present day Farmington, Pennsylvania. Washington's troops were victorious. Washington shortly thereafter learned how to lead in defeat, when his forces were attacked at Fort Necessity and defeated by a much larger French and allied Indian force.

Needless to say, Washington served Virginia well and at great personal sacrifice. Even though suffering from serious illness, Washington insisted on leading his Virginians in battle against the French during the disastrous campaign against Fort Duquesne conducted by Major General Edward Braddock in 1755. When, ambushed by the French and their Indian allies on the Monongahela River, the regular British troops panicked and ran, Washington rallied the Virginia troops to make a stand. As he described the battle in a letter to his mother:

The Virginia Troops shew'd a good deal of Bravery, and were near all kill'd; for I believe out of 3 Companys that were there, there is scarce 30 Men left alive. . . . I luckily escap'd [without] a wound, tho' I had four Bullets through my Coat, and two Horses shot under me.

Frustrated in their efforts to dislodge the French from the Ohio Valley, the Virginia Regiment returned home. As he had led them on the offensive, Washington, now a colonel at the age of twenty-three, led them in defense of the Virginia frontier.

When Colonel Washington later resigned from military service in 1758, he returned to Mount Vernon and immersed himself in family and the world of a Virginia planter. (Mount Vernon would not actually become George's until he inherited it upon the death of Lawrence's widow, Ann, in 1761; until that time, he paid an annual rent of fifteen thousand pounds of tobacco.) George was no exception to the rule that we all marry up. On January 6, 1759, right after he resigned his commission, George married the, by the standards of that time, quite wealthy Martha Dandridge, the widow of Daniel Parke Custis. Martha's holdings, which became George's, included about fifteen thousand acres, much of it prime real estate located near Williamsburg. But perhaps the most treasured thing that Martha brought with her were two stepchildren, John Parke "Jacky" and Martha Parke "Patsy" Custis, who at the time of the marriage were six and four, respectively. George, who never had children of his own, immediately became attached to these two and lavished affection upon them.

As a planter, Washington was in his element. By this time, that being the 1760s, he could boast of substantial estates, and he would continue to expand the borders of Mount Vernon throughout his life. Six days a week, he worked hard managing the farm, sometimes even rolling up his shirtsleeves and performing manual labor, and on the seventh he rested and attended church. (Washington was a devout Episcopalian.) As for his crops, he began with tobacco, but, when that proved less profitable than desired, he added wheat. He had his own water-powered flour mill, a blacksmith shop, brick and charcoal kilns, carpenters, and masons. He also had a fishery, which produced shad, bass, and herring. He experimented in cattle breeding, kept stallions at stud, and flirted with bison farming.

If Washington worked hard, then he played hard as well. He attended picnics, barbecues, and clambakes. He greatly enjoyed dancing, fox hunting, duck hunting, fishing, cockfighting, horse racing, boat racing, and card playing. Mount Vernon was a haven for guests, where tea and cards were always at the ready. In the seven years prior to 1775, it is estimated that some two thousand guests passed through Mount Vernon, many of whom stayed for dinner and overnight. On June 30, 1785, after the Revolution, Washington wrote in his diary that he "dined with only Mrs. Washington which I believe is the first instance of it since my retirement from public life."

The hospitality of Mount Vernon and the generosity of its master were not restricted to other planters or members of the Virginia aristocracy. Washington lent sizable sums to those in financial distress, even at the risk of his own solvency. "Let the Hospitality of the House with respect to the Poor, be kept up," he instructed Lund Washington, his second cousin and the manager of his plantations. "Let no one go hungry away," and let some "money in Charity to the Amount of Forty or Fifty Pounds a Year" also be given to assist the indigent and afflicted.

Though retired from military service for the time being, Washington continued to serve the people of Virginia. From 1759 to 1775, he served in the Virginia House of Burgesses, first as a burgess from Frederick in Western Virginia, and later as a burgess from Fairfax. In his first successful election in Frederick, Washington instructed his supporters to provide entertainment to the electorate, which was successfully accomplished through 66 gallons and 10 bowls of rum punch, 58 gallons of beer, 35 gallons of wine, 8 quarts of hard cider, and 3½ pints of brandy. Upon taking his seat, Washington received an excellent appointment to the Committee of Propositions and Grievances, one of the four principal instruments of the House. And later he was appointed to the influential Committee of Privileges and Elections, and to the Committee for Religion. The legislation Washington sponsored as a burgess was of intense interest to his constituents, and probably of very little interest to anyone else. For example, one of his first projects was a bill to preserve the water supply of Winchester by preventing hogs from running at large therein.

In a time when long-winded speeches were the norm in legislative debates, George Washington mostly kept quiet, a habit that earned him the respect (and, no doubt, the appreciation) of his colleagues. Though it seems strange in this age of celebrity, Washington did not relish the spotlight. In his first year as a burgess, Washington was honored by the General Assembly for his military service to Virginia. By order of the Assembly, Speaker Robinson delivered a speech praising Washington. When the speech was over, Washington rose to give his thanks for the honor, but was so tongue-tied that he was unable to articulate a single word. When it appeared that Washington could not make reply, the Speaker gracefully interjected: "Sit down, Mr. Washington, your modesty equals your valor, and that surpasses the power of any language that I possess." When he did speak, Washington's few words went a long way. As Thomas Jefferson said, "I served with General Washington in the legislature of Virginia before the revolution, and, during it, with Dr. Franklin in Congress. I never heard either of them speak ten minutes at a time, nor to any but the main point which was to decide the question. They laid their shoulders to the great points, knowing that the little ones would follow of themselves." So great was the respect of Washington's colleagues that, when the time came to appoint representatives to the First Continental Congress, he received the third-most votes among the seven appointed to attend. A year later, he received the second-most votes for the Second Continental Congress, coming in behind Peyton Randolph, the president of the First Continental Congress, by only one vote.

Washington also was active in local civic activities. He was elected a vestryman of his local parish, Truro, in 1762, and he continued to serve actively until he left to attend the First Continental Congress in 1774. He did not tender his formal resignation until 1784. In those days before church and state went their separate ways, the vestry in Virginia governed not only the affairs of the Church of England, but also undertook several functions that are today performed by local government. Vestries would supervise the construction of churches, the maintenance of ecclesiastical property, the supervision of spiritual affairs, the employment of ministers, the processing of land, the fixing of tithes, and the care of the local poor. It is a measure of its importance that, in the years immediately before the Revolution, Truro Parish had a larger budget than the budget for Fairfax County, in which it was located. Each year, the vestry selected two of its members to serve as churchwardens, and Washington was chosen for this task three times. A churchwarden had special duties, such as binding out orphans and indigent children as apprentices and presenting cases of blasphemy, profanity, drunkenness, adultery, and fornication to the county court.

In 1768, Washington was appointed by the governor to serve on the county court of Fairfax County. These courts considered civil as well as criminal cases (though capital cases were outside their jurisdiction); they also had a variety of administrative duties, including supervision of public buildings, laying out and improving roads, and levying taxes. (I, for one, am thankful that our modern, robust notion of separation of powers has removed such administrative duties from the courts' dockets.) Along with George Washington, George Mason, Washington's country neighbor at Gunston Hall, also served as a justice of Fairfax County and vestryman of Truro Parish. Mason and Washington were also trustees of the town of Alexandria, a position that carried essentially the same power as that of a county magistrate.

Washington had a local (and pecuniary) interest in the navigability of the Potomac. In 1769, Washington and Richard Henry Lee introduced a bill before the House of Burgesses for clearing the Potomac to make it navigable from the great falls of the river, which are a little above Washington, D.C., to Fort Cumberland, which was located in western Maryland, about 130 miles from modern-day D.C. Nothing came of the project at the time. But Washington, along with Thomas Johnson of Annapolis, Maryland, and George Mason, gave much thought to the project and, after the Revolution, they helped to found the Potomac Company, of which Washington was president. In addition to actively addressing physical problems associated with the river, Washington worked hard to address legal conflicts that were no less threatening to those who depended on the river for their livelihood. For years, Virginia and Maryland had staked out conflicting claims to ownership of the river. In 1785, Virginia and Maryland appointed commissioners to address this problem, and they met at Mount Vernon at the invitation of Washington. The commissioners agreed upon a compact, a set of rules that would govern usage of the river by each state and its members. The compact, unfortunately, did not end all disagreement between the two states over the river. This very term, my court was called upon to decide a case, *Virginia v. Maryland*, that involved the very compact hammered out at Mount Vernon. (Washington's home state prevailed, by the way.)

And even after his retirement from the presidency Washington continued to be a model citizen of the commonwealth. He served on a grand jury, and before this he had several times acted as petit juror. When at Mount Vernon, he invariably attended the election, though it was a ride of ten miles to the polling town. All told, excluding his boyhood, there were but seven years of his life in which Washington was not engaged in the public service.

Throughout his many adventures, George Washington never lost his love for Mount Vernon and it was to here that he always returned when his work allowed. He is buried here in the family tomb, along with Martha. His final words, a characteristically pithy and yet accurate summation of his life: " 'Tis well."

ABRAHAM LINCOLN

Justice Scalia's keynote speech highlighted the centennial celebration of the Illinois Supreme Court building at the Abraham Lincoln Presidential Museum in Springfield on May 20, 2008. On "a night I will never forget," Illinois supreme court justice Robert R. Thomas relishes having been there to "watch and listen as one of our nation's greatest jurists celebrated the legal legacy of one of its greatest presidents."

———

It is a particular pleasure to celebrate the renovation of this courthouse among members of the Illinois bar. It is a bar for which I have special reverence because it produced one of the finest American lawyers in our history. I speak, of course, of Abraham Lincoln. Before Lincoln became the president of our nation, before he became known as the Great Emancipator, he was a lawyer in the courts of this state and a member of this bar, with a practice that may in many respects have been not much different from your own. After he was elected to Congress in 1846, he was asked to identify himself in the *Dictionary of Congress*. He wrote, with characteristic simplicity and bluntness: "Education, defective. Profession, a lawyer."

Speaking in 1896, just over thirty years after President Lincoln's assassination, President William McKinley said that "[t]he best training [Lincoln] had for the Presidency . . . was his twenty-three years' arduous experience as a lawyer traveling the circuits of the courts of his district and State. Here he met in forensic conflict, and frequently defeated, some of the most powerful legal minds of the West. In the higher courts he won still greater distinction in the important cases coming to his charge." It is very difficult today to imagine a larger-than-life figure such as Lincoln ever being a small-town lawyer, undergoing the arduous task of riding circuit from town to town in the state, horse-shedding witnesses, arguing cases for five to fifty dollars. But that is what he once was and what he once did.

Lincoln was a self-taught frontier attorney, who reportedly received his initial training in the law from a borrowed copy of the *Revised Statutes of Indiana* and from a copy of Blackstone's *Commentaries* that he discovered in an old barrel. His admission to the Illinois bar occurred before the circuit court of this county (Sangamon County), where, on March 24, 1836, a state judge entered an order certifying that Lincoln was a person of "good moral character." We appear to have no record of his having sat for an examination for admission to the bar, which apparently was oral in all states until Massachusetts instituted a written test in 1855. Some things were different at that time.

Illinois was just emerging from being a pure frontier state. Shortly before Lincoln entered his legal practice, the courthouses of the states were log-built, and "in some districts the sessions were held in bar room taverns." Springfield "was a mere village" when Lincoln started his law practice here. The first Springfield courthouse "was erected at a cost of forty-two dollars and fifty cents. It was built of rough logs and consisted of one room."* Lincoln's first law office consisted of a table, some chairs, a lounge, a bench, an old woodstove, and his library of five *Illinois Reports* and about twenty volumes of law books, legislative reports, and congressional documents.

In his twenty-three years as a member of the Illinois bar, Lincoln would argue 172 cases before the Illinois Supreme Court. He frequently appeared before the United States circuit and district courts, and of course the Eighth Circuit of Illinois, where he tried more cases than any other member of the bar of his day. He was

---

* The quotations are from Frederick Trevor Hill's 1906 book *Lincoln the Lawyer*, as are many of the other details of Lincoln's legal career.

counsel to the Illinois Central Railroad, the largest corporation in the state, and the Rock Island Railroad. He argued cases before his future rival for the Senate and the presidency, Stephen Arnold Douglas, who had been elected judge for the Fifth Circuit. In fact, in one case, *Grubb v. Crane*, then-Judge Douglas delivered an opinion for the court in Lincoln's favor.

Lincoln left us some "Notes for a Law Lecture," which scholars suggest were the basis of an address he gave at Ohio State and Union Law College during the 1850s. His lecture focuses on what we might describe as the mundane aspects of being a lawyer: he advised his audience to "leave nothing for tomorrow which can be done today"; to "make all examinations of" legal documents; to avoid overcharging for services; and to cultivate and practice extemporaneous speaking, for "it is the lawyer's avenue to the public." His advice also touched upon the issue of professional ethics: "If in your judgment, you cannot be an honest lawyer, resolve to be honest without being a lawyer," he wrote. "Choose some other occupation rather than one in the choosing of which you do, in advance, consent to be a knave."* It is not for nothing that we call him "Honest Abe."

Lincoln was also counsel in at least one case before the United States Supreme Court, *Lewis v. Lewis*, in which ironically Chief Justice Taney delivered the opinion of the Court. I say ironically because Lincoln would have more to say about Taney during one of the defining periods of his career. I refer, of course, to his famous speeches on Taney's opinion in the *Dred Scott* case, one of which he delivered on June 26, 1857, in this very city.

Dred Scott, you will remember, was a slave whose Missouri owner, after a detour through Illinois, had moved with Scott into what was then the Wisconsin Territory (and is now the state of Minnesota), and, after residing there for some time, had returned to Missouri with Scott. Scott sued in a Missouri court, claiming that his residence in the free state of Illinois and the free Territory of Wisconsin had emancipated him. He won at the trial court

---

* This paragraph draws from Brian Dirck's *Lincoln the Lawyer* (2007).

level, but the decision was reversed on appeal. Scott was then sold to a man in New York and began another lawsuit in the federal courts of St. Louis, which ruled against him.

Scott took his case to the United States Supreme Court. He was, at this point, represented by Montgomery Blair (later a member of Lincoln's cabinet) and George Custis, an eminent lawyer and legal historian. Scott's owner was represented by Reverdy Johnson, a former attorney general of the United States. After two hearings, the Court declared Scott to be a slave, decreeing that slave owners enjoyed a constitutionally protected property right in their slaves. The Court reasoned that descendants of African slaves were not citizens of the United States under the Constitution (and thus had no authority to file lawsuits under the Constitution in federal courts). Though this holding deprived the Court of jurisdiction to adjudicate the dispute, the Court went on to hold that Congress lacked the power to declare any territory to be free (as it had done in the provisions of the Missouri Compromise) because the Fifth Amendment's Due Process Clause barred any law that would deprive a slaveholder of his property, such as his slaves, merely because he had brought them into a free territory.

The Court also went on to state that the territorial legislatures had no authority to ban slavery. Its critical language on the constitutional question was this: "An act of Congress which deprives a citizen of the United States of his liberty or property, merely because he came himself or brought his property into a particular Territory of the United States, and who had committed no offence against the laws, could hardly be dignified with the name of due process of law." (By the way, this is the first instance of the Supreme Court's use of what has become known as the doctrine of substantive due process—that is, the notion that the Due Process Clause guarantees not merely certain procedures, but certain absolute rights to be identified by the Court. I do not believe in that doctrine, and it is good to know that it has such questionable parentage.) The dissenting opinion responded that "when a strict interpretation of the Constitution, according to the fixed rules which govern the interpretation of laws, is abandoned, and the theoretical opinions of individuals are allowed to control its meaning, we have no longer a Constitution; we are under the government of individual men, who for the time being have power to declare what the Constitution is, according to their own views of what it ought to mean." It was only the second time—the first being *Marbury v. Madison*—that the Court had explicitly held that an act of Congress was unconstitutional.

Lincoln's June 26 Springfield speech on *Dred Scott* responded to a speech that Stephen Douglas had given two weeks earlier. Lincoln's speech began with a side issue—Lincoln's criticism of Douglas's position that the people of Utah were in open rebellion because of their desire to form a state constitution tolerating polygamy. That position, as Lincoln deftly showed, cut against Douglas's stated principle that the territories possessed the "sacred right of self-government." Far from being a neutral principle that Douglas applied consistently across all cases, Douglas's "sacred right" was according to Lincoln a "mere deceitful pretense for the benefit of slavery."

Though coming from a budding politician giving a political speech, Lincoln's criticism of Douglas's position illustrates one of the fundamental precepts of the legal system—consistency and logical rigor are required above all things. It will not do for a lawyer, or for a court, to rely on a legal principle in one case, only to abandon it in another without explanation, simply because the underlying merits of the case seem more sympathetic. If you abandon an overarching legal principle, you have to explain why you are doing so. According to Lincoln, Douglas was not able to make any such explanation of his abandonment of the principle of territorial self-government, to which he strongly adhered in the context of slavery, when it came to Utah.

Lincoln's speech continued by discussing *Dred Scott* specifically and, more generally, his views on the relevance of judicial opinions as precedents. Douglas had, two weeks earlier, condemned any person who criticized the correctness of the *Dred Scott* decision as, in Lincoln's terms, "offering violent resistance to it." Douglas had announced a view of judicial supremacy in the interpretation of the

Constitution: according to his view, "the courts are the tribunals prescribed by the Constitution and created by the authority of the people to determine, expound and enforce the law. Hence, whoever resists the final decision of the highest judicial tribunal, aims a deadly blow to our whole Republican system of government." He stated that "if resistance to the decisions of the Supreme Court of the United States, in a matter like the points decided in the *Dred Scott* case . . . shall be forced upon the country as a political issue, it will become a distinct and naked issue between the friends and the enemies of the Constitution."

But Lincoln explained that "judicial decisions have two uses—first, to absolutely determine the case decided, and secondly, to indicate to the public how other similar cases will be decided when they arise. For the latter use, they are called precedents and authorities." In other words, while a judicial decision resolved conclusively the particular controversy before it, the decision stood as a precedent or authority only with respect to similar cases that may arise in the future. Any person who, like Lincoln, believed in obedience to and respect for the judicial branch could thus criticize the reasoning of an opinion without being branded an enemy of the Constitution. Of course, a constitutional question, according to Lincoln, "when fully settled, should control, not only the particular cases decided, but the general policy of the country, subject to be disturbed only by amendments of the Constitution as provided in that instrument itself." But Lincoln did not believe that this principle extended to *Dred Scott*: "We think the *Dred Scott* decision is erroneous," he said. "We know that the court that made it"—the Supreme Court, my court—"has often overruled its own decisions, and we shall do what we can to have it to overrule this."

As Lincoln explained, his views offered no "resistance" to the Court because "judicial decisions are of greater or less authority as precedents, according to circumstances. That this should be so, accords both with common sense, and the customary understanding of the legal profession." He continued by saying: "If this important decision had been made by the unanimous concurrence of the judges, and without any apparent partisan bias, and in accordance with legal public expectation, and with the steady practice of the departments throughout our history, and had been in no part, based on assumed historical facts which are not really true; or, if wanting in some of these, it had been before the court more than once, and had there been affirmed and re-affirmed through a course of years, it then might be, perhaps would be" wrong not to "acquiesce in it as a precedent." But that was not the case with *Dred Scott*.

Not only was the principle of judicial supremacy in constitutional interpretation that Douglas announced wrong, Lincoln explained, but Douglas applied the principle inconsistently (much as he applied his principle of territorial self-government inconsistently). How could Douglas demand immediate acquiescence in the *Dred Scott* opinion when he had previously denounced the Court's opinion finding the national bank to be constitutional and applauded President Jackson for vetoing Congress's recharter of it because he believed it to be unconstitutional? As Lincoln approvingly quoted, Jackson had in his veto message said that "[m]ere precedent is a dangerous source of authority, and should not be regarded as deciding questions of constitutional power, except where the acquiescence of the people and the States can be considered as well-settled."

Any current observer of the confirmation process for United States Supreme Court justices will recognize that President Lincoln speaks, in these passages, of the principle of *stare decisis*, the principle that courts will stand by prior decisions and not disturb what is settled. In our time, it has become *de rigueur* to grill nominees for judicial office about their views on this principle. For my part, I have not discovered a better way of putting the point than Lincoln's *Dred Scott* speech.

Lincoln's *Dred Scott* speech is notable for one other reason—his explanation of why he believed the *Dred Scott* opinion to be wrongly decided. Chief Justice Taney, in his opinion for the majority, had admitted that the language of the Declaration of Independence was "broad enough to include the whole human family," but both the chief justice and Douglas argued that "the authors of that instrument did not *intend* to include negroes." But for Lincoln this was blatant error, which did "obvious violence to the *plain unmistakable language* of the Declaration."

Here we see the age-old debate over interpretation of the text of a document and whether, in giving a legal text meaning, one must accept the plain language of the document or rather is free to discern intentions of the authors that contradict the text. Leaving aside for current purposes the merits of the argument between Lincoln and Douglas on the meaning of the Declaration of Independence, the underlying issue is the following: Should legal interpreters apply the language of a particular provision by sticking to the words of that provision, or should they attempt to discern the underlying purpose of the provision and interpret the provision in light of that purpose—by reading in exceptions to the provision or by extending the provision more broadly than its language would otherwise permit? The critical point here, as the debate between Lincoln and Douglas suggests, is that the proper interpretive technique is in important respects outcome-neutral. A desire by legal interpreters to arrive at the intentions and purposes of the enactors of a provision, as opposed to merely interpreting the words as they are enacted, can as easily lead to injustice as it can to justice.

Lincoln had an additional remark to make on interpreting legal documents. He noted that he understood the *Dred Scott* decision to be "based on assumed historical facts which were not really true." Though Chief Justice Taney insisted in his opinion for the majority that Americans descended from Africans "were no part of the people who made, or for whom was made, the Declaration of Independence or the Constitution of the United States," Lincoln agreed with the dissenting opinion, which showed that in five of the initial thirteen states (New Hampshire, Massachusetts, New York, New Jersey, and North Carolina) free blacks were voters and played a role in making the Constitution.

Lincoln amplified this argument in his masterful Cooper Union Address to the New York Young Men's Republican Union three years later, which carefully examined the views of the thirty-nine signers of the Constitution and determined that at least twenty-one of them believed that Congress could control slavery in the territories of the United States and prohibit slavery's expansion. The speech was, according to Lincoln's law partner, "devoid of all rhetorical imagery," but rather "constructed with a view to accuracy of statement, simplicity of language, and unity of thought. In some respects like a lawyer's brief, it was logical, temperate in tone, powerful—irresistibly driving conviction home to men's reasons and their souls." In the speech, Lincoln began by agreeing entirely with Douglas's statement that, in the case of constitutional interpretation, "our fathers, when they framed the Government under which we live, understood this question"—namely, whether the federal Constitution forbade the federal government from controlling slavery in the federal territories—"just as well, and even better, than we do now."

Lincoln demonstrated that the Framers of the Constitution believed that the Constitution did not bar the federal government from prohibiting slavery in the territories by examining the votes of the "39." Twenty of the signers of the Constitution had voted to prohibit slavery in the Northwestern, Mississippi, Louisiana, and other territories in Congress (some before the Constitution's adoption), thus showing that in their understanding nothing forbade the federal government from controlling slavery in federal territory. President Washington, another of the thirty-nine signers of the Constitution, had approved and signed such a bill, thus indicating that he did not believe that the Constitution forbade the federal government from controlling slavery in federal territory. Lincoln concluded that the text of the Constitution and their actions "affirm[ed] that they understood the question *better than we*."

Some defenders of *Dred Scott*, Lincoln observed, argued that amendments to the Constitution contradicted his view, specifically the Fifth Amendment's prohibition against depriving a person of "life, liberty, or property without due process of law" and the Tenth Amendment's statement that "the powers not delegated to the United States by the Constitution . . . are reserved to the States respectively, or to the people." But that could not be: those same amendments were, as Lincoln observed, "framed by the first

Congress which sat under the Constitution—the identical Congress which passed" an act enforcing the prohibition of slavery in the Northwestern Territory.

Lincoln asked rhetorically, and I stress his words:

> Is it not a little presumptuous [for] any one at this day to affirm that the two things which that Congress deliberately framed, and carried to maturity at the same time, are absolutely inconsistent with each other? And does not such affirmation become impudently absurd when coupled with the other affirmation, from the same mouth, that those who did the two things alleged to be inconsistent, understood whether they really were inconsistent better than we—better than he who affirms that they are inconsistent?

That was enough in Lincoln's view. Though we cannot know for certain the tone of his speech at the Cooper Union that day, I have little trouble imagining him, towering over his audience at six foot four inches, thundering:

> I defy any man to show that any one of [the Framers] ever, in his whole life, declared that, in his understanding, any proper division of local from federal authority, or any part of the Constitution, forbade the federal government to control as to slavery in the federal Territories. I go a step further. I defy any one to show that any living man in the whole world ever did, prior to the beginning of the present century.

That the Framers themselves approved of a measure, while perhaps not wholly dispositive of the point, was powerful evidence that the Constitution did not prohibit it. Lincoln's adversaries maintained that they had a constitutional right to keep slaves in the federal territories. But as Lincoln explained, "no such right is specifically written in the Constitution. That instrument is *literally silent* about any such right."

Lincoln's interpretive technique with respect to the Constitution can be criticized in some of its particulars. He announces in the Cooper Union speech that "[f]or the purpose of adhering rigidly to the text, I have purposely omitted whatever understanding may have been manifested by any person, however distinguished, other than the 39 fathers who framed the original Constitution." But why should that be the case? Why, in other words, must the views of the thirty-nine actual signers of the document be privileged above the ratifiers of the document in the several states, or even the common person on the street's understanding of it? This aspect of Lincoln's speech gets to whether, in interpreting a legal document such as the Constitution, we ought to determine the intentions of the Framers who signed it, or rather the meaning that the public would have given to it.

But this is a minor quibble with what is otherwise rightly viewed as one of the masterful orations of American history. For the time being, I wish to draw attention to how closely Lincoln's speeches hewed to the traditional tools of the American lawyer—the importance of precedent, the absolute requirement that one be honest and forthright in application of one's principles, and the value of text and history. In fact, the themes of the speeches are not too far removed from the grand mural in the Illinois Supreme Court courtroom, which reminds us to pay heed always to "precedent, justice, and record"—so long as we substitute proper interpretation of text and consistency and rigor in application of legal principles for doing justice in the courtroom context.

My brand of legal interpretation—which today is called, in some quarters derisively, originalism—is not too far removed from the principles that Lincoln articulates in these two speeches. It is the view that the Constitution, like other legal documents, must be interpreted fairly according to its text, in light of the history of its adoption, and the tradition of its application. And that while the Constitution may have to be applied to new phenomena, in its application to phenomena extant when it was adopted, *it does not change.*

I would hazard a guess that members and enthusiasts of a commission devoted to historical preservation—such as yourselves—

would be sympathetic to this method of interpretation. My interpretive method, after all, gives the appearance of being devoted to the preservation of the past by dwelling on what the authors of a legal document said in the past. Indeed, originalism is often confused with historical preservation. But I have to disappoint you. Truth be told, originalism is not necessarily about preserving the past, even when it refers to and relies on the words of our Framers.

Take the debate between Lincoln and Douglas, for example. Douglas, and the *Dred Scott* Court, sought to preserve and extend into the territories a morally repugnant tradition—that of slavery—by creative interpretation of the Constitution. Lincoln appealed to the original understanding of that document by determining how its Framers had acted while they were in Congress. If they themselves had authorized laws prohibiting the extension of slavery into the territories, how then could it be that the Constitution that they enacted forbade such laws? To state this question was to answer it. The Framers did not enact a Constitution at war with their own actions. Thus, the Constitution reserved space for social progress by permitting Congress to enact laws relating to slavery in the territories.

I will leave the merits of Lincoln's historical arguments in these speeches to other scholars and for another day. For now, it suffices to note that President McKinley was indeed correct that Lincoln's service as a lawyer in this jurisdiction provided the "best training" for his presidency. His speeches display the values of honesty, consistency, logical rigor, and fidelity to text and history that are the hallmarks of a great lawyer. As we celebrate the centennial of the Illinois Supreme Court's magnificent home, I propose a toast: May the "Land of Lincoln" never forget the institutions that fostered her most famous son, and may she always hold true to the essential principles, both legal and moral, that he advocated.

WILLIAM HOWARD TAFT

Justice Scalia was a great admirer of William Howard Taft—the only person ever to serve both as president and as a Supreme Court justice (indeed, as chief justice). As this speech to the University Club in Washington, D.C., in February 1995 makes clear, Scalia particularly admired Taft's "magisterial opinion" in Myers v. United States *(1926) on the president's constitutional authority to fire executive-branch officials.*

In his powerful solo dissent in Morrison v. Olson *(1988)—a strong candidate for his greatest opinion—Scalia built on Taft's analysis to explain why the independent-counsel statute, in placing restrictions on the president's power to remove the independent counsel, was unconstitutional. A mere decade later, a remarkable bipartisan consensus recognized Scalia's constitutional wisdom, and Congress refused to renew the statute.*

I am honored to be present as your guest speaker on the occasion of the ninety-first anniversary of the University Club. When a justice of the Supreme Court is invited to give remarks in celebration of "Founder's Day," I presume that a proper subject is the first president of the Club, Chief Justice William Howard Taft. He was an extraordinary man by any standards. A state trial judge at twenty-nine, solicitor general of the United States at thirty-two, a United States circuit judge at thirty-four, professor and dean at the University of Cincinnati Law School, high commissioner of the Philippines, secretary of war, president of the United States, chief justice of the United States.

Or perhaps I should say that he was *two* presidents of the United States. That is not (as I am sure some of you were thinking) a reference to Taft's physical stature, which was, to understate it a bit, ample. (A special bathtub was made for him at the White House; and Justice Brewer is reported to have wisecracked that on one occasion the chief justice got up to give his seat to three ladies on the trolley.) But in saying he was two presidents I was recalling an episode recounted by one of his biographers: One morning, when Chief Justice Taft was taking a walk near his home, a little girl planted herself in his path. The girl, all of six years old, announced to him, "I know who you are!" Taft chuckled and said, "Well now, who am I?," whereupon she called out: "Why, you are Chief Justice Taft and you used to be President Coolidge."

Of the two great offices that he held, president and chief justice, the latter was the one that Taft himself most valued, judging by a statement he made at the time of his nomination to the chief justiceship. Not only an appropriate modesty but even a fear of the Almighty gives me some pause at quoting this, but here goes. Taft said: "I love judges and I love courts. They are my ideals that typify on earth what we shall meet hereafter in heaven under a just God." I truly think he was not kidding. Taft's nomination to the chief justiceship represented the fulfillment of a hope he had openly expressed even after attaining the presidency. When considering whom to appoint in place of Chief Justice Fuller, President Taft remarked that "[i]t does seem strange that the one place in the government which I would have liked to fill myself I am forced to give to another." Taft ultimately selected for the chief justiceship the only Louisianan ever to be on the Court, Edward Douglass White, who of course shared Taft's essentially conservative philosophy.

Taft's associates always remarked on the man's devotion to the ideals of law; and that devotion was displayed in action as well as in talk. Once, during his presidency, when he was out on another of his walks, he decided to pick flowers for Mrs. Taft from a rose bed by the Washington Monument. An old watchman came upon the scene of the crime and arrested the whole presidential party. Upon recognizing the chief perpetrator, the watchman said, "I am put here for a purpose, and I have to obey my orders whether it is the president or not." (A good old American sentiment.) Taft replied, "Right you are. Do you want me to go to the station house with you? But I must ask you to let off these other gentlemen, as they were only acting under my orders."

Taft was an outstanding jurist. His opinion as a circuit judge on the Sixth Circuit, in *United States v. Addyston Pipe & Steel Co.* (1898), became the classic statement of what constitutes a restraint of trade under the (then new) Sherman Antitrust Act. But his reputation as a great chief justice rests not upon his opinions but upon his organizational and administrative skills—which he could indulge to an extraordinary degree because of his national popularity and unmatched political contacts. As described by one biographer, in his very first year as chief justice, Taft "launched his campaign for reform, making appeals in speeches across the continent, presenting his case in legal periodicals and in testimony before the House and Senate Judiciary Committees." He succeeded in obtaining passage of the Act of Congress, September 14, 1922, which established the Judicial Conference of the United States, and the Judiciary Act of 1925, which finally brought the Supreme Court's unmanageable docket under control by establishing the system of discretionary certiorari jurisdiction to replace appeals of right. He successfully opposed (and this should be of particular interest to modern lawyers, for the issue is still with us) Senator Norris's bill to eliminate the diversity jurisdiction of the federal courts. And I am tangibly in his debt more than most of you, since he obtained for the Court its first (and current) home, the Supreme Court building that is now the symbol of equal justice under law.

But Taft was, as I say, not just a great administrator but a great jurist; and if he is not famous for many of his opinions on the Court, that is only because many of them ran counter to the ultimate sweep of history. One commentator observes condescendingly:

Taft's Chief Justiceship might have been constructive, but for his haunting fear of progressivism. Had he maintained the

powerful position he assumed in his commerce cases and minimum wage dissent of 1923, he might have, with the backing
of Holmes, Brandeis, Stone, and possibly Sanford, swung the
Court along the line the great triumvirate was so eloquently
staking out.

Another complains:

Lacking in William Howard Taft was the quality Woodrow
Wilson suggested as an essential requirement of statesman-
ship—"a large vision of things to come."

This is the school of history that assesses the greatness of a
leader by his success in predicting where the men he is leading
want to go. That is perhaps the way the world ultimately evaluates
things—but one may think that Taft, having (as I have described)
a more celestial view of the judge's function, had a quite accurate
"vision of things to come," did not like them, and did his best,
with consummate skill but ultimate lack of success, to alter the
outcome.

I have to mention one legal opinion of the great chief justice,
because he was so right, though ultimately on the losing side. He
himself must have regarded it as his most significant opinion, judging by the amount of time he took to produce it, and by its sheer
length. Indeed, we need not rely upon that persuasive secondary
evidence, for Taft himself said of the case: "I never wrote an opinion that I felt to be so important in its effect." I refer to his opinion for the Court in *Myers v. United States* (1926), which declared
unconstitutional congressional attempts to restrict presidential removal of executive officers. Argument in that case was first heard
on December 5, 1924. It was set for reargument and heard again
on April 13 and 14, 1925. (In those days oral argument was, to understate the point, somewhat more protracted.) The chief justice's
seventy-page opinion for the Court, as well as a one-page dissent
by Justice Holmes, a sixty-one-page dissent by Justice McReynolds,
and a fifty-five-page dissent by Justice Brandeis, did not issue until

more than a year and a half after the second argument, on October 25, 1926. Taft's opinion was one that I myself might have written (which is of course what makes it so good), relying extensively upon historical materials to demonstrate the original understanding of what dismissal powers the president was to have.

Taft's magisterial opinion was essentially overruled about nine years later, after Charles Evans Hughes had succeeded Taft as chief justice, in a case called *Humphrey's Executor v. United States* (1935), which invalidated President Franklin Roosevelt's attempt to remove a member of the Federal Trade Commission. The contrast with *Myers*, not only in result but in process, was astounding: The case was argued on May 1, 1935, and the opinion issued twenty-six days later—the same day the Court declared unconstitutional Roosevelt's National Industrial Recovery Act. It contained almost no historical analysis and announced the existence of a branch of government that was neither Congress nor executive, but something in between—the headless fourth branch, as it came to be known. It did all this, overruling *Myers* in the process, in fourteen quick pages. Many (including President Roosevelt and his attorney general, Robert Jackson) thought that the rapid switch in legal analysis between *Myers* and *Humphrey's Executor* had little to do with the law and much to do with the justices' antagonism toward the New Deal. But surely the switch must also be attributed to loss of the great intellectual influence that Taft, an ex-president and hence a supporter of executive power, had exercised over his colleagues.

But enough of the law. I want to conclude my reminiscences of Taft with a tribute to those qualities of his that were most appropriate to his status as the first president of this Club, and that we should therefore most celebrate and honor tonight. William Howard Taft was a good-natured, good-hearted, affable, sociable man, just as all of us are. In perusing his biographies, it is really astounding how often he is reported to have "laughed heartily." Even his animosities were jovial. Samuel Gompers, with whom (as you can imagine) he had a good number of run-ins, recalls encountering him accidentally on a train ride. Taft came up, a broad smile on his face, warmly grasped the labor leader's hand and said: "How are you, my dear old enemy?" How much better that is than calling him, to take an example currently in the news, a reptilian bastard.

There used to be a large blown-up photograph of Chief Justice Taft in the basement of the Court. (I don't know if it's still there.) He stands there with his top hat on and overcoat open, a broad, amiable smile on his face and a vast expanse of body spreading out unashamedly below that smile. Not for him the unimorph culture of the 1990s, which causes me and my colleague Chief Judge Loren Smith[*] to starve and exercise ourselves, seeking, against all nature, to achieve sticklike physiques resembling Remington Steele, or Tiny Tim, or Twiggy. None of that for the great man. He stands there in the photograph, beaming out at the world, supremely confident and content in his identity and his nature, almost flaunting his corpulence. One can almost imagine coming forth from his lips the famous, profoundly philosophical words of Popeye: I yam what I yam. And in the case of Chief Justice Taft, that was something extraordinary indeed. Ladies and gentlemen, I propose another toast to our great and amiable first president, Chief Justice William Howard Taft.

---

[*]   Loren Smith, an active member of the University Club, was chief judge of the U.S. Court of Federal Claims from 1986 to 2000.

Ruth Bader Ginsburg

Justice Scalia and Justice Ginsburg forged their enduring friendship during the four years, from 1982 to 1986, in which they were colleagues on the D.C. Circuit. In 1990, Justice Scalia took part in a roast of then-Judge Ginsburg in celebration of her tenth anniversary on that court. She would join him on the Supreme Court three years later.

———

It was a great imposition on the part of Judge Ginsburg's law clerks to ask me to participate in this roast. It is not so much that the Court is busy this time of year, but that I do not have any law clerks who worked for Judge Ginsburg—so that I have had to engage in original composition, something I have not done for many years.

Some things do not roast very well. Roast kangaroo, for example. I doubt whether Ruth Ginsburg roasts very well. She's much too serious a person. It's rather like roasting Queen Victoria or Erwin Griswold.* So I'll say only a few things.

First of all, it's surprising that Ruth has come as far as she has. As everyone knows, she interviews very badly. Queen Victoria probably did, as well. Too serious, for Pete's sake.

Now those of us who know Ruth well understand that this is really not true. It is not the case that she has no sense of humor. No one who married Marty could be lacking in a sense of humor. (Maybe that did not come out as I intended.) It is just that Ruth is a very orderly person—all you have to do is walk into her immacu-

---

* Erwin Griswold was dean of Harvard Law School from 1946 to 1967.

late office to realize that. That's also why, in her academic days, she specialized in civil procedure, a field characterized by utterly pointless order. So, being an orderly person, Ruth tries to schedule her levity as she schedules everything else. That explains why it is sometimes as hard to get her to stop laughing as it is to get her to start. Marty has told me (I hope I'm not breaching any confidence here) that on alternate Tuesdays Ruth goes into the living room after dinner and just sits there giggling until bedtime. Alternate Wednesday mornings, as you have perhaps learned, are a very bad time to go in and see her.

Ruth and I were drawn together, of course, by our similar philosophical proclivities: she was an ardent feminist and a public-interest litigator; and I (in the days when I had policy views) opposed affirmative action and thought that standing to litigate should be constricted as narrowly as possible. We have formed a very close friendship, and one of us must be mistaken. Or perhaps both.

Ruth and I were also drawn together, I suppose, by the fact that we are both kibitzers. We like to kibitz and we don't mind being kibitzed. I often tell the story about my early days on the court of appeals, when Ed Tamm invited me up to his office for the first time—to talk about some administrative matter, as I recall. Ed had been a district judge for many years, and district judges get used to writing opinions that no one else butts in on. They tend to retain the attitude that that fosters even after they are demoted to the court of appeals. And Ed, as I learned that day, retained this attitude to a particularly high degree. He cupped his hand around my elbow, guided me over to the wall where his judicial commission hung, squinted up at it, and said: "You know, I've read this thing hundreds of times, and I can't find anything in it that authorizes me to be an editor." This was entirely unprovoked! I hadn't even had occasion to sit with Ed yet! Anyway, I took his message—and pretty much abided by it, as far as his opinions were concerned, over the years.

But to return to my point: Ruth was perhaps the only judge on the D.C. Circuit who needed that advice as much as I did. She's the only one from whom I recall regularly receiving comments for improvements rather than corrections. Not "this is wrong, Nino" but "the point would be even stronger if." And maybe I'm the only judge that appreciated receiving them. Ruth and I had developed something of a mutual improvement society—and I miss it.

That's all I have to say by way of roasting, but I will conclude with a few earnest comments. I have missed Ruth very much since leaving the court of appeals. She was the best of colleagues, as she is the best of friends. I wish her a hundred years.

FAREWELLS

Justice Scalia had a great capacity for friendship, including with many individuals whose political and religious beliefs differed from his own. His eulogies reveal a man who cared deeply about his friends, who found in them much to admire and appreciate, who savored their distinctive qualities, and whose strong faith instilled in him the hope of reuniting with them.

ITALO H. ABLONDI

(1929–2001)

Italo ("Al") Ablondi served on the U.S. International Trade Commission in the 1970s. He played professional basketball in the American Basketball League in the early 1950s.

I was a friend of Al Ablondi for about thirty years. I am not sure how we first met. It might have been through our wives. When Al was a commissioner on the International Trade Commission and I was chairman of the Administrative Conference of the United States, Maureen and Unalane belonged to an organization called—the name surely dates it—the Independent Agency Wives. Or perhaps Al and I met in connection with one or another of the Italian American organizations that we both took some part in. In any case, it was a long friendship, though not—in these later years at least—one that brought us together with any regularity. I did not even know of his last illness, and his death came to me as a surprise. And as a warning, perhaps, that good friends deserve constant attention.

All of us here have seen different sides of Al Ablondi and have seen him through the lens of our own experiences. Let me recite, in memoriam, the qualities of the man that struck me as distinctive.

First, there was a constant spirit of intellectual curiosity—about all things, great and small. A conversation with Al was likely to range (at his guidance) from gastronomy to sports to trade policy to historic preservation to Washington politics to the law practice to New York politics to any number of other subjects that I would never have thought of broaching myself, and knew little about. And the strange thing is, he would always seem to be listening rather than pontificating—to be acquiring information rather than imparting it. Surely a rare quality anywhere, but especially in this town.

Second—to my mind a most endearing quality—Al Ablondi was loyal, to all those people and all those institutions that had had a formative influence in his life. To his Italian heritage, which he was intensely proud of; to New York City, where he grew up and where I sometimes thought his heart still resided; to our common alma mater, Georgetown—which he attended on an athletic scholarship in the days when it was still pretty much a rich kids' school; and, of course, first and foremost to his wife, Unalane—his pride and affection for whom was apparent to anyone who saw them together—and to the children of their union, who have a lot to live up to.

Finally—I have saved it until last because to me it was the most notable—there was a quality to Al Ablondi that always reminded me of my father—who, like him, was born in Italy and raised in an Italian family. I refer to an almost quaint, Old World courtliness, courtesy, and gentility. He spoke softly and almost deferentially, listened attentively, and took an interest (as a good man should) in the lives and the doings of his friends. Al Ablondi elevated the civility level of any group he was in. I did not know him when he played basketball at Georgetown, and I frankly cannot imagine him throwing elbows under the basket. Perhaps it was a kinder, gentler game in those days.

I will miss Al Ablondi and am sorry I was so poor a friend as not to say goodbye. But I have the sure hope that I will see him again where old friends will have an eternity to catch up and make amends.

RICHARD CONWAY CASEY

(1933–2007)

Richard C. Casey served as a federal district judge for the Southern District of New York from 1997 until his death in 2007. He was the first blind federal trial judge.

Cardinal Egan, reverend clergy, colleagues on the Second Circuit and Southern District, members of their bar, friends of Richard Casey:

Dick Casey was a good friend. I would be here among the mourners today if my court were not sitting.

I do not recall when I first met Dick Casey. He was the sort of vivid personality that burns itself so deeply into your memory that you seem to have known him forever. It was, in any case, after his blindness, and after he became a federal judge.

Being stricken with such a disability late in life (Dick was about fifty-four, I believe) and in the midst of a successful career (Dick was a partner at Brown and Wood) is surely an acid test of character. Many people become embittered; a few become even better human beings, and an inspiration to others. As all who knew him can attest, Dick Casey fell into the latter category. It greatly understates the matter to say that he was *resolute* in the face of adversity; he was positively *joyful*. If you ever needed cheering up, spend an hour with Casey. Unlimited optimism and good cheer—even in the last year or so, when he was tried with additional illnesses. He made you ashamed of your own complaining and ingratitude.

Dick was a devout Catholic, receiving from Pope John Paul II the Blessed Hyacinth Cormier, O.P., Medal, for "outstanding leadership in the promotion of Gospel Values in the field of justice and ethics." I am sure Dick's faith was the principal factor in his ability to make lemonade out of lemons. He described a pilgrimage to Lourdes as a turning point in his life. He was touched by the story of a girl who went to the shrine, as he did, hoping to receive the miracle of sight. She did not, but her tombstone read: "What is important is not to see, but to understand."

I most admire, and will most miss, Dick Casey as a man. But I suppose I should say a few words about his qualities as judge. Although Dick presided over many important and high-profile trials, he received national recognition (or, in some quarters, notoriety), for presiding over a trial challenging the constitutionality of the federal Partial-Birth Abortion Ban Act. I cannot and do not comment on the merits of Dick's opinion, as this very issue is pending before my court. But I think it proper and unobjectionable to recount what Dick did. During the sixteen-day bench trial, he took an active role in questioning the medical experts, inquiring in great detail about the nature of the procedure, getting them to describe it in terms comprehensible to the layman, asking whether fetuses feel pain and whether patients are informed of that possibility. He came to the conclusion that partial-birth abortion is, and I quote his opinion directly now, "a gruesome, brutal, barbaric, and uncivilized medical procedure." And he ruled—he *ruled*—that my court's jurisprudence rendered the statute banning that procedure unconstitutional.

Dick Casey was a judge's judge. He did not confuse his personal views with the law; and he knew that he sat to pronounce the latter, not advance the former. Dick received some disappointed criticism, in Catholic circles, and anti-abortion circles generally, when his judgment issued. But I am entirely certain that before the only judgment seat that really matters he scored high points for unbending fidelity to his judicial oath. I can bestow no higher professional praise on a man whose religious values were such a pivotal part of his extraordinary life than to commend his humble recognition that there is a line between law and personal belief.

But I would not end on such a somber note. As I have said, I mainly loved Dick Casey the man, not the judge. I taught with him for a few weeks at several summer sessions of American law schools abroad. During one of them (in Nice) he went up parasailing over the Mediterranean. Just imagine! And he used to go on a skiing trip for the blind out West somewhere (Park City, I think).

I joked with him (one could joke with Dick about his disability; he made light of it himself) that he really could not be sure he was in Park City. For all he knew he was going up and down a big pile of snow on a parking lot in Jersey City. He acknowledged that I might be right, but said he enjoyed it anyway.

There used to be a feature in some popular magazine—the *Reader's Digest*, perhaps—entitled "The Most Unforgettable Character I Have Ever Met." For me, and I suspect for many others, Judge Richard Casey gets that award. He was a blessing to us all, and I hope to see him again. May he rest in peace.

MARTIN FEINSTEIN

(1921–2006)

Martin Feinstein was the first executive director of the John F. Kennedy Center for the Performing Arts. In 1980 he became general manager of the Washington National Opera.

It is the greatest curse of advancing years that our world contracts, as friends who cannot be replaced, with insights into life that are not elsewhere available to us, leave us behind. Martin Feinstein leaves a much bigger hole than most. Who now will give me a box seat in the glamorous world of opera, ballet, and music—with tales of Sol Hurok and temperamental divas and greedy tenors, all seen through the eyes and told in the accents of someone who grew up in lower-middle-class New York City, just like me? Who will turn the conversation in pre-poker-game bull sessions to matters far apart from, and infinitely more interesting than, the usual political chatter of Washington cocktail parties? Who, in distinctive life experience, distinctive warmth, distinctive wit, will replace my friend Martin Feinstein? The answer is no one.

I grieve for me, of course, and not for Martin. Death comes to us all, and I know of no one who had a fuller, more satisfying run than Martin Feinstein. He worked at what he loved—and what are the odds of making a career as an impresario, and then topping it off as a gentleman antiquarian? And he spent his life with people he loved and people worth loving—notably Bernice, who was his wife when I first met him, and Marcia, at whose wedding he gave me the honor of presiding. He leaves behind a legacy that makes all of us who knew him proud. I went to college in Washington, so I know what its artistic life was like BF—Before Feinstein. Washington was the North American equivalent of Brasilia, a capital city all the ambassadors deserted over the weekend to go up to our Rio de Janeiro, New York City. It was Martin who, as executive director for performing arts, made the Kennedy Center a success;

it was he who brought in Rostropovich to improve the quality of the National Symphony Orchestra; and most of all, it was he who established the Washington National Opera as a first-rate company. Martin, we miss you. Thanks for your talent; and most of all thanks for your irreplaceable friendship.

ROBERT H. JOOST

(1937–2008)

Robert Joost was a friend of Antonin Scalia from their days as classmates at Harvard Law School, where he arranged a momentous blind date for him.

Like it or not, life is a lot like cards. There's a good deal of luck involved (in life we call it fate or providence); and the test of a good player in cards or a good man in life is what you make of the hand you're dealt.

Bob Joost was in several respects dealt a really bad hand. He was in my class at Harvard Law School—we were co-editors on the law review—but he graduated not with my class, but eight years later, because he had an onset of the bipolar disorder that dogged him much of his life. In those days that disorder, and the treatments for it, were not well understood. And then, at the back end of his life, Bob was stricken with Alzheimer's.

Of course Bob was dealt some pretty good cards as well. For starters, a fine mind—good enough to graduate from Harvard Law School magna cum laude. A mother who scraped and saved, as he once told me—working nights as a cleaning woman in New York law firms—to give her son the best education. And, of course, for the last twenty years of his life, a loving wife, Elaine, who was his joy and support.

But how well he played the hand. Any lawyer would be proud of his record of accomplishment: a valued staff member of the Senate Commerce Committee, drafting legislation in many important fields; campaigner for no-fault insurance and author of the definitive book on the subject; service with the D.C. Law Revision Commission and the Commodity Futures Trading Commission; chairmanship of the Coast Guard Board for Correction of Military Records.

But most important of all, right until the end (I last saw him when he was in a fairly advanced stage of Alzheimer's) he retained his drive, his determination, his good spirits. (Don't you always wonder, when you see someone who has confronted adversity so nobly, whether you could measure up? I probably couldn't.)

So, Bob Joost's life was a life worth remembering and worth honoring. I haven't even mentioned what was, as far as I am concerned, his greatest accomplishment: when we were classmates at Harvard he fixed me up on a blind date with the Radcliffe student who has now been my wife for some forty-eight years.

Hail and farewell to a good friend and an admirable man.

Mary C. Lawton

(1935–1993)

Mary Lawton had such a distinguished career as a government lawyer that the American Bar Association's administrative-law group named its annual award for outstanding government service after her.

You have heard from Mary's family. I am here to say a few words on behalf of her friends—and particularly on behalf of her friends in the government of the United States, which was such a large part of her life.

I heard of Mary Lawton before I met her. And the context in which I heard of her would have amused her very much. I never told her about it. It was the summer of 1974, and I had just been appointed assistant attorney general in charge of the Office of Legal Counsel of the Department of Justice, the division for which Mary worked for so many years. I was told (by a person or persons who shall remain unnamed) that I would have full authority to restaff the division as I thought necessary—but I should give particular thought to getting rid of the second deputy, one Mary Lawton, who, this unnamed person or persons assured me, was thought by some to be too ideological, and of the wrong ideology.

I look back on this event with such amusement because, as I soon enough came to learn, if there was ever a public servant for all administrations—a lawyer devoted to doing her job skillfully, honestly, impartially, without fear and without favor—it was Mary Lawton. That is why she rose to become, at a very young age, the highest-ranking woman in the career civil service, and one of the most honored and respected civil servants of any shape or sex.

Mary joined the Office of Legal Counsel, as an attorney adviser, in 1960, after graduating (first in her class) from Georgetown Law Center. She worked in that office for nineteen years—three of them, to my great benefit, as one of my two deputy assistant attorneys general. By the time I arrived at OLC, there were few senior lawyers in the executive branch, I think, who did not know Mary Lawton. It was the task of the Office of Legal Counsel to provide legal advice to all the agencies of government, and for many years much of that advice came from or through Mary. She won the Department of Justice's John Marshall Award, and later the Attorney General's Exceptional Service Award. I never knew her to do a shoddy piece of work, to run from a fight, to shade the truth. She was a lawyer's lawyer, a counselor's counselor, an adviser's adviser.

I could tell a lot of stories about Mary's extraordinary competence, but I will tell only one, which reveals a lot about her character. The years I served in the Justice Department were years in which the Federal Bureau of Investigation and the intelligence agencies were being placed on what might be termed a more regularized basis—subjected to checks and oversights that other agencies had long endured, but from which they had been generally exempted. Understandably, they did not like this. During these years, Mary served as OLC's principal liaison with the Bureau. It was a troubled relationship at first. The Bureau's personnel had trouble coming to terms, for example, with the Freedom of Information Act. Despite Mary's best efforts, they tended to claim an exception from production with respect to every FOIA request. On one occasion, just to make a point, Mary herself filed a FOIA request for the Bureau's telephone book, which was widely available throughout the Justice Department. Sure enough, the request was denied.

Mary ultimately succeeded in bringing the Bureau along. Much beyond that, she ultimately succeeded in winning the Bureau's respect and admiration. By the time I left the Department, the agents looked upon her (as they should) as a valued adviser rather than an antagonist. Indeed, she became so respected by the intelligence community that she ended her career—after a sojourn as general counsel of the Corporation for Public Broadcasting and later as an administrative law officer at the White House—back at the Justice Department as counsel for intelligence policy in the Office of Intelligence Policy and Review.

But it is not because Mary was smart and hardworking that I

am here to honor her. It is because she was that good and irrepressible person who was Mary. Two of her qualities stand out in my memory. The first is her good humor. I have heard it said, and I believe it, that the Lord loves a cheerful countenance. Well, the Lord must have loved Mary Lawton. She was never a brooder, never a mope. Even her anger—and she could rise to wonderful degrees of anger at the latest stupidity of officials in one or another branch of government—was always an exuberant, hearty, cheerful anger. It was more fun to be in the company of an angry Mary than to be in the company of a satisfied and contented someone else. She loved her life, she loved her work—even, perhaps especially, the struggle of it—and it showed. Even in the years when she was suffering severe physical illness—she had a close scrape with cancer—I never recall seeing her anything but cheerful.

The other predominant characteristic of Mary, in my recollection, is closely related to her cheerfulness: more than most people, Mary Lawton knew who she was. She had a confidence, an assurance, an inner balance that comes from self-knowledge, from a grasp of her proper place in the whole scheme of things. Mary Lawton never gave the impression of being accidentally where she was; she was there because she was supposed to be there, and she seemed to know it.

That leads me to the last—and, at the end of the day, the most important—aspect of Mary Lawton's life. It would be improper to dwell upon it at a nonreligious memorial service; but it would be improper not to mention it at this requiem Mass. I have said a lot about Mary's professional accomplishments, but in the last analysis both they and the honor they bring are fleeting. Mary's fine work in developing government-wide procedures for implementing the Privacy Act, for example, will, like the best opinion I ever write, not likely be known fifty or one hundred or two hundred years from now. Mary herself, on the other hand, as I believe, and as she believed, will live forever.

Mary did not wear her faith on her sleeve—but, as I discovered when I attended her father's funeral, she was a devout Catholic. This church is familiar to her; she was an active member of the

Little Flower parish—and before that of Holy Redeemer parish in Kensington. For one who believes, nothing can give as much comfort upon the loss of a friend as does the assurance that that friend kept clearly in mind what was most important and died in the friendship of Christ.

For those of Mary's friends who share her faith, it will be easy to remember her death, and to be reminded to pray for her. She is being buried today on All Souls' Day, the day of the year on which all Masses throughout the world are offered in commemoration of the faithful departed, and on which the living faithful pray for their beloved dead—that if those departed souls be not yet in heaven the Lord may shorten the time they must spend in Purgatory. As things stand, I figure that I am more likely to be the beneficiary of Mary Lawton's intercessions than she is of mine, but just in case I pray for her today and will surely be reminded to keep her in my prayers whenever All Souls' Day comes back around.

I shall end my remarks with a reading that used to be the Epistle at all the first Masses on All Souls' Day. It is from the first letter of Paul to the Corinthians, and thanks to various musical settings is familiar even to many who are not Christians. It explains why our sadness today is mostly sadness for ourselves, for our own loss, rather than for Mary's. St. Paul wrote:

Behold, I tell you a mystery: we shall all indeed rise again, but we shall not all be changed. In a moment, in the twinkling of an eye, at the last trumpet; for the trumpet shall sound, and the dead shall rise again incorruptible, and we shall be changed. For this corruptible must put on incorruption, and this mortal must put on immortality. And when this mortal hath put on immortality, then shall come to pass the saying that is written: "Death is swallowed up in victory. O death, where is thy victory? O death, where is thy sting?" Now the sting of death is sin: and the power of sin is the law. But thanks be to God, who hath given us the victory through our Lord Jesus Christ.

Morris I. Leibman

(1911–1992)

In 1981, President Reagan awarded Morris Leibman the Presidential Medal of Freedom and cited him as "living proof that a full career in the private sector can flourish hand in hand with civic and humanitarian duties."

I guess that I first met Morris Leibman in the winter of 1977–78. I was a professor at the University of Chicago Law School, having accompanied my former boss, Attorney General Ed Levi, on his return there after the people threw us out in the '76 election. Morry was in the process of resuscitating the old ABA Committee on Americanism—on which he and Justice Powell had been so active—giving it a new name and a new mission. It was going to be called the Committee on Law and National Security, and one of the first areas Morry wanted it to look into was the realm of intelligence law. You all know the old bromide about military intelligence being an oxymoron. Well, in 1977 intelligence law really was an oxymoron. Until the years of the Ford administration, intelligence gathering was really what one might call an extralegal activity. That changed rather quickly, with the Church Committee and Pike Committee investigations of the CIA and of the COINTELPRO program of the FBI. New executive orders were framed, dealing with intelligence matters with an explicitness unprecedented in this country and in the world; and ultimately new legislation was enacted, such as the Foreign Intelligence Surveillance Act of 1978.

Morry Leibman, American patriot and Cold Warrior, saw these developments, and saw the need for some organization sympathetic to national-security interests to track and to guide the new regularization of intelligence. He knew that I had been deeply involved in many of the new developments as assistant attorney general in charge of the Office of Legal Counsel, so he called me at the University of Chicago (maybe Ed Levi sicced him on me, I don't recall) to get me involved. The next thing I knew I was attending a meeting of the reorganized ABA committee on Longboat Key, one of Morry's favorite hangouts.

So that is how I first got swept up into the vortex of Morry Leibman's causes. There was no reason for me to do that work. It was not in the area of my teaching interest, and it consumed a lot of time. It was the sheer force of Morry's enthusiasm for it, and his glowing optimism about all the good it could accomplish, that simply sucked me along, like some huge intellectual vacuum cleaner. That is my tale of how I first became a Leibman work slave. I am sure that many others here have similar stories. The man had an uncanny ability to get people to do things that, if they consulted their own selfish interests, their own personal cost-benefit analysis, they had absolutely no business doing. Vacuum cleaner is the wrong analogy. Morry was a dust devil. One of those tiny, head-high mini-tornados that you see out in Arizona—which appear out of nowhere, sweep up all the dust, paper, anything that is not glued down lying in their path, and move it all somewhere else. They disappear as quickly as they came. But you know they will be back, to move all the unattached debris somewhere else. We were the unattached debris to Morry's dust devil.

Morry Leibman was Jewish. Indeed, with the possible exception of Abraham, God never created anybody more Jewish than Morry Leibman. He had, moreover, what I consider a distinctively American delight in not only his own ethnicity but also everybody else's. He somehow enjoyed and celebrated my Italianness and my wife Maureen's Irishness as much as his own Jewishness. One had the impression that he would like to belong to each and every identifiable ethnic group, if he only could. He loved them all and understood that the America he and I knew would not be the same place without them.

I frankly don't know how smart Morry was. He was a spectacularly successful lawyer, of course, but I sometimes suspected that he would maybe have gotten a gentleman's C in Phil Kurland's constitutional law course at the University of Chicago. Now, I don't consider that speaking ill of the dead, because I have never thought that smarts counted for that much. My father used to tell me that brains are like muscles: they can be hired by the hour. It is character and judgment that are not for sale; and for sure Morry had unmatched quantities of those. Or to put the point more elegantly, in the words of William Penn:

> Knowledge is the Treasure, but Judgment the Treasurer of a Wise Man. He that has more Knowledge than Judgment, is made for another Man's use more than his own.

A lot of us held our knowledge for Morry Leibman's use. He was better than an intellectual or a scholar—he was an *impresario* of intellectuals and scholars, who would decide where their various talents were most needed and could best be employed.

Morry was a *good* man—with the kind of deep-down, fundamental, instinctive, irreplaceable goodness that provokes the description "salt of the earth." I never heard a mean-spirited word from him. (That is not to say I never heard a hate-filled word from him. Morry hated as exuberantly as he loved—but only evil things that deserve the hatred of good men.) Morry's basic decency and humanity were, I think, the greatest ingredient of his success. It may be true that nice guys don't win ball games—but it is also true that only genuinely good people come to have as many loyal friends as Morris Leibman.

I mentioned that Morry Leibman was an optimist. That really understates the point. He was an *irrepressible* optimist. Come to think of it, he was an irrepressible everything. If I had to pick a single epithet for Morry, it would be "irrepressible." The irrepressible Morry Leibman. He was always bursting out, brimming over, with hopes, with plans, with projects, with proposals. Brimming over to such a degree that it was quite impossible to get near him without getting wet.

I believe in life after death, so I hope to see Morris Leibman again. Indeed, a person like Morry is one of the most persuasive evidences of life after death. It seems unlikely that an intelligent spirit *that* full of life—such an energy force of mind and will—

simply comes to an end. Morry had a good life, as nice guys usually do. Indeed, he had two good lives, because marrying Mary was a sort of rebirth or rejuvenation. For us, his friends, it would never have been a good time for Morry to go—but there was something fitting about his leaving when, and only when, the final dissolution of the Evil Empire had been achieved, a result he helped perceptibly, through this committee and in other ways, to produce.

I am honored, then, to pay tribute to Morris Leibman: ardent patriot; tireless crusader; inspiring friend. Chicago, Washington, the United States are better places because we were lucky enough to have him here.

Emerson G. Spies

(1914–1990)

Emerson Spies joined the faculty of the University of Virginia law school in 1946 and served as the law school's dean from 1976 to 1980. He was "Uncle Emerson" to the Scalia children when the family lived in Charlottesville. (This tribute first appeared in the April 1991 issue of the Virginia Law Review.*)*

When participating in a program such as this, consisting of brief memorial tributes, one sometimes fears that he will paint a portrait of his departed friend that others will not recognize, that perhaps he saw or thought he saw colorations of character or personality that others did not—rose where they saw pink, or violet where they saw purple. That is not a problem when one stands up to talk about Emerson Spies. His colors were bright, and they neither changed nor were ever dissembled.

I first met Emerson in 1967 when I came to teach at the law school with Maureen and our by then four children. He was our landlord for a time, since we paid him monthly rent on the house in West Leigh that we had agreed to buy from him, until we could put together the money for the closing. That real-property relationship was my first extensive association with Emerson (which is appropriate enough, I suppose, given his field of specialty), and it was characteristic of all the rest. Despite the fact that Emerson as a real estate lawyer should have known better—and I, too, I suppose, since I was coming to Charlottesville to teach contracts—the whole contract between us was virtually a handshake deal until the closing occurred. Maureen just reminded me on the way up here that during that interim period, and before we had even come to Charlottesville to occupy the house, a major storm sent a tree limb right through the front window. The handshake took care of it.

We probably could not have afforded the house if Emerson had not quoted us a price clearly below what he could have gotten—

computed, as I recall, by taking the cost of the lot and adding to it what the builder had charged for the construction to date. The fact was, as Emerson explained and as I entirely believe, he simply wanted us to have that particular house, because he and his then recently deceased wife, Mary Ethel, had picked out the plans together and had taken pleasure in supervising the construction. He thought it would be nice to have it owned and occupied by somebody he knew. I learned later in my career at Charlottesville about Emerson's widely acclaimed business acumen, but business obviously was not what he put first.

That incident, I came to learn, was characteristic of Emerson—not only of his generosity but of his ability to see life as a whole, with all of its aspects related to one another. Emerson would not have said "business is business" with respect to the sale of that house, any more than he would have said "career advancement is career advancement" with respect to his work at the law school. More than any other person I have known, Emerson saw his life as a whole, and he lived it that way.

We were very lucky to have ended up living in West Leigh, not least because it gave us frequent occasion to go over and visit Emerson and his children Peggy and Rick (Sally was in college, as I recall) in their cottage on the shore of the West Leigh Lake. In those days, before the hurricane that silted it up, the lake was well stocked with eating-size bass, and I remember very fondly taking my family over for a congenial hamburger dinner and spending the twilight hour chatting with Emerson while casting from the patio into the water.

Emerson spent a lot of time with his family—as he later did with Julia and his new family. In those days, the venue of his domesticity was not only the West Leigh cottage but also the big house at the end of Rugby Road. There, those who are fortunate enough to have experienced it will recall another aspect of Emerson's life, Emerson the azalea grower. I suppose there are more impressive displays of azaleas somewhere, perhaps in the Arboretum in Washington. But I have never enjoyed anything as much as the spring party Emerson used to throw for the faculty, when we would stroll through several acres of resplendent azaleas, gin and tonics in hand, taking only slightly more pleasure in the flowers than we did in Emerson's childlike delight at having produced them.

Another aspect of Emerson's life that has of course been mentioned was athletics. He had, after all, been a Rhodes Scholar. I do not recall playing more than a game or two of tennis with Emerson—enough to establish that I was clearly not in his league. I used to excuse this by pointing out that I had taken up tennis many years after law school. On one occasion I recall complaining to Emerson about my misspent childhood, which had been devoted mostly to baseball and stickball. "What do you do with those sports later in life?" I asked, and suggested that I would be a much happier man if only I had devoted all that energy to tennis. Emerson, ever the philosopher, responded, as I recall: "Well, Nino, that's one way to look at it. On the other hand, I was a terrific tennis player at twenty-seven and every year I get a little worse." Whereas my terrible game, of course, was of necessity constantly improving.

Emerson would never forgive me if I did not tell you one other sports story that he often used to recount, one in which he is the hero and I am the goat. He would hate it to pass from memory: On one occasion he asked me what was this stickball that I kept blaming for my lack of tennis ability and said he'd like to try his hand at it. I told him he'd better not—that this was my native game and he'd be as mismatched as I was with him on the tennis court. But he insisted, so I described the game to him, after which we drew a box on the wall. I batted first and struck out three times, and Emerson came up and hit the ball out of sight. In defense of my performance, I may point out that the ball was a tennis ball, and not the regulation spaldeen.

A large part of Emerson's life, of course, and the reason we meet here today, was the law school. He devoted forty-four years to it, and it would have been a much different place without him. Many of you knew him as a dean. Generations of law students, and of faculty members such as I, knew him as an outstanding teacher, a friend, an adviser, a man for all committees. He was an essential element of glue that held this place together and caused it to remain the same even as it changed. Dean Ribble became Dean Dillard became Dean Paulsen—but the great factotum of the place, Emerson Spies, remained the same.

Emerson had a fine mind and could, I think, have made his mark in the highest ranks of published scholarship if he had chosen to do so. He chose another course, devoting himself to teaching and to the institution. The longer I am in the law, the wiser I realize he was. It is a rare law review or treatise, or for that matter even Supreme Court opinion, that is much cited fifty years later. But the institution that Emerson Spies helped to shape, the lawyers he helped to form, will continue to reflect his good work for many years to come.

It is hard to speak of any good friend who has died, but especially so of Emerson. It is not only difficult to contemplate him in death, it is difficult to contemplate him in repose. The students had him right: every year in the libel show, Emerson would be portrayed as an ebullient, enthusiastic, youthful figure with white wool sweater and tennis racket who would bounce about the stage during most of the performance. There was indeed a perpetually youthful, almost childlike quality about Emerson—the best qualities of youth and childhood: cheeriness, enthusiasm, energy, openness, utter lack of affectation. Bright, clear colors. We all miss them.

Acknowledgments

We have more people to thank than we have room to name them. Everyone we reached out to for assistance—from longtime friends and former law clerks of Justice Scalia to folks who just heard him speak on one occasion—responded generously. Even Chris's siblings cooperated, at least when Ed contacted them.

Justice Scalia's longtime assistant Angela Frank tirelessly sorted through the justice's electronic and paper files to locate various sets of his speeches and the travel itineraries that helped us nail down when and where he delivered the speeches. Sarah Shanoudy, Ed's assistant at the Ethics and Public Policy Center, organized all the speeches electronically and provided valuable and efficient logistical support throughout. A young summer intern of Ed's by the name of Antonin Scalia—grandson of the justice and nephew of Chris—tracked down often elusive information about the speeches and reviewed cited sources. Ed's research assistant, Yale law student Samuel Adkisson, carefully read through the entire manuscript.

We are grateful to Chris's mom, Maureen Scalia, for inviting us to work on the book; to Chris's brother Eugene for overseeing the project; to legendary lawyer and book broker Robert Barnett for connecting us with Crown Forum; and to Crown Forum's executive editor Mary Reynics for her deft guidance and excellent suggestions.

We are especially grateful to Justice Ruth Bader Ginsburg for contributing her beautiful foreword.

Finally, we would like to thank our wives, Adele Scalia and Deborah Whelan, for offering insightful comments on the speeches and headnotes, providing steadfast encouragement, and showing abundant patience. Without them, we probably wouldn't be doing this book—or if we were, it wouldn't have been nearly as much fun.

INDEX OF SPEECHES

This index identifies the occasion on which Justice Scalia delivered a particular speech or, for those speeches that he delivered more than once, one such occasion, and any title he used for the speech if it differs from the heading for the speech.

Index

About the Authors

ANTONIN GREGORY SCALIA was born on March 11, 1936, in Trenton, New Jersey, the only child of Eugene and Catherine Scalia. His father, who had emigrated from Sicily as a young man, was a professor of Romance languages at Brooklyn College. His mother, a schoolteacher, was one of eleven children of Italian immigrants. He grew up in Queens, where he played stickball, rooted for the Yankees, and joined the Boy Scouts. He was valedictorian of the Xavier High Class of 1953 and valedictorian of the Georgetown University class of 1957. He attended Harvard Law School, where he earned high honors and was a Notes Editor for the law review.

While at Harvard, Scalia went on a blind date with a Radcliffe student named Maureen McCarthy. They wed in 1960. Scalia then studied in Europe for a year as Sheldon Fellow of Harvard University before working at the law firm of Jones Day in Cleveland from 1961 to 1967. He left private practice to become a professor of law at the University of Virginia from 1967 to 1971, and then served in a number of government positions: general counsel of the Office of Telecommunications Policy from 1971 to 1972, chairman of the Administrative Conference of the United States from 1972 to 1974, and assistant attorney general for the Office of Legal Counsel in the U.S. Department of Justice from 1974 to 1977.

He returned to academic life in 1977, joining the faculty at the University of Chicago. He was also visiting professor of law at both Georgetown and Stanford, and was chairman of the American Bar Association's Section of Administrative Law from 1981 to 1982 and its Conference of Section chairman from 1982 to 1983.

In 1982, President Reagan nominated Scalia to join the U.S. Court of Appeals for the District of Columbia Circuit. Four years later, Reagan nominated him to the Supreme Court of the United States, to which he was confirmed by the Senate, 98–0. Justice Scalia took his seat on the bench on September 26, 1986.

As a Supreme Court justice, Scalia articulated and exercised the interpretive methods of originalism and textualism. He established himself as a forceful presence on the bench, a vivid and compelling writer, and a gregarious public presence. One of the most significant justices in the history of the Court, he served for nearly thirty years before his death on February 13, 2016.

Antonin Scalia was married to Maureen for fifty-five years. Together they had nine children and dozens of grandchildren. He was a loving husband, a devoted father, a devout Catholic, and a proud American.

CHRISTOPHER J. SCALIA is the eighth of Justice Scalia's nine children. He holds a PhD in English literature from the University of Wisconsin–Madison and was a professor of English at the University of Virginia's College at Wise from 2007 to 2015. His political commentary and book reviews have appeared in *The Wall Street Journal*, *The Weekly Standard*, *The Washington Post*, *The Times Literary Supplement*, and elsewhere. He works at a public relations firm in Northern Virginia, where he lives with his wife and three children.

EDWARD WHELAN was a law clerk for Justice Scalia during the Supreme Court's October 1991 term. A graduate of Harvard College and Harvard Law School, he has also served as general counsel to the U.S. Senate Committee on the Judiciary and as principal deputy assistant attorney general in the Office of Legal Counsel at the U.S. Department of Justice. Since 2004, he has been president of the Ethics and Public Policy Center. A father of four, he lives with his family near Washington, D.C.